The Consumer Revolution, 1650–1800

The production, acquisition, and use of consumer goods defines our daily lives, and yet consumerism is seen as increasingly controversial. Movements for sustainable and ethical consumerism are gaining momentum alongside an awareness of how our choices in the market-place can affect public issues. How did we get here? *The Consumer Revolution, 1650–1800* advances a bold new interpretation of the "consumer revolution" of the eighteenth century, when European elites, middling classes, and even certain laborers purchased unprecedented quantities of clothing, household goods, and colonial products. Michael Kwass adopts a global perspective that incorporates the expansion of European empires, the development of world trade, and the rise of plantation slavery in the Americas. Kwass analyses the emergence of Enlightenment material cultures, contentious philosophical debates on the morality of consumption, and new forms of consumer activism to offer a fresh interpretation of the politics of consumption in the age of abolitionism and the Atlantic Revolutions.

MICHAEL KWASS is a professor of history at The Johns Hopkins University. He is author of *Privilege and the Politics of Taxation in Eighteenth-Century France: Liberté, Égalité, Fiscalité* (Cambridge University Press, 2000), which received the David H. Pinkney Prize; and *Contraband: Louis Mandrin and the Making of a Global Underground* (Harvard University Press, 2014), which was awarded the J. Russell Major Prize, the Gilbert Chinard Prize, the Annibel Jenkins Prize, and the Oscar Kenshur Prize.

T0384714

NEW APPROACHES TO EUROPEAN HISTORY

New Approaches to European History is an important textbook series, which provides concise but authoritative surveys of major themes and problems in European history since the Renaissance. Written at a level and length accessible to advanced school students and undergraduates, each book in the series addresses topics or themes that students of European history encounter daily: the series embraces both some of the more 'traditional' subjects of study and those cultural and social issues to which increasing numbers of school and college courses are devoted. A particular effort is made to consider the wider international implications of the subject under scrutiny.

To aid the student reader, scholarly apparatus and annotation are light, but each work has full supplementary bibliographies and notes for further reading: where appropriate, chronologies, maps, diagrams, and other illustrative material are also provided.

For a complete list of titles published in the series, please see:
www.cambridge.org/newapproaches

The Consumer Revolution, 1650–1800

Michael Kwass

The Johns Hopkins University

CAMBRIDGE
UNIVERSITY PRESS

CAMBRIDGE
UNIVERSITY PRESS

University Printing House, Cambridge CB2 8BS, United Kingdom

One Liberty Plaza, 20th Floor, New York, NY 10006, USA

477 Williamstown Road, Port Melbourne, VIC 3207, Australia

314–321, 3rd Floor, Plot 3, Splendor Forum, Jasola District Centre, New Delhi – 110025, India

103 Penang Road, #05–06/07, Visioncrest Commercial, Singapore 238467

Cambridge University Press is part of the University of Cambridge.

It furthers the University's mission by disseminating knowledge in the pursuit of education, learning, and research at the highest international levels of excellence.

www.cambridge.org
Information on this title: www.cambridge.org/9780521198707
DOI: 10.1017/9780511979255

First published 2022

Printed in the United Kingdom by TJ Books Limited, Padstow Cornwall

A catalogue record for this publication is available from the British Library.

Library of Congress Cataloging-in-Publication Data
Names: Kwass, Michael, author.
Title: The consumer revolution, 1650-1800 / Michael Kwass, The Johns
    Hopkins University.
Description: New York, NY : Cambridge University Press, [2022] | Series: Euro
    new approaches to European history | Includes bibliographical references and
    index.
Identifiers: LCCN 2021041003 (print) | LCCN 2021041004 (ebook) |
    ISBN 9780521198707 (hardback) | ISBN 9780521139595 (paperback) |
    ISBN 9780511979255 (epub)
Subjects: LCSH: Consumption (Economics)–Europe–History. | Consumer
    goods–Europe–History.
Classification: LCC HC79.C6 K88 2022 (print) | LCC HC79.C6 (ebook) |
    DDC 339.4/7–dc23/eng/20211012
LC record available at https://lccn.loc.gov/2021041003
LC ebook record available at https://lccn.loc.gov/2021041004

ISBN 978-0-521-19870-7 Hardback
ISBN 978-0-521-13959-5 Paperback

For my parents

Contents

Illustrations

Acknowledgments

I would like to thank the many graduate students who participated in my seminar, Consumer Revolution in Global Perspective, over the years. Their insights have enormously enriched this book. I'm also grateful to Cambridge University Press' final reader, who provided invaluable feedback on every chapter; to Laura Mason, who read the entire manuscript and encouraged me to develop key ideas; and to my editor, Liz Friend-Smith, who expertly shepherded the text through the production process. Thanks to my parents, Phoebe and George Kwass, for their boundless love and support, and, finally, to Laura, Max, and Isabel for their love, friendship, and humor, gifts that made the years writing this book very happy ones indeed.

Abbreviations

AHR	*American Historical Review*
AHRF	*Annales historiques de la Révolution française*
EHR	*Economic History Review*
FH	*French History*
FHS	*French Historical Studies*
HJ	*Historical Journal*
JDH	*Journal of Design History*
JEH	*Journal of Economic History*
JMH	*Journal of Modern History*
JWH	*Journal of World History*
PP	*Past & Present*
SVEC	*Studies in Voltaire and the Eighteenth Century*
WMQ	*William and Mary Quarterly*

Introduction

"They kept shopping." So observed a dazed Kimberly Cribbs after a tragic incident at the Green Acres Mall Wal-Mart in Valley Stream, New York, the morning of "Black Friday," November 28, 2008. In the predawn darkness of the first day of the Christmas shopping season, customers gathered outside the entrance to the big-box chain store, eager to snatch up holiday bargains. At 4:55 a.m., five minutes before the store was set to open, an impatient crowd of 2,000 customers crashed through the sliding-glass doors and, rushing into the store toward discounted merchandise, stampeded over several employees who had been trying to hold back the throng. One of those employees was thirty-four-year-old Jdimytai Damour, a temporary worker from Queens, who was knocked onto the linoleum floor and killed as customers surged past him. Upon learning that an employee was fatally injured, managers attempted to close the store, but customers "kept shopping," determined to get what they came for.[1]

We live in an age of consumption. In high-income countries of the Global North and, increasingly, middle- and low-income countries of the Global South, the acquisition, circulation, and use of nonstaple consumer goods define much of daily life. Children grow up staring at advertisements on screens large and small. Adults go into debt to obtain cars, household appliances, and electronics. Internet users click on products selected for them by complex algorithms, leaving behind "taste fingerprints" to be processed for laser-targeted advertising. Small wonder that even wealthy Americans say that they cannot afford to buy everything that they "need," despite living in houses of unprecedented size crammed with stuff. According to M. J. Rosenthal, member of the

---

[1] After the tragedy, the US Occupational Safety and Health Administration fined Wal-Mart $7,000 for violations of employee safety rules. The corporate giant battled the ruling for years but ultimately gave up and paid the fine. "Wal-Mart Employee Trampled to Death," *New York Times*, November 28, 2008.

National Association of Professional Organizers, the average American home holds 300,000 items, from televisions to toothpicks.[2]

The COVID-19 pandemic laid bare the sheer force of consumption in contemporary society. Government restrictions and fear of infection sent consumer spending plunging in 2020, producing severe contractions in economies across the planet. As neighborhood restaurants closed and retailers shut their stores, many nations experienced declines in GDP not seen since the Great Depression of the 1930s. At the same time, however, the pandemic showed how eager people were to continue purchasing goods and services, even if it put their own and others' lives at risk. Months into the pandemic, consumers dismissed warnings from public health officials and blithely shopped and dined out, even as the retail and service workers who attended to them fell ill. Restaurants, bars, night-clubs, cafés, casinos, gyms, and big-box stores filled up once more in a stirring of expenditure lauded by business leaders around the world. To bet against the US consumer "is a loser's game," said Paul Schatz, president of Heritage Capital, who predicted America's "spending spirit" would power the economy forward once the crisis passed.[3] Meanwhile, corporations concerned about the optics of crassly promoting products in the midst of a public health crisis nimbly reframed consumption as an act of public service or familial duty. One commercial depicted a drone-equipped grandfather airlifting a box of Dunkin' donuts to his safely distant grandson, implicitly promising that the sweet pastry would keep families together during the pandemic.

If the force of consumption in the modern world is undeniable, so is our profound unease with that reality. In the twentieth century, intellectuals on both the left and right raised doubts about the moral implications of spending so much time and money on the acquisition of material objects. As consumption reached unprecedented heights in the postwar Global North, critics warned that an obsession with commercial products dulled moral sensibilities and eroded our humanity. "The people recognize themselves in their commodities," lamented Herbert Marcuse, one of the last century's fiercest critics of consumer capitalism, "they find their soul in their automobile, hi-fi set, split-level home, kitchen

[2] Robert Frank, *Luxury Fever: Money and Happiness in an Era of Excess* (New York, 1999); Juliet Schor, *The Overspent American: Upscaling, Downshifting, and the New Consumer* (New York, 1998); www.bostonglobe.com/magazine/2017/05/18/why-hard-stop-buying-more-stuff/TikBKa6hUCSN2UkKoSBSeL/story.html, accessed June 29, 2021.

[3] Callum Keown, "'Betting against the U.S. Economy and Consumer Is a Loser's Game – Why One Strategist Sees Dow 40,000 on the Horizon," www.marketwatch.com/story/betting-against-the-us-economy-and-consumer-is-a-losers-game-why-one-strategist-sees-dow-40000-on-the-horizon-2020-05-18, accessed June 29, 2021.

equipment. The very mechanism which ties the individual to society has changed, and social control is anchored in the new needs which it has produced."[4] The materialism of modern consumer society, Marcuse asserted, impeded independent critical thinking and prevented human beings from reaching their full social and political potential.

Today, a surfeit of books, magazines, and blogs offer advice to anxious consumers on "decluttering" their homes, "simplifying" their lifestyles, and "downshifting" their expenditure, even as the very same texts advertise the latest fashions. *The Life-Changing Magic of Tidying Up,* the bestseller by Japanese writer Marie Kondo,[5] has created a worldwide sensation. Kondo encourages her millions of readers to purge from their homes all material possessions that do not spark "joy." The ultimate goal is the creation of a clutter-free household in which every possession brings happiness. While such movements have failed to slow the furious growth of consumption, they suggest that many of the world's most privileged citizens are exploring ways (however superficially) to recast their relationship to commercial life.

And then – alarmingly – there is the climate crisis. The greatest threat facing humanity today, climate change is a direct result of the ceaseless consumption of fossil fuels, which provide the energy for consumers to live comfortably by heating and cooling buildings and powering cars and trucks. Environmental activists argue that we cannot solve the problem of climate change with technological advances alone. We will have to reduce consumption significantly by changing our everyday habits, habits centuries in the making but which now seem perfectly natural. For some, the dramatic fall in consumption following the COVID-19 pandemic demonstrates that it is possible, if the collective will is there, to escape the grip of modern consumer capitalism, mitigate its disastrous effects on the environment, and build a sustainable green economy. But the failure on the part of the consuming public to sustain lockdowns during the pandemic suggests how difficult this will be.

Meanwhile, concerns about the environment and other pressing issues have given rise to a variety of movements that social scientists call "political" or "ethical consumerism." Many consumers have come to believe that their daily purchases have significant implications for a whole host of major public issues: human and animal rights, corporate governance, fair trade, labor policy, industrial agriculture, and climate change. Accordingly, they refrain from buying certain goods (boycott) and

---

[4] Herbert Marcuse, *One-Dimensional Man: Studies in the Ideology of Advanced Industrial Society* (London, 2002), 11.
[5] Marie Kondo, *The Life-Changing Magic of Tidying Up* (London, 2014).

choose to buy others (buycott) under the assumption that their collective decisions will make a genuine difference in the world at large. Proponents of ethical consumerism believe that a new awareness of the global connections between production and consumption – a better understanding of where consumer goods come from and how their production effects communities near and far – will generate new patterns of demand, which will in turn discourage corporations and states from pursuing harmful labor, environmental, and political policies. We see this playing out in any number of ways, from the spread of vegetarianism and veganism (which are more sustainable than meat-eating) to boycotting fast-fashion (disposable garments made by child laborers and others working under terrible conditions in the Global South) to dropping subscriptions to Facebook (which amplifies hate speech on its platform). Indeed, the contemporary marketplace has become an ethical minefield for countless socially conscious consumers.

Histories of Consumption

How did we get here? It will be difficult to make enduring changes in consumption at either the personal or collective level without a better understanding of how humans developed a hunger for high levels of consumption in the first place. Delving into the history of consumption can help us comprehend contemporary predicaments and perhaps find ways to resolve them. The first step is to acknowledge that consumption has a history. The obsession with shopping is nothing new. Nor is the seemingly endless pursuit of novelty and fashion; the process of globalization with its attendant inequalities and international division of labor; or the attempt to build a better world through consumer activism. Historians are currently unearthing consumption's deep past, and it turns out to be a rich, complicated, and controversial story.

When did large numbers of people begin to expand their consumption beyond mere subsistence? Historians propose different chronologies. Some adopt a short-term perspective, spotlighting the development of post–World War II American and European consumer culture. In the 1950s and 1960s, the growth of suburbia and youth culture drove consumption to new levels as the West moved beyond the lean years of the Great Depression and the war. Even the dramatic social protest movements of the 1960s, as subversive as they were, were integral to a larger process of the commodification of youth culture. Looking deeper into the past, others trace the origins of modern consumer society to the nineteenth century, when the gains of the Industrial Revolution translated into remarkable profits for the bourgeoisie and (eventually) rising wages for the working classes. This was the age of factories, railroads, and steamships; of grandiose department stores and amply decorated bourgeois apartments; of cheap newspapers and popular entertainments for the working classes – an age that experienced "an immense accumulation of commodities," as Karl Marx famously wrote in the opening line of *Capital*.[6] Surely, these scholars conclude, the first age of mass production in the late nineteenth and early twentieth centuries gave rise to the first age of mass consumption.

Until fairly recently, most historians assumed that changes in consumption followed from changes in production. Production was the causal agent that mattered, setting the conditions for various patterns of consumption. Thus, the idea that the development of modern forms of consumption was only possible after the Industrial Revolution of the nineteenth century was virtually axiomatic.

In 1982, however, Neil McKendrick took a radically different approach. In a seminal work written with historians John Brewer and J. H. Plumb, *The Birth of a Consumer Society*, he claimed that there was a "consumer boom" of "revolutionary proportions" as far back as the eighteenth century. This "consumer revolution was the necessary analogue to the industrial revolution, the necessary convulsion on the demand side of the equation to match the convulsion on the supply side."[7] According to this hypothesis, the middling women and men of late eighteenth-century England bought an unprecedented quantity of goods, ushering in the first modern consumer society. For McKendrick, the "birth" of this consumer society, which was coterminous with the advent of industrial factories, constituted the first "stage" of a longer process that would ultimately lead to mass consumption in the twentieth century. Scholars had missed this first consumer revolution, he explained, because they so long focused on the history of production, particularly on the causes and consequences of the Industrial Revolution. McKendrick insisted that the Industrial Revolution had a semiautonomous demand-side counterpart, the consumer revolution, that was not merely a consequence of industrialization. The consumer revolution had a history all its own that paralleled that of industrialization.[8]

[6] Karl Marx, *Capital*, trans. Ben Fowkes (London, 1981), 25.
[7] Neil McKendrick, John Brewer, J. H. Plumb, *The Birth of a Consumer Society: The Commercialization of Eighteenth-Century England* (Bloomington, IN, 1982), 9.
[8] McKendrick, Brewer, and Plumb, *The Birth of a Consumer Society*. Joan Thirsk's *Economic Policy and Projects: The Development of a Consumer Society in Early Modern England* (Oxford, 1978) first articulated many of the themes discussed in *The Birth of a Consumer Society*.

For McKendrick, the consumer revolution could only have begun in England, where commercial society was developing more rapidly than in the rest of Europe and the structure of society was less rigidly hierarchical. He argued that the precocious existence in England of a prosperous middling class engendered a system of social emulation that encouraged the diffusion of fashionable goods. The wealthy aristocracy set standards of consumption, the robust middling ranks aped them, and the rest of society imitated the middling classes. First appearing in eighteenth-century England, he claimed, this sociocultural dynamic activated a robust new system of consumption. "Spurred on by social emulation and class competition, men and women surrendered eagerly to the pursuit of novelty, the hypnotic effects of fashion, and the enticements of persuasive commercial propaganda." As social inferiors emulated their social superiors, "many objects, once the prized possession of the rich, reached further and further down the social scale."[9] Consumer society was born.

The publication of *The Birth of a Consumer Society* triggered a veritable explosion of literature on consumption. Historians of England and British America dug into late seventeenth- and eighteenth-century probate inventories (lists of household goods drawn at the time of death) to add detail to the preliminary sketches of McKendrick, Brewer, and Plumb. After-death inventories showed that men and women dramatically expanded their wardrobes; splurged on a variety of personal accessories; adorned their homes with new types of furniture, tableware, and decorative objects; and ingested new psychoactive colonial products like tea, coffee, tobacco, and sugar – all well *before* the Industrial Revolution.[10] If McKendrick rendered the consumer revolution equal and opposite to the Industrial Revolution, the body of work his book spawned moved the growth of consumption even further back in time to predate industrialization.

Meanwhile, as the picture of British consumption became clearer, the geographic scale of the study of consumption broadened considerably. Casting the exceptionalism of the British case into doubt, historians of continental Europe discovered similar phenomena there. The pioneering work of Daniel Roche revealed that France, too, experienced

---

[9] McKendrick, Brewer, and Plumb, *The Birth of a Consumer Society*, 11.
[10] Studies that have effectively used probate inventories include Mark Overton et al., *Production and Consumption in English Households, 1600–1750* (New York, 2004); Carole Shammas, *The Pre-industrial Consumer in England and America* (LA, 1990); Lorna Weatherill, *Consumer Behaviour and Material Culture in Britain, 1660–1760* (London, 1988).

"a revolution in consumption" involving many of the same sorts of goods.[11] Others demonstrated that the Netherlands and parts of the German Lands enjoyed surges in consumption as well.[12] By the turn of the twenty-first century, something of a consensus had emerged that patterns of consumption changed dramatically in western and central Europe and in colonial America between the seventeenth and eighteenth centuries. Jan de Vries called this historiographical turn "the revolt of the early modernists," because it was a rebellion against an older historiographic tradition that had assumed that the economy of the early modern period (1500–1800) was stagnant and that any meaningful social change could have only occurred after the Industrial Revolution.[13] By contrast, the new interpretation of consumption was based on a more dynamic image of early modern society, a society shaped by vigorous migration, expanding commerce, robust urbanization, accelerating social mobility, vibrant print culture, and complex labor markets.[14] For Roche, the birth of consumption was essential to a vast cultural transformation whereby the traditional values of a stationary economy gave way to the egalitarianism and individualism of contemporary commodity culture. Challenging the twentieth-century critiques of Marcuse and others, Roche contended that the expansion of consumption was not completely negative, for it had liberating effects on society and culture. As early modern historians reevaluated the period on which they worked, moreover, historians of later eras began to emphasize the gradual rather than revolutionary pace of nineteenth-century industrialization, calling the very term "Industrial Revolution" into question. As a result, the once great chronological divide of industrialization no longer seemed quite so imposing. The consumer revolution thesis narrowed the gap between the preindustrial

---

[11] Daniel Roche, *The Culture of Clothing: Dress and Fashion in the Ancien Regime*, trans. Jean Birrell (Cambridge, 1996); Daniel Roche, *A History of Everyday Things: The Birth of Consumption in France, 1600–1800*, trans. Brian Pearce (Cambridge, 2000). See also, Annik Pardhailé-Galabrun, *The Birth of Intimacy: Privacy and Domestic Life in Early Modern Paris*, trans. Jocelyn Phelps (Philadelphia, 1991). To encourage further reading, the notes that follow give priority to English translations of foreign-language texts whenever possible.

[12] Notably, Simon Schama, *The Embarrassment of Riches: An Interpretation of Dutch Culture in the Golden Age* (New York, 1987).

[13] Jan de Vries, "The Industrial Revolution and the Industrious Revolution," *Journal of Economic History* (JEH) 54 (1994), 253.

[14] The early modern world beyond Europe, particularly East, South, and Southeast Asia, is now cast in more dynamic terms as well, though debate still rages over the question of the later divergence between the developed and developing worlds. See Victor Lieberman, *Beyond Binary Histories: Re-imagining Eurasia to c. 1830* (Ann Arbor, MI, 1999).

past, once seen as fundamentally alien – a world we have lost – and contemporary industrial and post-industrial society.

To say that some sort of consensus has been reached is not, however, to suggest that the consumer revolution thesis has gone unchallenged. Some historians are not comfortable using the term "revolution" to describe a transformation that was decades in the making and may not have significantly altered the lives of ordinary people.[15] They prefer the term "consumer evolution" since it evokes a gradual rate of change. Others, however, argue that while the growth of consumption may have been incremental, its cultural effects were indeed revolutionary.[16] They contend that the hothouse environment of rising consumption engendered new social and cultural practices, new forms of sociability and publicity, new kinds of political debate and contestation, and new ways of thinking about society and social progress. This book retains the expression consumer revolution because it conveys the transformative nature of consumption in the eighteenth century. However, it does so with some important caveats that acknowledge that the transformation unfolded over the course of a century or more; that it was not, in many respects, unique to Europe; and that large sections of the European population did not experience a dramatic increase in consumption even if elites, the middling classes, and, strikingly, some in the laboring classes undoubtedly did. Readers can judge for themselves whether the changes the book examines were truly revolutionary or merely evolutionary in scale.

[15] Weatherill, *Consumer Behaviour and Material Culture in Britain*, rejected words like "consumer society" and "consumerism." Shammas, *The Pre-industrial Consumer in England and America*, avoided the expression "consumer revolution." T. H. Breen, *The Marketplace of Revolution: How Consumer Politics Shaped American Independence* (Oxford, 2004), 81, suggests that "revolution" overstates the pace of change. More recently, contributors to "Les révolutions à l'épreuve du marché," *Annales historiques de la Révolution française* (AHRF) 370 (2012), 165–190, shied away from the term "consumer revolution."

[16] Daniel Roche consistently speaks of a "revolution of consumption." James Riley, "A Widening Market in Consumer Goods," in Euan Cameron, ed., *Early Modern Europe: An Oxford History* (Oxford, 1999), 257, suggests that "the process of growth in consumption was evolutionary, but its effect was revolutionary." Natacha Coquery, *Tenir boutique à Paris au XVIIIe siècle* (Paris, 2011), 24, denies the existence of a consumer revolution or society but acknowledges a "rise of a *culture* of consumption." Regina Grafe, *Distant Tyranny: Markets, Power, and Backwardness in Spain, 1650–1800* (Princeton, NJ, 2012), 208–209, distinguishes between the consumer revolution in northwestern Europe and a consumer evolution in Spain. Maxine Berg, *Luxury and Pleasure in Eighteenth-Century Britain* (Oxford, 2005), 5, speaks of a "product revolution." John Styles, *The Dress of the People: Everyday Fashion in Eighteenth-Century England* (New Haven, CT, 2007), 1–5, parses the debate between optimists and pessimists.

Indeed, although the book employs the term consumer revolution, it openly addresses questions about that revolution's speed, global reach, and social limits, inviting further debate. In terms of chronology, McKendrick portrayed the revolution as a strictly late eighteenth-century phenomenon, but many scholars claim that it began, in the Netherlands and England at least, in the middle of the seventeenth century, and perhaps even earlier. Some would claim the origins go as far back as the Italian Renaissance. When the growth of consumption really began remains an open question.

Geography is also at issue. If transformations in consumption took place most conspicuously in northwestern Europe, what of the rest of the continent? Did consumption accelerate in areas beyond the northwestern European core as well? And what of rural Europe? Did provincial nobles, farmers, and peasants partake of novel forms of consumption or was this primarily an urban phenomenon? Further, in the multipolar early modern world, regions beyond Europe were hardly static. Although Fernand Braudel once claimed that fashion first emerged as a dynamic force in the West, the modernity of which he contrasted with a purportedly fixed non-Western world, it is now clear that Europe was not the only part of the globe where fashion took hold and consumption was growing.[17] Elites in China during the Ming dynasty (1368–1644), for example, eagerly filled their homes with an abundance of new furnishings and other fashionable goods.[18] Kenneth Pomeranz suggests that before the middle of the eighteenth century, consumption in the bustling Yangzi delta was roughly on par with that of northwestern Europe.[19] Hence, this book, while it concentrates on Europe, does not make claims about the uniqueness of the European case. Instead, it places European consumption in a global perspective, underscoring connections between Europe

[17] Fernand Braudel, *Civilization and Capitalism, 15th–18th Century*, trans. Siân Reynolds (New York, 1982–1984).

[18] Craig Clunas, *Superfluous Things: Material Culture and Social Status in Early Modern China* (Cambridge, 1991); and "Things in Between: Splendour and Excess in Ming China," in Frank Trentmann, ed., *The Oxford Handbook of the History of Consumption* (Oxford, 2012), 47–63.

[19] Kenneth Pomeranz, *The Great Divergence: China, Europe, and the Making of the Modern World Economy* (Princeton, NJ, 2000). Alternatively, Carlo Marco Belfanti, "Was Fashion a European Invention?" *Journal of Global History* 3 (2008), 443, argues that, in Europe, consumption underwent a particularly deep transformation as fashion moved well beyond the orbit of royal courts, was treated extensively in the periodical press, and shaped the material lives of the middling and, to some degree, laboring classes. "Fashion was not a European invention, but it first fully developed as a social institution in Europe, while in India, China, and Japan it only evolved partially in pre-modern times, without being able to obtain full social recognition." See also the conclusion in Maxine Berg, Felicia Gottmann, Hanna Hodacs, and Chris Nierstrasz, eds., *Goods from the East, 1600–1800: Trading Eurasia* (New York, 2015).

and the wider world that dramatically shaped European consumption and altered, to a greater or lesser degree, the many regions with which Europe interacted.

Finally, and perhaps most problematically, there is the social question. It is difficult to determine how far down the social hierarchy new consumer practices spread. Did the laboring classes enjoy rising levels of consumption or was this an exclusively elite or perhaps middling affair? This is a crucially important question because depictions of the rise of consumption that do not carefully define its social limits risk giving a falsely sanguine impression of the eighteenth century. Rosy portrayals of consumption must be weighed against evidence of severe material constraints, persistent underemployment, and downward social mobility. After all, as we know well today, it is possible for downward and upward social mobility to occur simultaneously, allowing consumption to expand among elites while stagnating among the laboring classes. It is time to provide a more nuanced assessment of these changes and to explain the uneven rise of consumption.

Going beyond questions of chronology, geography, and social structure, this book will also consider a number of themes that, though addressed in the early literature, have since received much closer attention. Take shopping, for example. The early literature on the consumer revolution claimed that well before the advent of the great department stores of the nineteenth century, retailers pioneered new modes of marketing in an effort to heighten the desire for goods. But it did not explore in detail how merchants, shopkeepers, and peddlers sought to stoke consumer desire. How did they market their goods, and how did consumers respond to their appeals to create feedback loops between producers and consumers? Long before corporate focus groups and data collection, consumers and retailers exchanged information about taste and desire. Print advertising was an important part of this exchange, but so was the shop itself, which became a site of display and sociability. What did eighteenth-century shops look like, and when did shopping become a leisure activity for city-dwellers and tourists? Further, how did the concept of fashion enter into the picture? It is clear that fashion cycles accelerated over the course of the seventeenth and eighteenth centuries as men and women sought to stay "à la mode," but we are only beginning to understand the mechanisms behind the spread of fashion and fashion's impact on capitalism.

Fashion raises difficult questions about what goods meant to those who acquired them. Originally, McKendrick and others who subscribed to the emulation thesis suggested the main function of nonsubsistence goods was to signal social status. Consumers displayed luxurious or fashionable items to claim that they belonged to certain social groups. Yet, upon closer examination, it seems that men and women attributed a remarkably wide range of meanings to the goods with which they surrounded themselves. Shifting from the social emulation paradigm to more open questions of material culture and consumer practices, a move initiated by Roche, allows us to see how eighteenth-century retailers, consumers, and commentators developed a host of modern consumer values, some of which are still with us today. Not that social status was unimportant, but approaches that stress material culture and practice provide an opportunity to examine how individuals, families, and social groups, far from reflexively imitating social superiors, actively invested meanings in objects as the world of goods expanded around them. To study how goods were imbued with meaning is to connect cultural and economic history, illuminating the cultural construction of economic demand.

Gender, which was treated superficially in the first generation of scholarship, has recently received a great deal of attention. The eighteenth-century philosopher Jean-Jacques Rousseau claimed that women were particularly susceptible to the frivolity of luxury consumption. Why did Rousseau associate luxury with femininity? Did women and men approach the world of goods differently? Was consumption gendered? Some historians argue that the pursuit of fashion increasingly became seen as a feminine activity in this period, as women accumulated more clothing and were targeted by fashion journals. Others suggest that men were hardly deaf to the siren of fashion; they bought watches, coaches, and furniture, and drank coffee and smoked tobacco in cafés. Both sexes participated in the consumer revolution. Rather than focus on the question of which gender consumed more, it may be more fruitful to investigate how changing consumption patterns affected the concept of gender itself or redefined the boundary between the masculine and the feminine. We have already asked if consumption conditioned changing social boundaries in this period; the same question should be put to the issue of gender boundaries.

Rousseau's ideas about gender were part of a wider eighteenth-century debate on consumption. Just as new consumer goods filled the spaces of Enlightenment sociability, so did Enlightenment thinkers reflect on the proliferation of goods. Indeed, the eighteenth century spawned the first modern debate on consumption, dubbed the "luxury debate." This debate, which has now been analyzed by intellectual historians, is the ancestor of our own public controversies over consumption. On one side, a group of important Enlightenment philosophers defended rising levels of consumption, arguing that the growth of luxury reflected long-term social progress. On the other side, moralists attacked new consumer practices, claiming that such "luxury" gave rise to decadence, the feminization of men, and, ultimately, the downfall of nations. Political economists, meanwhile, attempted to carve out a third position that would open the way for a prosperous yet morally stable economy. This debate was more than an abstract intellectual exercise. It was a way to think through the dramatic changes in consumption that were shaping European empires at the time.

While marketing, gender, and luxury were discussed in at least a preliminary fashion by the first generation of consumption scholars, other subjects and themes never even saw the light of day. A whole series of new questions have arisen since McKendrick, Brewer, and Plumb first articulated their bold thesis. If the first generation of work emerged in the 1980s and 1990s, a moment of neoliberal optimism marked by the fall of the Berlin Wall in 1989 and a surge in global trade at the end of the century, the next generation of scholarship came of age in the era of 9/11 and the "war on terror" (2001–), the financial crisis and the Great Recession (2007–2012), and the COVID-19 pandemic (2020–). Exposing the glaring socioeconomic and racial inequalities of the post-Fordist global order, the Great Recession stoked long-standing, virulent strains of white supremacy, racism, and xenophobia to incite intense populist backlashes, replete with calls to build walls, wage trade wars, block migration, police people of color, and reject traditional party politics. The stunning election of Donald Trump in the USA, the relentless "Brexit" dispute in the UK, and the unexpected mobilization of the "gilets jaunes" in France all support Adam Tooze's contention that "the financial and economic crisis of 2007–2012 morphed between 2013 and 2017 into a comprehensive political and geopolitical crisis of the post-cold war order."[20] The rise of state capitalism in China and growing awareness of the threat of climate change further challenged that liberal order. In the crucible of twenty-first century uncertainty, scholars are employing new methodologies to rethink the history of consumption and relate it to a number of pressing contemporary problems.

One such problem is empire and globalization. It is no coincidence that the growth of European consumption in the long eighteenth century occurred simultaneously with the dramatic expansion of European overseas empire and trade. In the early modern period, a truly global circuit of commerce formed that, for the first time in the history of the world, directly linked Asia, Africa, the Americas, and Europe. Mediated

[20] Adam Tooze, *Crashed: How a Decade of Financial Crises Changed the World* (New York, 2018), 20.

principally by European merchants, this new period of global commerce depended on aggressive European imperialism in Asia, where state-sponsored companies conducted "armed trading," and in the Americas, where colonialism decimated indigenous populations. Early modern globalization also entailed the largest forced migration in human history as European traders coercively transported millions of African captives (6 million in the eighteenth century alone) across the Atlantic to the Americas. Enslaved and forced to work on plantations under brutal conditions, Africans and their descendants toiled to produce unprecedented supplies of tropical goods for distant European consumers. This piece of the story of the consumer revolution was absent from much of the early scholarship, and it is high time to integrate it fully into general accounts.

Although the global context of European consumption has not always been stressed, its significance suggests the need for scholars to connect consumption back to production. It is entirely understandable why McKendrick and others focused exclusively on consumption, because the study of consumption had for so long been overshadowed by that of production. But this myopic view of consumption is no longer justifiable at a time when the study of consumption has come into its own across the social sciences and humanities. We no longer need to be defensive about incorporating problems of production and exchange into the history of consumption.

There is another reason to bring production back into the picture. Some consumers in the Global North, who are becoming increasingly aware that many of the goods that they enjoy are produced under extremely poor labor conditions in the Global South, are eager to bridge the cognitive disconnect between consumption at home and production abroad. Accordingly, they are curious to learn how this international system of global production, consumption, and exchange developed in the first place. The large-scale exploitation of overseas labor for the purposes of producing consumer goods for rich countries began with the consumer revolution of the seventeenth and eighteenth centuries. That is more than enough reason to adopt a global perspective on the history of consumption and to widen our lens to take in the commodity chains that belted the planet and bound distant consumers and producers in often profoundly unequal ways.

A second major issue that was ignored in early consumption studies is politics.[21] What do changing patterns of consumption have to do with

---

[21] Despite John Brewer's innovative chapter on the subject, "Commercialization and Politics," in McKendrick, Brewer, and Plumb, *The Birth of a Consumer Society*.

power, governments, and political movements? Was there a connection between the consumer revolution (lowercase "r") and the American, French, Haitian, and Latin American Revolutions (capital "R") of the late eighteenth and early nineteenth centuries? After decades of astonishingly apolitical histories of consumption, these questions are only now beginning to be addressed. This book seeks to advance the field by examining various aspects of the relationship between politics and consumption. It considers how new forms of consumption contributed to the development of the public sphere, focusing on the book trade, the material dimensions of Enlightenment sociability, and the production of public opinion. Not only were books extraordinarily important objects of consumption during the Enlightenment, but sites of Enlightenment sociability and knowledge production (salons, cafés, restaurants, theaters, public gardens) were centers of consumption themselves. This study also places consumption in the context of political economy. In the seventeenth and eighteenth centuries, powerful fiscal-military states in Europe intervened in global commerce in an attempt to regulate the flow of consumer goods across the world. Later termed "mercantilism," this mixed bundle of military and economic policies, all of which aimed to boost imperial economic power, left a deep imprint on the consumer practices of millions of Europeans. It also stimulated the growth of a massive and sometimes violent underground economy, as smugglers secreted prohibited goods across national and imperial borders to eager consumers.

Further, the Age of Revolution gave rise to new forms of consumer politics in the Atlantic world. Citizens on both sides of the Atlantic experimented with consumer activism: American revolutionaries boycotted British imports; French revolutionaries burned down customs gates; and British abolitionists called for the end of the Atlantic slave trade by boycotting Caribbean sugar. Political and ethical consumption may have deeper historical roots than previously imagined, for they appear to have become an integral part of a wider repertoire of political and social activism during the Age of Revolution. Moreover, revolutionary activists consciously created new material cultures to express their political aspirations. Novel architecture, product design, and modes of dress marked ruptures with the past and enabled revolutionaries to broadcast political agendas while reinforcing horizontal bonds of citizenship. In France, the sans-culotte, the archetypal figure of the French Revolution, was defined by the trousers he wore (and the breeches he did not). In an age when consumption was becoming more fluid and commercialized, revolutionary leaders and activists sought to animate political movements by mobilizing material culture. Such revolutionary experiments were not always successful, but they reflected an ardent desire to construct a new relationship between politics and consumption.

Third and lastly, early work on consumption did not dwell on environmental questions. The climate crisis invites us to reflect more deeply on the long-term origins of expanding consumption and on possible ways to change today's consumer habits. Since one of the most obvious and effective solutions to climate change is to reduce levels of consumption, historians have something to contribute by denaturalizing practices of consumption and demonstrating how "needs" are socially and historically constructed. As eighteenth-century thinkers pondered the changing material conditions around them, they became increasingly aware of the history of their own material culture. Some realized that their habits of consumption were not innate but rather historically conditioned. We need a similar burst of consciousness today to gain critical distance on what we consider "natural" needs, comforts, and desires. One way to achieve that critical distance is to seek a better understanding of the history of consumption and to learn how various consumer values and practices were invented in the past. Making ourselves aware of the invention of new forms of consumption may make it easier to change practices of consumption in the present and future.

With that goal in mind, this book provides a transimperial synthesis of the consumer revolution, reviewing recent debates, assessing the latest research, drawing fresh conclusions, and, where possible, advancing new hypotheses. By approaching the subject in an open-ended fashion, it aims to put readers in a position to interpret for themselves the social, cultural, and political implications of European consumption before the age of the Industrial Revolution, stimulating debate that will drive the field forward.

1   Consumer Revolution

	L	s	d
In the Hall a Clock & Case	1	10	0
A Looking Glass	0	10	0
A Writing Desk and Table & Stand	2	10	0
A Doz of Sedge Chairs	0	6	0
a grate	0	8	0
In the Parlour A Corner Cupboard & China & a Tea Table	0	17	6
An Oval Table a Tea Table a Card Table a dressing Table and a Hand Board	1	2	6
twelve Cane Chairs	2	8	0[1]

Linen shirts, calico skirts, and silk stockings; pocket watches, colorful ribbons, and silver buttons; armchairs, earthenware dishes, and decorative pictures; hot coffee, tea, and chocolate laden with sugar – these are just some of the consumer goods that increasingly filled the material world of Europe and its colonies over the course of the long eighteenth century (1650–1800). Subsequent chapters will consider the social, economic, political, intellectual, and cultural ramifications of the dramatic rise in consumption during this period. Here, we will plunge into the world of goods itself, taking the measure of its growth, tracking the emergence of particular commodities, and gauging who had access to them. To provide a balanced account, this chapter also traces the social and geographical limits to the efflorescence of consumption, underscoring the many groups that did not have access to the relative abundance of the eighteenth century. Finally, it addresses chronology and periodization. Well before the eighteenth century, urban growth and the rise of court culture created vibrant markets in luxury goods. Such markets were important precursors to the consumer revolution, but they did not generate the levels of consumption that many Europeans would experience in the age of Enlightenment.

[1] Inventory of estate of Thomas Heath of Shelton, potter, 1742, in Lorna Weatherill, *Consumer Behaviour and Material Culture in Britain, 1660–1760* (London, 1988), 34.

The Growth of Consumption

While *The Birth of a Consumer Society* by McKendrick, Brewer, and Plumb sketched an image of a new material world coming into being in the eighteenth century, it was only after its publication that historians would become intimately familiar with that world. Putting aside the literary and commercial accounts on which that book was largely based, historians went into the archives to unearth tens of thousands of precious legal documents called probate inventories, like the one in the epigraph at the start of this chapter. Inventories opened a new window onto the world of goods. They revealed that between the rarefied society of the court and the subsistence-oriented sphere of countless rural peasants and urban day laborers, an intermediate zone of consumption widened to include a multitude of new goods. Inventories demonstrated in rich, quantifiable detail that Europe experienced an unprecedented expansion in consumption that touched not only aristocrats and wealthy bourgeois but men, women, and children of the middling and, to some extent, laboring classes.

Drawn up at the behest of heirs to settle matters of inheritance, inventories were relatively precise lists of a dead person's material possessions and their estimated value. However, there are many reasons to approach this type of primary source with caution. Wealthier families were more prone than poorer ones to have them composed, a problem that skews data toward the middling and upper reaches of the social order. Inventories were typically incomplete; perishable and ephemeral items like food, cheap print material, and trinkets were often omitted, while expenditure on services (entertainment, education) and fuel went unrecorded. Nor do they track change over time with respect to a given household. Rather, they provide snapshots of goods at the end of a life, revealing little about when goods had been acquired in a person's life-cycle, where they came from, who produced them, and what path they took before reaching their owner. Nonetheless, despite all of these shortcomings, historians have turned to inventories more than any other single source to demonstrate the expansion of European and colonial consumption in the seventeenth and eighteenth centuries.

Taken together, studies of inventories show that three types of goods proliferated with particular speed over the course of the long eighteenth century: clothing and personal accessories, household objects, and paraphernalia for various articles of ingestion such as food, drink, and tobacco (see Figure 1.1). For each of these areas, it is important to ask what specific items increased in number, which socioeconomic groups consumed them, and how consumption was gendered.

Figure 1.1 William Hogarth, *Portrait of a Family*, c. 1735.
Copyright Getty Images. Set in an opulent living room, this scene of domestic life
features fashionable clothing, fine furnishings (including a card table), and a
porcelain tea service

The case for a consumer revolution is perhaps most obvious with
respect to clothing, the second costliest item, after food, in the household
budgets of ordinary people. Because English inventories frequently omitted clothing or grouped it with other categories, the richest data come
from France, which has been deeply studied by Daniel Roche. Roche
found that from the turn of the eighteenth century to 1789, the value of
linens and clothes in a broad sample of Parisian inventories rose by
80 percent (accounting for inflation), an increase that far outpaced that
of other categories of goods.

What sorts of people accumulated clothing? To be sure, the nobility
participated heavily in clothing consumption. By 1789, an individual
noble could boast an average of eighty garments, with some of the
wealthiest and most fashionable aristocrats possessing hundreds of
expensive pieces. But the growth of wardrobes also occurred lower down
the social hierarchy among professionals, merchants, shopkeepers, artisans, domestic servants, and even wage earners. Indeed, the laboring
classes began to accumulate clothing for the first time ever and, given

their relatively modest starting point, did so at a faster rate than the nobility. The value of clothes owned by Parisian wage earners and domestic servants tripled over the eighteenth century. It may not be all that surprising that well-placed domestic servants indulged in clothing, for their elegant working environments may have encouraged them to be particularly sensitive to appearances, but wage earners acquired many more clothes as well.[2]

Gender played a decisive role in shaping patterns of clothing consumption. After the fourteenth century, the sexually ambiguous, loose-fitting, draped dress of the Middle Ages gave way to tighter-fitting, shaped clothing for each gender. Men and women signaled their gender identity by wearing ever more distinct types of garments. By the eighteenth century, the norm was that men wore breeches and women skirts or gowns. Equally important, however, Roche found that men and women accumulated clothing at strikingly different rates, a pattern he called "sexual dimorphism." Women, it turned out, were vanguard consumers of clothing. Over the course of the century, the average male Parisian day laborer doubled the value of his clothes, while his wife enjoyed nothing less than a sixfold increase. By the end of the period, a woman of the laboring classes typically owned more than a dozen garments, including petticoats, shirts or camisoles, a dress, an apron, several pairs of stockings, one or two pairs of shoes, and perhaps a jacket. Women in the clothing trade were particularly enthusiastic textile consumers.[3] However, the sexual dimorphism Roche discovered in Paris did not necessarily occur elsewhere. Englishman William Hutton recalled that when he was a young bachelor of sixteen, he began to think of clothing as a "powerful mode" to win over the opposite sex. Dress "is a passport to the heart, a key to unlock the passions, and guide them in our favour."[4] Based on one set of English accounts, John Styles observes that husbands, too, spent a good deal of money on their clothes, even more than their wives.[5] Thus, different national trends present a mixed picture of

[2] Daniel Roche, *The People of Paris*, trans. Marie Evans (Berkeley, CA, 1987), ch. 6; Daniel Roche, *Culture of Clothing: Dress and Fashion in the Ancien Regime*, trans. Jean Birrell (Cambridge, 1996). See also Cissie Fairchilds, "The Production and Marketing of Populuxe Goods in Eighteenth-Century Paris," in John Brewer and Roy Porter, eds., *Consumption and the World of Goods* (London, 1993), 228–248.
[3] Clare Haru Crowston, *Fabricating Women: The Seamstresses of Old Regime France, 1675–1791* (Durham, NC, 2001); Jennifer Jones, *Sexing la Mode: Gender, Fashion, and Commercial Culture in Old Regime France* (Oxford, 2004).
[4] Quoted in Styles, *The Dress of the People: Everyday Fashion in Eighteenth-Century England* (New Haven, CT, 2007), 58.
[5] Styles, *The Dress of the People*, 218 and 241. Men had no trouble spending money on accessories like wigs, watches, and canes. See Margot Finn, "Men's Things: Masculine

gender. We need more transnational research – and more work on consumer decision-making within households – to clarify this issue.

Apart from his findings on gender in England, Styles' evidence dovetails with that of Roche. Having examined newspaper advertisements, trial records, and lists of goods saved from the 1789 Brandon fire, Styles concludes that plebeian men in England wore "shirt, breeches, coat and waistcoat, supplemented by shoes, stockings, hat and neckcloth," while women wore "petticoat and gown over stays and shift, supplemented by shoes, stockings, apron, cap, hat and neckcloth."[6] The volume of garments rose steeply as ordinary people accumulated multiple changes of clothing, especially white linen and cotton shirts and undergarments. In England, France, the Netherlands, and Germany, what now distinguished the wardrobe of elites was not so much the types of garments they owned as their quantity and quality.[7]

Accessories were almost as important as clothing itself. We might think of accessories as frivolous trifles, but they were essential to the rise of consumption in the eighteenth century because they provided laboring people an inexpensive way to participate in the acquisition and display of fashionable goods. Many accessories were designed for bodily adornment, such as wigs for men and jewelry for women. The concern for bodily appearance that continued to permeate court culture had an analogue among middling and ordinary people, which is why one historian has identified cheap knockoffs of high-end products as "populuxe" goods.[8] Other accessories, such as bonnets, ribbons, lace, *cravates*, buttons, buckles, pins, and the ubiquitous handkerchief, enabled consumers to add a splash of color and sparkle to their wardrobe. Accessories could lend a fashionable air to otherwise mundane apparel.

The portable utilitarian object was yet another type of accessory that provided its owners with a degree of distinction. Snuffboxes, canes, fans, umbrellas, toothpick cases, pocket watches, and, in Catholic countries,

Possession in the Consumer Revolution," *Social History* 25 (May 2000), 133–155; Michael Kwass, "Big Hair: A Wig History of Consumption in Eighteenth-Century France," *The American Historical Review* (AHR)111 (June 2006), 631–659; John Styles and Amanda Vickery, eds., *Gender, Taste, and Material Culture in Britain and North America, 1700–1830* (New Haven, CT, 2006).

[6] Styles, *The Dress of the People*, 55.

[7] For the Netherlands, see Jan de Vries, *The First Modern Economy: Success, Failure, and Perseverance of the Dutch Economy, 1500–1815* (Cambridge, 1997); Simon Schama, *The Embarrassment of Riches: An Interpretation of Dutch Culture in the Golden Age* (New York, 1987). For Germany, see Michael North, *"Material Delight and the Joy of Living": Cultural Consumption in the Age of Enlightenment in Germany*, trans. Pamela Selwyn (New York, 2008).

[8] Fairchilds, "The Production and Marketing of Populuxe Goods in Eighteenth-Century Paris."

rosary beads proliferated in this period. Indeed, pockets *themselves* became a popular accessory for holding other accessories. As Adam Smith observed, the pockets of toy lovers "are stuffed with little conveniences. They contrive new pockets, unknown in the clothes of other people, in order to carry a great number [and] walk about loaded with a multitude of baubles."[9] Such baubles tempted consumers of all social levels. At the upper end, an English lord cautioned his son: "A fool cannot withstand the charms of a toy-shop ... snuff boxes, watches, heads of canes, etc. are his destruction."[10] At the lower end, snuffboxes, fans, and gold watches, while virtually nonexistent among Paris' laboring classes in 1725, showed up in 33 percent, 34 percent, and 55 percent of their inventories, respectively, sixty years later.[11] The enormous success of these accessories cannot be overemphasized. Essential to plebeian fashion, they enabled artisans, domestic servants, and petty traders to participate in a transformation of personal appearance that would otherwise have been beyond their means.

What of clothing and accessories in European overseas empires? Although the first generation of scholarship on the consumer revolution neglected European colonies, except for British North America, historians are now examining practices of dress in a variety of imperial spaces. Recall that, by the eighteenth century, several European seaborne empires had, through a protracted process of plunder, settlement, coercion, and commercial exchange, developed vast colonies in the Americas and extensive networks of coastal trading posts and military forts in Africa and Asia. In the Americas, as elsewhere, the Iberian powers led the way. Spain laid claim to much of South America, Central America, southern North America, and the Caribbean, while Portugal colonized the large territory of Brazil. Eager to reap the benefits of empire, the Dutch, British, and French followed suit, encroaching on Spanish lands to carve out their own empires in the Caribbean and eastern half of North America. As a result, heterogeneous societies emerged from the mixing of indigenous Americans, European-descended settlers, African-descended slaves, and free people of color, giving rise to rich, new cultural forms (see Figure 1.2).

[9] Adam Smith, *The Theory of Moral Sentiments,* D. D. Raphael and A. L. Macfie, eds. (Indianapolis, 1982), 180.
[10] Quoted in Styles and Vickery, *Gender, Taste, and Material Culture in Britain and North America, 1700–1830,* 5.
[11] Fairchilds, "The Production and Marketing of Populuxe Goods in Eighteenth-Century Paris," 230. Ordinary Parisians also carried many small items on their persons (knives, dice, scissors, mugs, cardboard boxes, and all manner of cases) that may not have shown up in inventories. Arlette Farge, *Fragile Lives: Violence, Power, and Solidarity in Eighteenth-Century Paris,* trans. Carol Shelton (Cambridge, MA, 1993), 210–211.

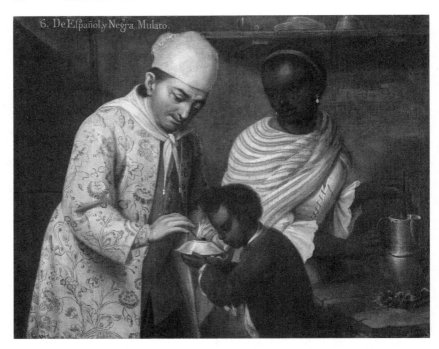

Figure 1.2 José de Alcíbar, *From Spaniard and Black, Mulatto,* Mexico, c. 1760.

Denver Art Museum Collection: Gift of the Collection of Frederick and Jan Mayer, 2014.217. Photo © James O. Milmoe. Photograph courtesy of the Denver Art Museum. Casta paintings from Spanish America not only depicted but classified mixed-race people. This image from eighteenth-century Mexico shows a Spanish father clad in an Asian banyan, an African-descended mother in an American shawl preparing hot chocolate, and their son in a European coat holding a brazier from which his father lights a cigarette

Recent work stresses the hybridity of material cultures that reflected varying degrees of agency and self-fashioning among different groups.

European settlers acquired clothing as eagerly as their peers in the metropole. In the Americas, free white settlers of European descent who considered themselves "civilized" strove to distinguish themselves from the "nakedness" of the Amerindians and enslaved Africans by following metropolitan fashions. This concept of civilization undergirded European ideas of cultural, religious, and racial superiority, legitimizing colonization and the exploitation of non-European peoples. Mankind was divided into sorts, explained Roger Williams, the founder of Rhode

Island: "first, the wild and pagan ... and second, 'the civil,' who were brought to clothes, to laws, &c, from barbarism."[12] Propping up such hierarchies, imported fabric from Europe flooded North America, where ordinary people possessed "so many of the conveniences of life."[13] Even in remote areas such as backcountry Virginia, local retailers offered farmers all manner of European-made cloth and accessories. In the Shenandoah Valley of the 1770s, John Hook's country store sold textiles, linens, buttons, hats, and handkerchiefs to planters and their families.[14] In tropical zones, colonists adapted to the climate by wearing lighter fabrics, but they too hewed to European fashion. Settlers in Spanish America "maintained social distance between themselves and the population of Amerindians, slaves and free people of colour" by wearing Spanish dress and eating Spanish food.[15] Across the Americas, "a trans-imperial but European-inflected" style defined settlers' dress among both women and men.[16]

The introduction of European woven fabrics into the Americas fundamentally changed the way indigenous Americans dressed. Even as the Old World diseases that Europeans brought with them to the New World decimated the Native American population, Christian missionaries eager to civilize "barbarous" peoples attempted to dress them in European clothes.[17] Although the project to clothe indigenous peoples never fully succeeded, Amerindians did mix traditional dress with imported European textiles to create new hybrid styles (see Figure 1.3). Amerindians increasingly wore cotton and woolen fabric, for example. Yet their appropriation of gendered European dress remained uneven and incomplete throughout the period. Jesuit missionaries in Río de la Plato, Brazil, provided the indigenous Guaraní with cotton cloth for shirts and trousers for men, and tunic gowns, hats, and sandals for women, but it remains unclear whether the Guaraní actually adopted the gendered apparel. In North America, colonists likewise sought to "civilize" indigenous peoples by imposing European-style linen, woolen,

---

[12] Quoted in Keith Thomas, *In Pursuit of Civility: Manners and Civilization in Early Modern England* (New Haven, CT, 2018), 116.

[13] William Burke, quoted in J. H. Elliott, *Empires of the Atlantic World: Britain and Spain in America, 1492–1830* (New Haven, CT, 2006), 314.

[14] Anne Smart Martin, *Buying into the World of Goods: Early Consumers in Backcountry Virginia* (Baltimore, 2008).

[15] Rebecca Earle, *The Body of the Conquistador: Food, Race and the Colonial Experience in Spanish America, 1492–1700* (Cambridge, 2012), 14.

[16] Robert DuPlessis, *The Material Atlantic: Clothing, Commerce, and Colonization in the Atlantic World, 1650–1800* (Cambridge, 2016), 171. The same could be said for food since early colonists sought to import or reproduce Old World agriculture and livestock.

[17] Some European writers, like Daniel Defoe, thought that "civilizing" Native Americans stimulated their consumption and increased Atlantic commerce. Thomas, *In Pursuit of Civility*, 225.

Figure 1.3 Catherine Tekaküita Iroquoise du saut S. Louis de
Montreal, *Histoire de L'Amérique septentrionale ...*, 4 vols.
(Paris, 1722), I, 351.
Courtesy of the George Peabody Library, the Sheridan Libraries, Johns Hopkins
University. In this image of hybridity, Catherine Tekakwitha (1656–1680), a
Mohawk and Catholic convert from the area of present-day New York State,
combines clothing characteristic of European nuns – a dark outer garment
covering a long white chemise – with an Indian-style skirt, leggings, and
moccasins

and cotton clothing. Northern settlers regularly gifted and traded European cloth with Amerindians, yet, as in South America, Amerindians only partially appropriated the new dress, creating hybrid peltry–textile fashions. A 1736 drawing of a Yuchi "King" wearing a woolen breechclout and leggings in addition to a buffalo skin illustrates this sartorial syncretism.[18] Of course, hybridity ran in the opposite direction too; French fur trappers and British Americans in the backcountry adopted leggings, moccasins, snowshoes, and many other accessories of indigenous origin. Sartorial hybridity was pervasive.

Most enslaved peoples of African descent in the Americas had little choice but to dress in the cheap, rough, imported linen and woolen cloth provided by their masters, a form of "involuntary consumption" that marked them as chattel.[19] (White indentured servants received clothing from their masters too but were given higher-quality, often finished products.) The horrific conditions of slavery severely constrained the dress of the enslaved, but some nonetheless exercised a degree of sartorial autonomy by acquiring clothing through petty trade and other means. In Virginia, John Hook sold goods to the enslaved, whose purchases challenged the civilized/uncivilized divide. In colonial Louisiana, textiles, handkerchiefs, ribbons, and shirts circulated in second-hand markets, licit and illicit, in which enslaved Africans, Indians, and Europeans all participated.[20] Among communities of the enslaved, what one wore depended largely on the type of work one did. Rural field hands did not have as much access to clothing and accessories as those who labored in plantation houses or in towns. Indeed, the diversity of apparel worn by the urban enslaved so alarmed whites in colonial cities that many cities sought to police sartorial boundaries by issuing racialized sumptuary laws that limited what the enslaved could wear. Such laws were not always strictly enforced, however, as descriptions of runaways in newspapers suggest.[21] Tom, an enslaved carpenter in South Carolina, ran away from his master with an ozenbrig shirt and breeches, a green jacket, and a surtout coat. Baptiste, a wigmaker in Saint-Domingue, fled wearing

[18] DuPlessis, *The Material Atlantic*, ch. 3.
[19] Styles, *The Dress of the People*, chaps. 15–17, emphasizes the importance of involuntary consumption through gifting, payment in kind, charity, and poor relief. Frank Trentmann, *Empire of Things: How We Became a World of Consumers, from the Fifteenth Century to the Twenty-First* (New York, 2016), further stresses the "institutional consumption" of armies, schools, and hospitals, a concept that is particularly useful for the nineteenth and twentieth centuries.
[20] Sophie White, "Geographies of Slave Consumption: French Colonial Louisiana and a World of Goods," *Winterthur Portfolio* 45 (June 2011), 229–248.
[21] DuPlessis, *The Material Atlantic*, ch. 4; Philip Morgan, *Slave Counterpoint: Black Culture in the Eighteenth-Century Chesapeake and Lowcountry* (Chapel Hill, NC, 1998), 125–134.

a pair of black velvet breeches and a jacket.[22] Within the stringent limits imposed by slaveholders, some enslaved men and women found ways to appropriate European-style clothing in more or less subversive acts of self-fashioning.[23]

Sumptuary laws in the Americas also targeted free people of color, whom white settlers accused of dressing too extravagantly. In Brazil, free blacks who violated prohibitions against wearing silk, fine wool, and jewelry risked confiscations, fines, and even exile to São Tomé off the coast of Africa.[24] In French Saint-Domingue, colonial authorities prohibited free people of color from affecting "the dress, hairstyles, style, or bearing of whites," though sumptuary law there was often subverted.[25] Faced with the mandate that they keep their hair covered in public, free women of color turned kerchiefs into elaborate adornments that would soon become fashionable among white women. In the end, free people of color wore clothing and accessories quite similar to those of whites, including the omnipresent handkerchief, rendering dress "a relatively weak marker of racial identity" (see Figure 1.4).[26]

After clothing and accessories, the second major category of goods that historians of consumption have focused on is household furnishings. Here probate inventories yield by far the most information. A substantial amount of evidence from western and central Europe makes it clear that elites and the middling classes were enlarging their homes, subdividing space into specialized rooms, and filling those rooms with more and more stuff. Although laborers were rarely in a position to expand their homes or buy expensive furniture, many embellished their interiors in modest ways.

From the Middle Ages through the sixteenth century, most European households consisted of a single room with a bed, a table, a few stools or benches, and a chest or two for storing linen and other valuables. In the seventeenth and eighteenth centuries, however, men and women

[22] DuPlessis, *The Material Atlantic*, ch. 4.
[23] Tamara J. Walker, *Exquisite Slaves: Race, Clothing, and Status in Colonial Lima* (Cambridge, 2017). Some enslaved people in British North America and the Caribbean may have had access to European-style ceramics as well. Ashli White, *Revolutionary Things* (New Haven, CT, forthcoming).
[24] Gabriel Paquette, *The European Seaborne Empires from the Thirty Years' War to the Age of Revolutions* (New Haven, CT, 2019), 167.
[25] Quoted in Laurent Dubois, *Avengers of the New World: The Story of the Haitian Revolution* (Cambridge, MA, 2004), 62. See also Meredith Gaffield, "Whiteness on Credit: Migration, Race, and Social Capital in France and the Caribbean, 1763–1791" (Ph.D. dissertation, Johns Hopkins University, 2021), 64–67.
[26] DuPlessis, *The Material Atlantic*, 171 and 193. Just as Caribbean white creoles criticized free people of color for their purported extravagance, metropolitan writers often criticized Caribbean creoles for their excessive concern with dress.

Figure 1.4 Augustin Brunias, *Linen Market, Dominica.*
Photo courtesy of the Yale Center for British Art. The free women of color
depicted in this painting of a Caribbean market mix European fashion with
African-style head wraps

acquired new kinds of furniture, kitchenware, tableware, books, and
decorative objects. Although the bed remained the single most valuable
piece of furniture in the home, new pieces multiplied, such as chests of
drawers, cabinets, cupboards, tables, and chairs. In Kent, England, a
commercialized county southeast of London, the number of pieces of
household furniture (excluding beds) doubled between 1600 and 1750.
Chests had long been used for storage and as makeshift tables, but they
were steadily replaced by more elaborate chests of drawers, which had
scarcely existed before 1650. By the mid-eighteenth century, chests of
drawers showed up in nearly 60 percent of households. Chairs, increasingly upholstered in wealthy residences, likewise replaced benches and
stools; the numbers of chairs more than quadrupled in Kent.[27]

---

[27] Mark Overton, Jane Whittle, Darron Dean, and Andrew Hann, *Production and
Consumption in English Households, 1600–1750* (New York, 2012), 90–98; Daniel
Roche, *A History of Everyday Things: The Birth of Consumption in France, 1600–1800,*
trans. Brian Pearce (Cambridge, 2000), ch. 7; Raffaella Sarti, *Europe at Home: Family
and Material Culture 1500–1800,* trans. Allan Cameron (New Haven, CT, 2002);

Kitchenware, tableware, and table linens were also on the rise. Families increasingly equipped their homes with stoves, pots and pans, and utensils. Dining involved more cutlery, glassware, and plates (first pewter, then ceramic). Once a rarity found only at table in European courts, the fork became ubiquitous, silver ones gracing wealthy households while tin ones appeared in modest homes. Even in a city on the decline like Antwerp, the use of the fork had become widespread by 1730.[28] Meanwhile, fragile but inexpensive earthenware pots, platters, and cups proliferated, as did drinking glasses and pitchers.[29]

Finally, a plethora of new decorative objects filled the home. Mirrors and pictures (both secular and sacred) hung on the wall, facing clocks on mantle pieces. White linens lined beds and covered tables while curtains shrouded windows. For those who could afford to buy such goods, homes became significantly more plush, comfortable, and private. Wealthy aristocrats and bourgeois could take such comforts on the road by travelling in well-appointed carriages.

Which social groups acquired the new household furnishings? In general, the wealthy bought more than the poor, nobles more than commoners, and men more than women (because the purchase of expensive furniture usually required the approval of the head of household). As Lorna Weatherill first pointed out with respect to Britain, however, wealth and status were not the only factors at play, since men and women in certain urban occupations – merchants, professionals, and craftspeople – often possessed more home furnishings than rural groups who stood above them in the social hierarchy. A recent study of inventories confirms Weatherill's thesis but, taking in a longer sweep of time from 1600 to 1750, suggests that the participation of different social groups evolved over time. Initially, in the first half of the seventeenth century, the English gentry pioneered the appropriation of new household goods, such as mirrors, upholstered furniture, chests of drawers, tables, and window curtains.[30] Later, urban men and women – professionals,

Weatherill, *Consumer Behaviour and Material Culture in Britain*. North, *"Material Delight and the Joy of Living,"* ch. 4., describes similar developments in Germany, though they occurred later there.

[28] Bruno Blondé, "Cities in Decline and the Dawn of a Consumer Society: Antwerp in the 17th–18th Centuries," in Bruno Blondé and Natacha Coquery, eds., *Retailers and Consumer Changes in Early Modern Europe: England, France, Italy and the Low Countries* (Tours, 2005), 37–52.

[29] Annik Pardailhé-Galabrun, *The Birth of Intimacy: Privacy and Domestic Life in Early Modern Paris*, trans. Jocelyn Phelps (Philadelphia,1991), ch. 4.

[30] Overton, Whittle, Dean, and Hann, *Production and Consumption in English Households*; Maxine Berg, *Luxury and Pleasure in Eighteenth-Century Britain* (Oxford, 2005) also brings the story back to the early seventeenth century.

traders, and retailers – took the lead, ultimately outpacing the gentry and yeomanry in almost every aspect of household consumption save the acquisition of clocks, which farmers acquired with singular enthusiasm. Throughout Europe, townspeople were particularly eager to buy the equipment necessary for serving hot drinks, and urban professionals and merchants played disproportionately large roles in the consumption of home furnishings, though prosperous farmers outside of cities like Paris and Florence participated as well.[31] The same could be said of British colonies in North America, where "even those at the lowest levels of wealth had chairs and bedsteads, knives and forks, bed and table linen, teapots, and ceramic tableware."[32]

The third area of consumption that expanded dramatically in the long eighteenth century consisted of products for bodily ingestion, namely food, drink, and tobacco. Food evolved more slowly than drink in this period. Bread remained the center of the European diet, providing between 75 and 90 percent of the lower classes' daily calories.[33] In towns, people generally ate wheat-based white bread, the whitest shades (the most thoroughly sifted and, we now know, least nutritious) going to the wealthiest eaters. In the countryside, peasants ate stale brown bread made from rye, barley, and oats, and grain-based gruels, porridges, and mashes. To soften the stale dark bread, rural folk dipped it in vegetable soup made with a touch of butter, lard, or oil; protein-rich meat remained a rare luxury for all but the wealthiest, who savored fresh fowl in the country and beef in the city. Apart from feasting at the occasional wedding or religious holiday, food was all too scarce for most Europeans, even if more affluent city-dwellers had access to an ever wider range of goods coming from distant provinces, countries, and even continents. Indeed, thanks to specialized market gardening, better transport, and foreign imports, the variety of food available to the urban propertied broadened considerably.[34]

But it was drink that changed the most. To wash down food, Europeans traditionally drank weak alcoholic beverages such as beer, wine, and cider, which provided much-needed calories and were often

[31] Paolo Malanima, *Il lusso dei contadini: consumi e industrie nelle campagne toscane des Sei e Settecento* (Bologna, 1990); Jean-Marc Moriceau, *Les fermiers de l'Île-de-France* (Paris, 1994); North, *"Material Delight and the Joy of Living,"* 166; Pardailhé-Galabrun, *The Birth of Intimacy.* Dominique Margairaz, "City and Country," in Frank Trentmann, ed., *The Oxford Handbook of the History of Consumption* (Oxford, 2012), 193, argues for a more balanced portrait of European urban and rural consumption.

[32] Berg, *Luxury and Pleasure in Eighteenth-Century Britain*, 303.

[33] Sarti, *Europe at Home*, 178.

[34] Reynald Abad, *Le grand marché: L'approvisionnement alimentaire de Paris sous l'ancien régime* (Paris, 2002).

less polluted than water. Between 1650 and 1800, however, three new hot drinks – chocolate, coffee, and tea, all psychoactive products taken with sugar – radically altered the European diet. Europeans had for centuries ingested products that affected their mental state, such as alcohol and local herbs, but with the expansion of global trade, first in the Iberian world and then beyond, consumers were exposed to an array of powerful psychoactive substances. So swiftly did hot drinks and tobacco disseminate, one historian suggests, that a "psychoactive revolution" unfolded at the heart of the broader consumer revolution.[35] Although inventories omitted perishable groceries like coffee beans and tea leaves, they did register a battery of paraphernalia used in the service of such hot drinks. Across western Europe, in the space of two or three generations, specialized roasting pans, mills, storage tins, caddies, kettles, pots, cups, saucers, and spoons became common. Among the lower-class in Paris, where drinking coffee became part of the morning routine, the proportion of inventories that listed specialized tea and coffee accessories climbed from 19 percent in 1725 to 45 percent in 1785. Shopkeepers sold such equipment in various materials (silver, stoneware, tin) to offer socially stratified clienteles a range of price points.[36]

In England, tea prevailed. The doubling of its consumption between the 1730s and 1740s shows up very clearly in Kent's inventories, 74 percent of which included tea and coffee paraphernalia.[37] Tea in particular became associated with British female domesticity, though historians debate the extent to which its consumption was in fact gendered.[38] Anthropologist Sydney Mintz argued that sweetened tea and other "drug foods" boosted the energy of English laborers who had to work long hours on farms and in factories, even though replacing beer with such empty calories meant a steep loss of nutrition, not to mention severe tooth decay.[39] In the Dutch Republic, tea and coffee accessories were

[35] David T. Courtwright, *Forces of Habit: Drugs and the Making of the Modern World* (Cambridge, MA, 2001).

[36] North, *"Material Delight and the Joy of Living,"* ch. 9; Pardailhé-Galabrun, *The Birth of Intimacy*, ch. 4; Weatherill, *Consumer Behaviour and Material Culture in Britain*, 230. Paris data is from Fairchilds, "The Production and Marketing of Populuxe Goods in Eighteenth-Century Paris," 230 (table 11.1).

[37] Overton, Whittle, Dean, and Hann, *Production and Consumption in English Households*, 106. See also Carole Shammas, *The Pre-industrial Consumer in England and America* (LA, 1990).

[38] The gendered interpretation in Woodruff Smith, *Consumption and the Making of Respectability* (New York, 2002) has been challenged by Jon Stobart, *Sugar and Spice: Grocers and Groceries in Provincial England, 1650–1830* (Oxford, 2013). Gendered understandings of consumption are further addressed in Chapters 4–6.

[39] Sydney Mintz, *Sweetness and Power: The Place of Sugar in Modern History* (New York, 1985), 180.

equally widespread by 1750, appearing in inventories of the poor who purchased used tea leaves and coffee grounds in second-hand markets.[40] Hot chocolate remained a more expensive elite beverage, but all three colonial drinks were taken with prodigious quantities of processed sugar, which entered the Western diet in precisely this period. Trade statistics reveal that by the late eighteenth century, Europeans were importing half a billion pounds of sugar, which was produced by enslaved men and women of African descent in the Americas. As the next chapter will show, the consumption of sugary drinks in Europe depended on a brutal system of plantation slavery across the Atlantic.

In addition to colonial beverages, new and potent alcoholic drinks entered the European diet in the eighteenth century. Gin, vodka, rum, grappa, and whiskey became dangerously popular, contributing to a steep rise in alcoholism. An array of psychoactive beverages thus became available in this period from stimulants like coffee to distilled spirits like gin.

Tobacco, the first major consumer import from the Americas, was a particularly important psychoactive product. The American leaf would more thoroughly pervade European society than any other colonial good. As early as the beginning of the seventeenth century, Spanish sailors who had encountered tobacco among Amerindians started to smoke it in European ports, spreading the custom to urban artisans, laborers, migrants, and soldiers. Atlantic merchants further shared the herb with fellow traders and nobles, who introduced it to European courts. Encouraging the trend, the Dutch city of Gouda produced millions of cheap ceramic clay pipes, one of the first disposable consumer items ever manufactured.[41] In the eighteenth century, as more and more men – and women – ingested tobacco by snorting rather than smoking, snuffboxes, handkerchiefs, and tiny spoons appeared in increasing numbers of inventories. Elites across Europe collected ornate silver and gold boxes, but in France even the laboring classes took snuff; a third of middling- and lower-class Parisian inventories recorded snuffboxes.[42] No matter how it was ingested, tobacco became so popular among western European laboring classes that one historian did not hesitate to characterize it as an article of "mass consumption."[43]

---

[40] Anne McCants, "Exotic Goods, Popular Consumption, and the Standard of Living: Thinking about Globalization in the Early Modern World," *Journal of World History* (JWH) 18 (December 2007), 433–462.

[41] Jan de Vries, *The Industrious Revolution: Consumer Behavior and the Household Economy, 1650 to the Present* (Cambridge, 2008), 157.

[42] Fairchilds, "The Production and Marketing of Populuxe Goods in Eighteenth-Century Paris," 230.

[43] Shammas, *The Pre-industrial Consumer in England and America*, 95–98.

Because inventories simply list items without describing their use, they make the acquisition of so many different kinds of clothing, furnishings, and ingestible products seem somewhat arbitrary. But products were not purchased at random or in isolation from one another. They were bought in particular combinations, which explains distinct patterns in their diffusion. "Goods do not travel alone," the economist Marina Bianchi notes, for "they are always part of an intricate network of relations with other goods."[44] Thus, new oval and round tables required chairs instead of benches. Wardrobes stored increasing volumes of linen while sideboards held dishes and kitchen utensils. Hot drinks were served in ceramic cups on new occasional tables (now described as "side" or "corner" tables). Forks were adopted as plates replaced trenchers. Glassware proliferated to accommodate different kinds of wine. Mirrors reflected new fashions in hair, cosmetics, and jewelry, and diffused light from candleholders. Snuff takers and coffee drinkers cleaned their noses and mouths with handkerchiefs. Beer drinkers smoked in taverns. Pens, paper, and inkstands adorned newly designed writing desks, often placed in special private rooms. The upswing of consumption hinged on the proliferation of clusters of goods, the cultural meanings of which we will explore in Chapter 4.

Consumer Revolution or Evolution?

Any claim that the growth of consumption in the eighteenth century was "revolutionary" has to acknowledge two powerful objections: (1) that there were social and geographic limits to the development of consumption in this period and (2) that the growth of consumption was less sudden than it appears, having deep roots in the urban life and court society of preceding centuries. Historians must take these objections seriously, lest they paint an exaggerated, overly optimistic portrait of the eighteenth century. We must therefore come to grips with a series of thorny questions. How broadly across Europe and how far down the social hierarchy did new practices of consumption spread? Were certain groups excluded from participating in the accumulation of goods and, if so, where do we draw the line between those who participated and those who did not? Did the vibrant consumer culture of the eighteenth century have antecedents?

There is no doubt that the rise of consumption was most pronounced in northwestern Europe, particularly the region around the North Sea

---

[44] Marina Bianchi, *The Active Consumer: Novelty and Surprise in Consumer Choice* (London, 1998), 75; de Vries, *The Industrious Revolution*, 31–37.

(southern England, northern France, the Netherlands, the Rhine valley, northern Germany) and along the Atlantic coasts of Britain and France. Southern Europe had benefited from a resurgence of Mediterranean trade and domestic craft production during the Renaissance (1400–1600), but thereafter the economic center of the continent shifted north. Recent work on Spain suggests that the country experienced a moderate rise in consumption during the eighteenth century, yet the expansion was not on par with countries to the north, Regina Grafe insists, making an explicit distinction between consumer "evolution" in Spain and consumer "revolution" elsewhere.[45] Divisions between east and west were also significant. Large cities in Central and Eastern Europe like Vienna and Moscow experienced some of the transformations of Western towns, but as a whole, Eastern Europe, which remained a largely rural society populated by peasants and serfs, did not participate in anything close to a consumer revolution.

And what of the poor in Western Europe? Perhaps a third or more of Western Europeans were indigent or lived precariously on the edge of poverty and could not afford to indulge in consumption beyond what we would consider the barest levels of subsistence (see Figure 1.5). In France, whose domestic market was more rural and less well integrated than England's, poverty persisted in isolated provinces. Even in Paris, one historian remarked,

being poor meant having enough to eat only in the good times. It meant dressing in rags, in the cast-offs of others. It meant living in a single room, with inadequate heating. And it implied being at the mercy of other people for credit or for alms, sometimes for shelter, even for tolerance of expedients like begging and gleaning that might inconvenience the better-off and therefore be illegal.[46]

Is it fair to speak of a revolution in consumption when so much of the population remained trapped in poverty?

One way to sort out which groups were included or excluded from new forms of consumption is to look at the social structure of eighteenth-century rural and urban communities. The assumption that towns enjoyed categorically higher levels of consumption than the countryside

---

[45] Belén Moreno Claverías, "L'inégalité comme norme: Modèles de consommation dans l'Espagne préindustrielle," in *Consommateurs & consommation XVIIe–XXIe siècle: Regards franco-espagnols* (Perpignan, 2015), 15–46; Regina Grafe, *Distant Tyranny: Markets, Power, and Backwardness in Spain, 1650–1800* (Princeton, NJ, 2012), 208–209. See also J. Torras and B. Yun, eds., *Consumo, Condiciones de Vida y Commercializacion: Catauna y Castillo, Siglos XVII–XIX* (Valladolid, 1999).

[46] David Garrioch, *The Making of Revolutionary Paris* (Berkeley, CA, 2004), 47. Jean-Yves Grenier, *L'économie d'ancien régime: Un monde de l'échange et de l'incertitude* (Paris, 1996), stresses the fragmentary character of the French economy.

Figure 1.5 John Coakley Lettsom, *A Morning Walk in the Metropolis*, 1797. https://wellcomecollection.org/works/j88yrgsg. Although poverty was widespread in this period, depictions of it were relatively rare. Note the one bed for a family of five, the tattered clothing on the shoeless boy, the bare walls and mantelpiece, and the storage trunk, which wealthier households replaced with the chest of drawers.

has been sharply contested. The difference was often one of degree as peddlers, traders at rural fairs, domestic servants, and village shopkeepers diffused goods from town to country.[47] Better to consider the steep social hierarchies that defined both rural and urban consumption. In the countryside, aristocrats, gentry, and better-off farmers, all of whom owned a great deal of land and could take advantage of rising rents and grain prices, accumulated substantial quantities of goods, but below the level of wealthier farmers, the standard of living dropped off quickly. Studying the English case, Lorna Weatherill underscored the existence of a large body of poor husbandmen whose consumption stagnated. On the continent, the lower strata of the peasantry were in even worse shape as population increases put pressure on small subsistence holdings, dividing them further and creating the conditions for mounting pauperism.

[47] Margairaz, "City and Country." Grafe, *Distant Tyranny*, 207, notes that rural Spaniards were increasingly "plugged into" transregional markets.

Yet towns, too, were defined by steep social hierarchies. An ever widening range of urban social groups enjoyed fashionable consumption in the eighteenth century, including nobles, financiers, wholesale merchants, professionals, well-off retailers, and skilled artisans, but a large group of urban poor – unincorporated artisans, day laborers, the under- and un-employed, and homeless migrants – were manifestly excluded from the consumer boom.

A more precise way to assess inequalities of consumption is to trace the social trajectories of particular goods. Growth in the consumption of clothing, for instance, was far from universal. While elites and middling classes of urban and rural Europe accumulated larger and more diverse wardrobes in the seventeenth and eighteenth centuries, a number of social groups seem to have been locked out of this process. Lower-level peasants, unskilled artisans, day laborers, and widows with minimal resources might have purchased an accessory or two – a ribbon here, a handkerchief there – but they lacked the wherewithal to expand their wardrobes in substantial ways. Even if they managed to come up with a bit of disposable income, the abject urban poor could not store clothing in crowded rented rooms or on the street without running the risk of it being stolen, which is why they were known to walk around with everything they owned on their back. It can hardly be said that these unfortunates – or those who did not even have a small stock of clothing to guard – participated in anything like a consumer revolution.

The social limits of consumption were even more clearly demarcated in the case of household furniture and furnishings, many of which were expensive. Among the poorest of inventoried households, we find families living in a single room with a shared bed and perhaps a mirror, table linens, and a cheap print for decoration. This group did not have the purchasing power to acquire the kinds of furniture and decorative objects found in wealthier homes, such as armchairs, cupboards, and porcelain.[48] By the end of the eighteenth century, ordinary Londoners who rented furnished lodgings could expect to find a bed with curtains, quilts, and counterpanes as well as mirrors and teakettles, but it would be a stretch to say such rooms were fashionably appointed. Even in the better rooms, furnishings were usually second-hand and damaged.[49]

In the countryside, all but the wealthiest peasants were excluded from the acquisition of new furnishings. The chairs, tables, chests of drawers,

---

[48] Pardailhé-Galabrun, *The Birth of Intimacy*; Sarti, *Europe at Home*, 101; Weatherill, *Consumer Behaviour and Material Culture in Britain*, 109.

[49] John Styles, "Lodging at the Old Bailey," in Styles and Vickery, eds., *Gender, Taste, and Material Culture in Britain and North America*, 61–80.

ceramic dishes, and cutlery that were piling up in the multiroom homes of well-off landholders remained notably absent in the interiors of the rural poor. Girolamo Cirelli, an affluent citizen of Rimini, was shocked when he visited a peasant family in the country and discovered that they

do not use a table cloth, but only a coarse cloth, which is really only a piece of canvass with a hem coloured dark blue that does not even cover the table. They have no napkins, and wipe their mouths with the sleeve of their jackets or shirts. They eat with neither fork nor spoon, in place of which they use a slice of bread taken from the table where they eat, which is covered with pots still filthy with ashes, and even the cauldron. They keep the bread in a pile in the middle of the table ... They put meat in the plate used for their soup, and they break it up with their hands ... Similarly, they put the wine in the middle of the table and they all indiscriminately drink from the same jug.[50]

In the case of food and drink, the picture is mixed as well. To be sure, some of the most widely diffused items of the consumer revolution were colonial products such as coffee, tea, sugar, and tobacco. In the bustling port of Amsterdam, adding sugar to hot drinks became so entrenched in the common diet that the City Orphanage provided ever greater quantities of the sweet crystal to its destitute charges as part of a minimum standard of food provision. Even more than hot drinks mixed with sugar, tobacco became a plebeian good, a sociable wonder drug shared in taverns that could stave off hunger, thirst, and cold, a miraculous effect for soldiers, peasants, and artisans who could not depend on a steady supply of calories and were often exposed to the elements. And yet, even the limits to the consumption of these colonial products were evident. The poor usually ingested low-quality, adulterated, or second-hand versions of these commodities. They purchased used coffee grounds in secondary markets and made do with contraband tea and tobacco cut with everything from ash to dirt. The use of elaborate porcelain and silver equipment associated with the new hot drinks and snuff did not extend beyond the elites and middling classes who were sure to employ such props in elaborate performances of polite sociability.

In some ways, consumption was growing in a society that was becoming *more* unequal, not less (as McKendrick had originally argued). The social polarization that had intensified during the century and half before 1650 may have attenuated between 1650 and 1750, but it would return

---

[50] Quoted in Sarti, *Europe at Home*, 148–149. Alexander Hamilton was similarly disgusted by the crude dining habits of a ferry keeper's family: "They had no cloth upon the table, and the mess was in a dirty, deep wooden dish which they evacuated with their hands ... They used neither knife, fork, spoon, plate, or napkin because, I suppose, they had none to use." Quoted in Kathleen Brown, *Foul Bodies: Cleanliness in Early America* (New Haven, CT, 2009), 118.

thereafter. In the countryside, large landowners exploited rising grain prices, while the lesser peasantry struggled to maintain its position on the land.[51] In cities, wealthy aristocrats and financiers moved to new neighborhoods, built stylish residences, and installed the latest furnishings, while increasing numbers of ordinary people crowded into one-room dwellings in poor areas. The divide between those who participated in the rise of consumption and those who did not appears to have been widening, a troubling dimension of the "consumer revolution" that, overlooked by earlier celebratory accounts, strongly resonates today.

The second potent objection to the consumer revolution thesis is that the sudden changes we associate with the eighteenth century had in fact been developing for two or three centuries. Much of the historical literature on eighteenth-century consumption implicitly contrasts the dynamism of that century with the purportedly stagnant eras that preceded it. Indeed, the very metaphor of a "revolution" is predicated on the notion of a preceding "old regime" of consumption. However, it would be a grave mistake to assume that all was immobile and unchanging prior to 1700 or 1650. Long before the turn of the eighteenth century, two powerful agents of change – urban development and court culture – were already generating new forms of consumption. Historians disagree on which of these two agents of change was more consequential. Jan de Vries makes a distinction between a fading "old luxury," which took the form of aristocratic conspicuous consumption, and an intensifying "new luxury," which was an urban phenomenon defined by privacy and comfort.[52] Linda Levy Peck rejects this distinction, emphasizing the overlap between the two types of consumption.[53] I would argue that the categories of "old" and "new" luxury – or what I call courtly and modern forms of consumption – overlapped but are still useful concepts.

In the rural society of the Middle Ages (500–1400), the world of goods was relatively small. Only the wealthiest landowners owned luxury goods. High clerics in the Roman Catholic Church wore colorful, sumptuous clothing to project holiness and power; their gold and silver vestments set them apart from the rest of society. Some feudal lords owned jewels and expensive garments, but they spent most of their wealth on service and hospitality, shoring up their status by maintaining large

---

[51] Philip Hoffman, David S. Jacks, Patricia A. Levin, and Peter H. Lindert, "Sketching the Rise of Real Inequality in Early Modern Europe," in Robert Allen, Tommy Bengtsson, and Martin Dribe, eds., *Living Standards in the Past: New Perspectives on Well-Being in Asia and Europe* (Oxford, 2005), 131–172.

[52] de Vries, *The Industrious Revolution*, 44–45.

[53] Linda Levy Peck, *Consuming Splendor: Society and Culture in Seventeenth-Century England* (Cambridge, 2005).

numbers of retainers and honoring guests with extravagant feasts of fresh game cooked with exotic spices. Such potlatch-style splurges reinforced social bonds more effectively than the steady accumulation of durable goods. Furniture was sparse when portability was a priority. What few durable goods existed were handed down through the generations.

During the Renaissance, service and hospitality continued to define elite expenditure in many rural areas, but the process of urbanization and the expansion of trade stimulated the circulation of consumer goods. If the term Renaissance evokes the rebirth of the arts in the age of da Vinci and Michelangelo, that art was an integral part of a wider mercantile culture that reveled in the consumption of fine objects. Thanks to the spread of urban markets and to increasing concentrations of merchants, professionals, and artisans, towns provided greater access to goods and stimulated the growth of a material culture based on fine craftsmanship. The skills with which artisans created objects came to mean just as much, if not more, than the value of the raw materials from which such objects were made. In northern Italy, nobles privatized the ancient principle of public "magnificence" by abandoning fortress homes and joining the newly rich in spending lavishly on residential architecture. They also accumulated large quantities of exquisitely crafted durable goods (including works of art) that radiated splendor. In the textile town of Florence, where wool and silk producers abounded, fashion-conscious elites invested huge sums of money in their wardrobes. In the middle of the fifteenth century, almost 40 percent of the inventoried property belonging to one well-connected clan, the Pucci family, consisted of clothing and jewelry worn for special occasions.[54] Thus, one historian of material culture concludes, "The seeds of our own ... bravura consumerism were planted in the European Renaissance."[55]

A similar concern for dress would soon appear north of the Alps in the German lands, the Netherlands, northern France, and England, which imported luxury goods from Italy and began making many of their own. Even in northern Protestant towns where, according to German sociologist Max Weber, Protestant values prescribed austerity, wealthy burgers did not hesitate to wear fashionable clothes as long as their appearance remained within the bounds of decency.[56] In the seventeenth century, urban luxury markets thrived in the Protestant north. Holland could

---

[54] Carole Collier Frick, *Dressing Renaissance Florence: Families, Fortunes, and Fine Clothing* (Baltimore, 2002), 111.

[55] Lisa Jardine, *Wordly Goods: A New History of the Renaissance* (London, 1996), 34. It must be added, however, that such consumerism provoked a major backlash in the form of sumptuary laws.

[56] Ulinka Rublack, *Dressing Up: Cultural Identity in Renaissance Europe* (Oxford, 2010).

hardly have enjoyed a "Golden Age" had Dutch consumers adhered strictly to Calvinistic anti-luxury rhetoric. Meanwhile, London merchants tailored foreign goods from Europe and Asia for an elite home market; even the English Civil War seems not to have weakened demand for finery.[57] Undoubtedly, the flowering of urban life before the eighteenth century established patterns in consumption that anticipated the transformations to come.[58]

In addition to the burgeoning of urban life during the Renaissance, the emergence of sumptuous royal courts in the sixteenth and seventeenth centuries unleashed a burst of luxury consumption. The development of royal courts in Europe has long attracted the attention of sociologists. In 1912, Werner Sombart argued that modern capitalism was born in the courts of early modern Europe – the "child of luxury."[59] Norbert Elias advanced an equally court-centered but different line of argument that would become enormously influential once his work was translated into French and English in the 1970s.[60] In *The Court Society*, Elias borrowed the concept of "conspicuous consumption" from Thorstein Veblen, an American sociologist who had coined the term to describe how the nouveau riche of late nineteenth-century America flagrantly (and, for Veblen, crassly) displayed their extravagant consumption in order to gain social status.[61] Veblen had also suggested, following sociologist Georg Simmel's theory of fashion, that upper-class norms of consumption extended their influence "down through the social structure to the lowest strata. The result is that members of each stratum accept as their ideal of decency the scheme of life in vogue in the next higher stratum, and bend their energies to live up to that ideal."[62] Elias applied these ideas to the court of Louis XIV, where conspicuous consumption was "an indispensable instrument in maintaining social position, especially when – as is actually the case in this court society – all members of the society are involved in a ceaseless struggle for status and privilege." For Elias, forms

[57] Levy Peck, *Consuming Splendor*, ch. 6.
[58] For works calling attention to changes in consumption before the eighteenth century, see Levy Peck, *Consuming Splendor*; Rublack, *Dressing Up*; Schama, *The Embarrassment of Riches*; and, for Italy, Collier Frick, *Dressing Renaissance Florence*; Richard Goldthwaite, *Wealth and the Demand for Art in Italy, 1300–1600* (Baltimore, 1993); Jardine, *Wordly Goods*; Evelyn Welch, *Shopping in the Renaissance: Consumer Cultures in Italy 1400–1600* (New Haven, CT, 2005).
[59] Werner Sombart, *Luxury and Capitalism*, trans. W. R. Dittmar (Ann Arbor, MI, 1967).
[60] Norbert Elias, *The Civilizing Process: The History of Manners*, trans. Edmund Jephcott (Oxford, 2000).
[61] Norbert Elias, *The Court Society*, trans. Edmund Jephcott (New York, 1983); Thorstein Veblen, *The Theory of the Leisure Class* (1899; New York, 1975).
[62] Veblen, *The Theory of the Leisure Class*, 84.

of courtly consumption "constantly percolated downwards" to inferior groups who attempted to imitate their superiors.[63] This theory of social emulation had a powerful impact on the field. As we have seen, McKendrick adopted a version of it in the 1980s to explain why England experienced a consumer revolution in the eighteenth century.

We will have occasion to reconsider the emulation thesis in Chapter 4, for this model of cultural trickle-down only partially explains the development of middling-class consumption in the eighteenth century. The point here is that royal courts played a key role in early modern luxury consumption. In the Middle Ages, medieval kings had been surrounded by small circles of vassals and clerics, while the rest of the nobility remained on their countryside estates. This began to change in the sixteenth century when Italian and Burgundian ducal courts began to patronize the arts, broaden their circles of courtiers, and instill new codes of civilized behavior. Civility manuals like Castiglione's *Book of the Courtier* (1528) instructed readers on how to dress, converse, and dine gracefully in polite company. Such attention to appearance and bodily control intensified over the course of the seventeenth century, culminating in the French royal palace at Versailles, where Louis XIV (r. 1643–1715) surrounded himself with as many as 5,000 nobles, including ambassadors from all over Europe and several hundred of France's highest aristocrats (see Figure 1.6). The scale and social dynamics of this court were qualitatively different from the small French and Italian courts that had preceded it.

The luxury on display at Versailles was, and still is, legendary. The largest and most magnificent secular building in Europe when it was built, the palace abounded with elegant tapestries, wondrous mirrors, and allegorical paintings – all glorifying the king. "Everything is divinely furnished; everything is magnificent," enthused courtier Madame de Sévigné of the king's "beautiful apartment."[64] Surrounding the palace were elaborate gardens where sumptuously clad nobles strolled amidst majestic fountains. Dress was taken very seriously. Louis XIV designated a corps of special officers to take care of his clothing and shoes, which were kept in three rooms on the ground floor of the château. Every morning, in the first of many of the day's ceremonies, the grand master of the wardrobe ritualistically dressed the king before a crowd of nobles, handing the sovereign his doublet, jacket, coat, and sword, while the masters of the wardrobe gave him his handkerchief, gloves, hat, cane,

---

[63] Elias, *The Court Society*, 56 n.30, 63–65.
[64] Madame de Sévigné to Madame de Grignan, July 29, 1676, in Project Gutenberg's Lettres de Madame de Sévigné, www.gutenberg.org/files/43901/43901-h/43901-h.htm, accessed July 8, 2021.

Figure 1.6 After Hyacinthe Rigaud, *Portrait of Louis XIV*.
Copyright Getty Images. The Sun King, shown here displaying a sumptuous robe, a flowing wig, elegant stockings, and brilliant accessories (sword, scepter, crown, and silver-buckled shoes with bright red talons), set the standard for fashion at the French court and beyond

Pl. I.

LE SEIGNEUR ET LA DAME DE COUR.

Figure 1.7 Nicolas Dupin, *Le seigneur et la dame de cour*, from *Costumes François*, 1776. Bibliothèque nationale de France. The caption of this etching reminded viewers that only high born lords with titles have the right to wear refined clothes, and that ladies of the court "are always obliged to appear in the most brilliant radiance. The richest cloth, the most elegant gold, stones, and carriages are her domain."

and, in cool weather, his muff and scarf. The king's courtiers attended in turn to their own wardrobes, making sure that they were dressed in fashionable styles with the finest textiles (see Figure 1.7). Men wore the silk or velvet coat known as the *habit habillé*, adorned with jewelry and embroidery, while women donned the *grand habit de cour*, an embroidered dress with a whale-boned bodice (to impose erect posture), puffy sleeves, a skirt worn over a hoop, and a train whose length was determined by the wearer's rank. Such material display did not merely reflect status, it constituted it.

The purpose of such extravagance was not comfort. Hot and humid in the summer, cold and drafty in the winter, Versailles could be a surprisingly *un*comfortable place to live. The aim of such splendor was to project the power and glory of Louis XIV across Europe, to elevate the court above the rest of society, and to establish a hierarchy of status that the king could manipulate for his own political benefit.

Court life contributed to broader developments in consumption in three basic ways. First, courtly consumption stimulated a preoccupation for fashion as a marker of social status. In the competitive political environment of Versailles and other European courts (in Madrid, Vienna, St. Petersburg, etc.), courtiers put a premium on dressing in the latest styles. The cultural credit derived from fashion could be quickly converted into political power. According to one seventeenth-century court manual, fine dress that gained the approval of high-ranking grandées could "open doors often closed to those of high status."[65] For the would-be courtier, the trick was to follow the dictates of fashion while avoiding extremes that could invite ridicule. This dangerous game required insider information, the kind of knowledge provided by well-placed patrons at court. As Antoine de Courtin noted, "fashion has two vicious extremes: the excess of negligence and the excess of affectation; both make people appear ridiculous. To avoid this inconvenient peculiarity, one must go back to the source of fashion which is the Court."[66]

Second, courtly consumption led to a boom in the luxury trades. Thanks to its skilled craftsmen and access to eastern markets in the Levant, Italy had dominated the luxury trades during the Renaissance. But as the French court blossomed in the seventeenth century, France displaced Italy to become Europe's leading producer of luxury goods, which ranged from clothing and jewelry to furniture and decorative objects to a host of what we would today call "personal care" products (cosmetics, perfumes, wigs, etc.). Under the energetic direction of Jean-Baptiste Colbert, Louis XIV's powerful finance minister, the French state actively promoted a process of import substitution by which highly skilled foreign artisans were recruited to work in well-subsidized royal

---

[65] Quoted in Clare Haru Crowston, *Credit, Fashion, Sex: Economies of Regard in Old Regime France* (Durham, NC, 2013), 100.

[66] Quoted in Frédérique Leferme-Falguières, "Corps modelé, corps contraint: les courtisans et les normes du paraître à Versailles," in Mathieu da Vinha, Catherine Lanoë, and Bruno Laurioux, eds., *Cultures de cour, cultures du corps, XIVe–XVIIIe siècle* (Paris, 2011), 132.

manufactories in France to produce high-end brands (Sèvres porcelain, Gobelins tapestries, Saint-Gobain mirrors, etc.). As European sovereigns embellished their courts in the eighteenth century, luxury production spread across the continent. In Neuwied on the Rhine, Abraham and David Roentgen ran one of Europe's most successful cabinetmaking enterprises, producing intricate furniture for eminent kings and queens, including Louis XVI and Marie Antoinette of France, Frederick William II of Prussia, and Catherine the Great of Russia.

Third, courtly consumption spilled over into cities in the late seventeenth and eighteenth centuries, which propelled luxury consumption to new heights. During the period of the Regency (1715–1723), the French royal court moved to the capital, galvanizing the city's luxury markets. As aristocrats who frequented the court settled in Paris, they built stone townhouses in fashionable neighborhoods, bought clothing from specialized fashion retailers, and liberally provisioned their households with an enormous variety of food.[67] In Germany, the influence of princely courts likewise extended to nobles and wealthier bourgeois in towns and the surrounding countryside.[68] Ultimately, with the passage of time, some of the "civilized" luxuries invented at European courts reached the urban laboring classes. In Antwerp, as noted earlier, the use of the fork was widespread among craftsmen and skilled laborers by the 1730s.[69] Thus, courtly consumption did spread to urban environments, although, as we shall see, townspeople often attributed meanings to goods that were different from those originally created at court.

The steady growth of urban and courtly consumption before 1700 belies any notion of a clean rupture between consumption in the eighteenth century and the preceding period. This is why some historians prefer the adjective "evolution" to "revolution" when describing long-term changes in early modern consumption. While scholars certainly need to give earlier developments their due, they should not lose sight of the distinctive features of the late seventeenth and eighteenth centuries. In the earlier period, from 1500 to 1650, the cost of housing and food staples in many European countries rose much faster than the price of nonstaple luxury goods, deepening the inequalities inherited from the Middle Ages. As the European population climbed, competition for work increased and real wages declined, a process that hurt the poor

---

[67] Natacha Coquery, *L'hôtel aristocratique: Le marché du luxe à Paris au XVIIIe siècle* (Paris, 1998); Natacha Coquery, *Tenir Boutique à Paris au XVIIIe siècle* (Paris, 2011); Robert Fox and Anthony Turner, eds., *Luxury Trades and Consumerism in Ancien Régime Paris* (Aldershot, 1998).

[68] North, *"Material Delight and the Joy of Living,"* 76.

[69] Blondé, "Cities in Decline and the Dawn of a Consumer Society."

even as it benefited the rich, who could now more easily afford to hire workers and servants. The result was that the wealthy who rented out excess land and urban property enjoyed a greater capacity to consume, whereas the poor had to devote higher shares of their meager income to food. In this particular economic environment, which was hampered by the strongest phase of the Little Ice Age, a period of cooling that impeded the growth of crops and the survival of livestock, the social limits to expanding consumption were considerable. Consumption certainly grew by medieval standards but only among a relatively small proportion of the population, a group dominated by courtiers, nobles, financiers, and wealthier merchants.[70]

As we explore in the next chapter, many of these economic constraints would ease between 1650 and 1800, enabling a more thoroughgoing transformation in consumption as the volume of goods increased, their variety widened, and their social reach deepened. More kinds of consumer goods circulated than ever before, touching a broader swathe of society. As nobles, financiers, and merchants continued to acquire luxuries, a throng of professionals, lesser traders, skilled artisans, independent farmers, and upper-strata peasants began to consume a host of goods beyond the usual staples. Some of these goods originated at court such as the fork; others were introduced at middling or plebeian social levels such as the tobacco pipe. Taken together, they significantly expanded an intermediate zone of consumption situated between aristocratic luxury and popular necessity. Although many urban and rural laborers remained excluded from this zone of consumption, it nevertheless grew dramatically in the eighteenth century as production and trade flourished in Europe and across many parts of the globe.

---

[70] Hoffman, Jacks, Levin, and Lindert, "Sketching the Rise of Real Inequality in Early Modern Europe." Even Goldthwaite, *Wealth and the Demand for Art in Italy*, 47–48, who emphasizes the relatively broad distribution of wealth in Renaissance Italy, carefully states that Italy did not experience "the kind of effective demand that produced the consumer revolution in eighteenth-century England and France."

There has never been any event as important for the human race in general and for the peoples of Europe in particular, as the discovery of the new world and the passage to the Indies around the Cape of Good Hope. It was then that began a revolution in commerce, in the power of nations, in morals, industry, and government of all the peoples. It was at this moment that men in the most distant countries became necessary to one another: the produce of equatorial regions were consumed by those in polar climes; northern industry was transported to the south; the cloths of the Orient dressed the west, and everywhere men exchanged their opinions, their laws, their customs, their medicines, their illnesses, their virtues and their vices. Everything has changed and must go on changing.[1]

How to explain the surge of consumption from 1650 to 1800? The simplest possible explanation – that a full-blown revolution in the mode of production suddenly improved living standards – must be ruled out. Mechanized, steam-powered production appeared only at the tail end of the period, and factory workers did not reap major benefits from industrialization until the final third of the nineteenth century. During the early modern period, gains in productivity (the rate of economic output) were limited because much production, though not all, continued to be based on age-old agricultural and artisanal techniques. No revolution in production brought about the revolution in consumption.

If the growth of consumption cannot be attributed to a revolution in productivity, then what did cause it? Historians have yet to settle on a firm answer, but they agree that the early modern economy was anything but static. A combination of factors appears to have stimulated European consumption. Incremental but important developments in agriculture, industry, and intra-European commerce, together with remarkably

---

[1] Guillaume-Thomas-François Raynal, *Histoire philosophique et politique des établissements et du commerce des Européens dans les deux Indes*, vol. 1 (Amsterdam, 1770), 1–2. Adam Smith borrowed from this passage in *The Wealth of Nations*, vol. 2, R. H. Campbell and A. S. Skinner, eds. (Indianapolis, IN, 1981), 626.

strong growth in one initially minor sector – overseas trade – dramatically expanded the volume and variety of goods available to consumers.

Incremental Change

Economic change depended in part on the relationship between towns and the countryside. Although rates of urbanization remained low throughout the early modern period – only 12 percent of Europeans lived in urban areas by 1800 – a number of large cities developed over the course of the seventeenth and eighteenth centuries as the European population increased to 190 million people. Once concentrated in the Mediterranean region (notably Italy), the continent's urban population shifted north to the Netherlands, England, Belgium, northern France, and the western German lands. Over the course of the seventeenth century, Amsterdam soared from a town of 60,000 to a city of 235,000. In the following century, Moscow grew to 300,000, Vienna swelled to 247,000, Paris nearly doubled to 700,000–800,000, and London skyrocketed to a staggering 950,000. Meanwhile, port cities on the North Sea and Atlantic (Hamburg, Bristol, Bordeaux, etc.) mushroomed.

In rural areas surrounding cities, towns, and ports, agriculture became increasingly specialized as peasants and farmers concentrated their efforts on a single activity, say, growing grain or raising livestock, rather than following traditional risk-averse customs of supplying their families with a variety of necessities. More capital-intensive and oriented to urban and foreign markets, such specialization led to gains in agricultural productivity and freed up labor for industry in towns. Thus, even if the rate of urban development rose slowly across Europe and even though no full-scale agricultural revolution took place, a new urban–rural dynamic favorable to both agricultural and industrial production – and to maritime commerce – appears to have been taking shape in many regions of Europe.[2]

If, thanks to specialization and the reclamation of land, agricultural output was able to keep pace with a rising population, industrial production and trade fared better. By one estimate, per capita GDP rose 25 percent between 1500 and 1800, thanks mostly to the development

---

[2] Robert Allen, "Progress and Poverty in Early Modern Europe," *The Economic History Review* (EHR)56 (August 2003), 403–443; Philip Hoffman, *Growth in a Traditional Society: The French Countryside, 1450–1815* (Princeton, NJ, 1996). Even in Spain, where the consumption of new goods rose more slowly than in northwestern Europe, "the countryside became more integrated with larger networks of distribution." Regina Grafe, *Distant Tyranny: Markets, Power, and Backwardness in Spain, 1650–1800* (Princeton, NJ, 2012), 208.

of nonagricultural sectors of the economy.[3] In the industrial sector, the industries that would go on to play an important role in the Industrial Revolution – textiles, metalwork, and coal mining – all underwent gradual expansion in the eighteenth century. But equally important was the manufacture of luxury and semiluxury goods in towns. Laboring in workshops and often organized into guilds, a slew of artisans, from cabinetmakers to seamstresses, offered an increasingly wide array of goods to their customers. Daniel Roche estimates that in eighteenth-century Paris alone as many as 15,000 craftsmasters and 20,000 workers were engaged in the manufacture of clothing.[4] Words like "guild" and "craftsman" may evoke romantic images of premodern artisans making things in small shops in an uncompetitive commercial environment, but the production of many goods, such as carriages (now seen in towns all over Europe), involved sophisticated systems of credit, subcontracting, and marketing. The skilled craft production that had taken root in Renaissance Italy flowered in the commercial centers of eighteenth-century Europe before the onset of industrialization.

Industry also grew because of changes in the labor market. There is an old debate among economic historians about wage growth during the early decades of the Industrial Revolution. Optimists argued that wages were rising in the late eighteenth and early nineteenth century as industrialization benefited workers. Pessimists claimed that wages remained stagnant as workers were subjected to miserable working conditions. Today, it is fair to say that the pessimists have not only won the debate but have pushed the chronology of stagnation back into the early modern era. Aggregating large sets of data, economic historians have demonstrated that real wages – the value of pay after accounting for inflation – largely stagnated across Europe from the sixteenth to the eighteenth centuries.[5] But if pessimists have won the battle, they seem to have lost the war, for households were accumulating more and more stuff over the course of this very period, especially from the second half of the seventeenth century onward.

[3] Jan Luiten van Zanden, "Early Modern Economic Growth: A Survey of the European Economy, 1500–1800," in Maarten Prak, ed., *Early Modern Capitalism: Economic and Social Change in Europe, 1400–1800* (London, 2001), 79–80.
[4] Daniel Roche, *The Culture of Clothing: Dress and Fashion in the Ancien Régime*, trans. Jean Birrell (Cambridge, 1996), 279.
[5] Jan de Vries, *The Industrious Revolution: Consumer Behavior and the Household Economy, 1650 to the Present* (Cambridge, 2008). For a more optimistic picture in the case of France, see Colin Jones and Rebecca Spang, "*Sans-culottes, sans café, sans tabac*: Shifting Realms of Necessity and Luxury in Eighteenth-Century France," in Maxine Berg and Helen Clifford, eds., *Consumers and Luxury: Consumer Culture in Europe 1650–1850* (Manchester, 1999), 37–62.

Such evidence begs the question: How could consumption rise among the middling and laboring classes while wages remained frozen and households continued to devote roughly the same proportion of their budgets to goods?[6] One possible answer, proposed by Jan de Vries, is that Europe experienced an "industrious revolution" in the eighteenth century.[7] Even if wages were not going up, he argues, it was possible for households to acquire more things because members of households – especially women and children – began to do more paid labor. First, the number of work days in a year rose following the Protestant Reformation as countries reduced the number of religious holidays. Even in Catholic areas, the number of saint's days gradually declined, as did the popular tradition of taking "Saint Monday" off from work. The elimination of holidays "*enabled* the expansion of the work year by more than 20 percent, from 250–60 to a maximum of 307 days per year."[8] Another development that encouraged industriousness was proto-industry, a form of production by which rural laborers did industrial work in their homes. Proto-industry became widespread in the textile industry, where merchants paid country folk to spin and weave wool, cotton, and flax at home, bringing countless women and children into the paid labor force. Rural women and children, who had always worked in farming, now became increasingly engaged in market labor, earning extra cash for the household.

Driving this intensification of labor, de Vries contends, was the lure of consumption. It was the desire for new fashionable goods that led households to make the collective decision to earn more (but not necessarily higher) wages in order to expand their purchasing power. Take the example of the Lathams of Scarisbrick in southwest Lancashire, England.[9] Small farmers with nineteen acres of land, Richard and Nany Latham spent very little money when their daughters were young.

---

[6] Carole Shammas, "Changes in English and Anglo-American Consumption from 1550 to 1800," in John Brewer and Roy Porter, eds., *Consumption and the World of Goods* (London, 1994), 188, concludes that the proportion of wealth in consumer goods of English households remained constant in the eighteenth century.

[7] The so-called industrious revolution was one of many revolutions attributed to the early modern period, including the military, scientific, agricultural, financial, reading, retail, and of course consumer revolutions. Whether or not the term revolution applies in all cases, its proliferation in the historiography reflects what historians now see as the dynamism of the early modern period – what de Vries aptly called "the revolt of the early modernists."

[8] de Vries, *The Industrious Revolution*, 88. See also Hans-Joachim Voth, "Work and the Sirens of Consumption in Eighteenth-Century London," in Marina Bianchi, ed., *The Active Consumer: Novelty and Surprise in Consumer Choice* (London, 1998), 143–173.

[9] John Styles, *The Dress of the People: Everyday Fashion in Eighteenth-Century England* (New Haven, CT, 2007), ch. 14.

But when the children entered adolescence, the couple bought three wheels for spinning cotton, presumably for Nany and her daughters, and the family's income and expenditure increased. Although the couple shied away from buying luxuries like the fancy tea sets that they must have seen in shops, they did purchase a few high-quality gowns of damask and printed cotton for their two eldest daughters. They also bought sundry accessories for the entire family, from shag hats, silk handkerchiefs, and white aprons to books, tobacco pipes, and cutlery. Such consumption-driven proto-industry seems to have been happening on a broad scale in rural areas of western Europe where the textile industry was developing.

In addition to agriculture and industry, trade in raw materials, manufactured goods, and services within Europe also modestly expanded. Several products circulated across the expanse of Europe. The breadbasket that stretched from Ukraine to Poland to Prussia provisioned northwestern Europe with grain by way of the southern Baltic. Herds of cattle were also driven east to west, from the plains of Poland and western Russia through the German lands to France and the Netherlands. The Baltic states sent wood to western European countries to supply their growing navies, while western Europeans sent back salt for the preservation of fish. French wines passed to the Dutch Republic and northern Germany, as Spanish wool was shipped to France and Holland. Along the European coast, captains piloted innumerable small ships from port to port, from Livorno to Bordeaux to Hamburg, just as watermen navigated the great rivers of Europe from the Gironde to the Danube to connect distant provinces. Thousands of periodic rural fairs and regular urban markets assured a vital wholesale trade, while unprecedented numbers of retail outlets proliferated to deliver goods and services to consumers. In towns, permanent shops offering everything from shoe buckles to ribbons competed with market stalls; in the countryside, peddlers brought a variety of urban wares to rural villages and farmhouses. Despite the persistence of formidable geographical constraints to trade before the age of the railroad, steamship, and telegraph, the circulation of goods within Europe gradually expanded to widen the range of consumer goods on offer.

Global Trade

Still, the incremental growth of the intra-European economy between 1650 and 1800 cannot fully explain the rise of consumption. Neither the modest expansion of agricultural and industrial production nor the pick-up in trade between European nations can sufficiently account for the panoply of goods that merchants and retailers peddled. The industrious revolution was certainly important. Increases in paid labor boosted household purchasing power in an age of relatively stagnant wages, but even the industrious revolution, as powerful a theory as it is, does not explain everything. In central, southern, and Nordic Europe, where institutions reinforced the authority of husbands, women's engagement with the market labor remained circumscribed.[10] And, in an age of enduring poverty with rising rents and food costs, many families were working harder just to stay afloat. One Dutch historian found that for certain households, the extra wages wives earned could "mean the difference between starvation and survival." These households were indeed laboring harder in apparent conformity to the "industrious revolution" model but they were doing so merely to scrape by "rather than to increase their consumption."[11] Far from participating in new forms of consumption, a substantial fraction of the population, including farmhands and unskilled urban laborers, may have been working harder simply to subsist. We do not know exactly what fraction of the population fell into this unfortunate category, but it may have been as high as a third in northwestern Europe and even higher in other parts of the continent.

One additional factor that helps to explain the growth of consumption has recently received a great deal of attention: globalization.[12] While

---

[10] Sheilagh Ogilvie, "Consumption, Social Capital, and the 'Industrious Revolution' in Early Modern Germany," JEH 70 (June 2010), 287–325. But see Deborah Simonton, "Toleration, Liberty, and Privileges – Gender and Commerce in Eighteenth-Century European Towns," in Deborah Simonton, ed., *The Routledge History Handbook of Gender and the Urban Experience* (New York, 2017), 33–47.

[11] Elise van Nederveen Meerkerk, "Couples Cooperating? Dutch Textile Workers, Family Labour and the 'Industrious Revolution,' c. 1600–1800," *Continuity and Change* 23 (August 2008), 256, 261. See also, Belén Moreno Claverías, "L'inégalité comme norme: Modèles de consommation dans l'Espagne préindustrielle," in Antonio Escudero and Nicolas Marty, eds., *Consommateurs & consommation XVIIe–XXIe siècle: Regards franco-espagnols* (Perpignan, 2015), 18–19; Craig Muldrew, *Food, Energy, and the Creation of Industriousness: Work and Material Culture in Agrarian England, 1550–1780* (Cambridge, 2011); Julie Hardwick, "Fractured Domesticity in the Old Regime: Families and Global Goods in Eighteenth-Century France," AHR 124 (October 2019), 1267–1277, which emphasizes the fragility of households that labored to produce goods.

[12] Neil McKendrick, John Brewer, J. H. Plumb, *The Birth of a Consumer Society: The Commercialization of Eighteenth-Century England* (Bloomington, IN, 1982), hardly mentioned overseas trade, but Carole Shammas made it a focal point of *The Preindustrial Consumer in England and America* (Los Angeles, 1990). Recent syntheses include Pim de Zwart and Jan Luiten van Zanden, *The Origins of Globalization: World Trade and the Making of the Global Economy* (Cambridge, 2018); Anne Gerritsen and Giorgio Riello, eds., *The Global Lives of Things: The Material Culture of Connections in the Early Modern World* (New York, 2016); Beverly Lemire, *Global Trade and the Transformation of Consumer Cultures: The Material World Remade, c. 1500–1820* (Cambridge, 2018); Ina Baghdiantz McCabe, *A History of Global Consumption,*

agriculture, industry, and intra-European trade expanded gradually from 1650 to 1800, intercontinental trade between Europe, Asia, Africa, and the Americas grew by leaps and bounds, dramatically expanding the horizons of the European material world. Global trade introduced consumers to an array of products from distant lands: delicate porcelain and pungent tea from China; colorful cotton cloth from India; and mind-altering tobacco and coffee – taken with heaps of sugar – from the Americas (see Figure 2.1).

As the epigraph to this chapter suggests, the Abbé Raynal believed that globalization began with the arrival of Europeans in the Americas in 1492 and the opening of a direct sea route between Europe and Asia in 1501. But economic historians disagree with Raynal (and each other) about the exact chronology of world trade. Kevin O'Rourke and Jeffrey Williamson insist that globalization as measured by price convergence – the convergence of the prices of identical commodities in different markets around the world – did not occur until the nineteenth century with the transport and communications revolutions.[13] Alternatively, Dennis Flynn and Arturo Giráldez claim that globalization began in 1571, the year the city of Manila was founded and with it the establishment of an entrepôt that facilitated Pacific Ocean trade between Asia and the Americas, thereby completing the global circuit begun by the Atlantic crossing and the rounding of the Cape of Good Hope.[14] For Flynn and Giráldez, trade routes connecting the continents are what counts.

Following O'Rourke and Williamson, there is reason to be cautious about making too much of early modern world trade, for the value of intra-European and intra-Asian trade remained much higher than that of intercontinental trade throughout the period. Further, the wealthiest Europeans had for centuries enjoyed access to South and East Asian luxuries, thanks to the Silk Road that ran from Java and China to the Levant in the eastern Mediterranean to southern Europe. Nonetheless, between 1500 and 1800, rival European seaborne powers aggressively and often violently intervened in the Atlantic and Indian Ocean worlds to create long-distance maritime trade routes that circled the globe and connected the Americas, Europe, Asia, and Africa as never before.

1500–1800 (New York, 2015); Frank Trentmann, *Empire of Things: How We Became a World of Consumers, from the Fifteenth Century to the Twenty-First* (New York, 2016).

[13] Kevin O'Rourke and Jeffrey Gale Williamson, "When Did Globalisation Begin?" *European Review of Economic History* 6 (April 2002), 23–50.

[14] Dennis Flynn and Arturo Giráldez, "'Born with a Silver Spoon': The Origin of World Trade in 1571," JWH 6 (1995), 201–221. See also C. A. Baily, *The Birth of the Modern World, 1780–1914* (Malden, MA, 2004); and A. G. Hopkins, ed., *Globalization in World History* (New York, 2002).

Figure 2.1 François Boucher, *Le déjeuner*, 1739.
Copyright Getty Images. In a rococo sitting room bathed in morning light, a
limonadier (coffee-seller) serves coffee or chocolate to an affectionate bourgeois
family who are indulging in a breakfast ritual that is fast taking shape in the
eighteenth century. The Chinese statuette and teapot against the rear wall, the
red lacquered table holding porcelain cups and saucers, and the blue and white
Chinese-style vase (far left) evince an interest in the exotic

"For the first time in human history regular commercial contact connected the world's continents directly," creating new patterns in the flow of transcontinental goods.[15] Over the course of the early modern period, the growth rate of intercontinental trade was not merely higher than that of world population probably for the first time in history; it was four-times higher.[16] During the eighteenth century, in particular, European overseas trade reached new heights as it shifted from rare luxury goods to more popular semiluxuries and as it increasingly revolved around the plantation complex in the Americas. English exports and reexports to Africa and the Americas increased sixfold, while French overseas trade jumped tenfold. Although what Fernand Braudel aptly described as the "tyranny of distance" continued to throttle intercontinental trade, it is nevertheless possible to speak of a process of early modern globalization during which commercial connections across the planet both ramified and intensified.[17]

This is how it worked. From the sixteenth to the eighteenth century, a truly global circuit of trade formed after the discovery of silver deposits in the Spanish empire in the Americas (in the lands we call today Mexico, Peru, and Bolivia). Spanish colonists forced and paid indigenous Americans, Africans, and mixed-race creoles to mine silver, hefty cargoes of which were shipped to Europe where the precious metal added liquidity to a species-starved economy. However, most of the American silver that reached Europe did not remain there for long. European merchants – first the Iberians and then the Dutch, English, and French – were eager to circumvent the Italian and Mamluk middlemen who had long controlled European imports of Asian goods via the Mediterranean, so they opened an alternative long-distance sea route to Asia that ran around the African continent and across the Indian Ocean. Along this route they transported massive quantities of American silver to Asia, where they traded it for spices, raw silk, cotton textiles, porcelain, and tea. These

[15] Jan de Vries, "Connecting Europe and Asia: A Quantitative Analysis of the Cape-Route Trade, 1497–1795," in Dennis Flynn, Arturo Giráldez, and Richard von Glahn, eds., *Global Connections and Monetary History, 1470–1800* (Aldershot, 2003), 36.
[16] Ronald Findlay and Kevin O'Rourke, "Commodity Market Integration, 1500–2000," NBER Working Paper No. 8579 (November 2001), 16.
[17] Indeed, one did not have to wait for the nineteenth-century steamship for global integration, as Steven Topik argues with reference to the world coffee economy in "The Integration of the World Coffee Market," in William Gervase Clarence-Smith and Steven Topik, eds., *The Global Coffee Economy in Africa, Asia, and Latin America, 1500–1989* (Cambridge, 2003), 29. See de Zwart and van Zanden, *The Origins of Globalization*.

Asian goods were in turn shipped back around the Cape of Good Hope to Europe, where they were sold at great profit (see Figure 2.2).[18]

The links between continents did not stop there. Although many Asian imports were consumed in Europe, much of the Indian cloth that arrived there only grazed the continent's shores before being reexported to the Americas and Africa. On the west coast of Africa, discerning African rulers, merchants, and consumers coveted the cloth every bit as much as their European counterparts. In fact, at the height of the Atlantic slave trade in the eighteenth century, when some 6 million people were forced to leave Africa, British and French merchants used Indian cloth more than any other single item of trade to acquire African captives.[19] Exchanged for calico and other goods, African captives were shipped to American plantations, where they were enslaved and forced to produce large quantities of tropical commodities (sugar, tobacco, chocolate, and coffee) for European consumers. Fueled by a forced migration unprecedented in its scale and horror, the American plantation complex expanded so rapidly that by the middle of the eighteenth century, transatlantic commerce dwarfed that between Europe and Asia.

We are only beginning to take the full measure of the impact of globalization on European consumption. In the early days of the Euro-Asian trade, European merchants specialized in rare luxury products such as spices and silk, which had been consumed in Europe long before the sea route to Asia was established. Late medieval European elites had consumed large quantities of Southeast Asian spices, such as pepper, ginger, cinnamon, nutmeg, and cloves. More than simply enhancing flavor, the use of spices conferred social distinction, evoked fantasies of an "oriental" paradise, and were thought to provide medicinal benefits like improved digestion. Silk was also a late medieval Asian import. Imported from the Mongol empire, which spanned from China to Persia, exotic Asian silk graced the wardrobes of European monarchs

---

[18] There was also a direct silver route across the Pacific to Asia, but its volume did not match the one that ran through Europe.

[19] Philippe Haudrère, *La Compagnie française des Indes au XVIIIe siècle* (Paris, 2005); Joseph E. Inikori, "English versus Indian Cotton Textiles: The Impact of Imports on Cotton Textile Production in West Africa," in Giorgio Riello and Tirthankar Roy, eds., *How India Clothed the World: The World of South Asian Textiles, 1500–1800* (Leiden, 2009), 85–114; Herbert S. Klein, *The Atlantic Slave Trade* (Cambridge, 1999), 86–89; Colleen E. Kriger, "Guinea Cloth: Production and Consumption of Cotton Textiles in West Africa before and during the Atlantic Slave Trade," in Giorgio Riello and Prasannan Parthasarathi, eds., *The Spinning World: A Global History of Cotton Textiles, 1200–1850* (Oxford, 2011), 105–126; Anne Elizabeth Ruderman, "Supplying the Slave Trade: How Europeans Met African Demand for European Manufactured Products, Commodities and Re-exports, 1670–1790" (Dissertation, Yale University, 2016).

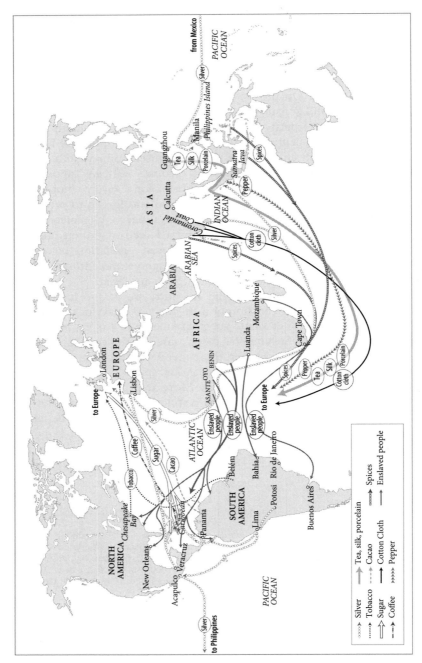

Figure 2.2 World Trade circa 1750: routes of select goods and enslaved human beings.

and elites, signaling power, status, and wealth. Silk was *the* quintessential luxury good.

Global trade changed over the course of the seventeenth and eighteenth centuries when the majority of the Asian trade was carried out by European East India Companies, state-sponsored trading companies that were precursors of today's multinational corporations. Established in 1602, the Dutch East India Company (VOC), a joint-stock company invested with formidable powers and monopolistic rights, aggressively overtook its rival, the Portuguese company, and built an empire in Indonesia. As a contemporary observer remarked, the VOC's success lay in "its being absolute, and invested with a kind of sovereignty and dominion, ... [it] makes peace and war at pleasure, and by its own authority; administers justice to all; ... settles colonies, builds fortifications, levies troops, maintains numerous armies and garrisons, fits out fleets, and coins money."[20] In a similar fashion, the British East India Company (EIC), founded by government charter in 1599, concentrated on expanding trade beyond the Cape of Good Hope, as did French, Danish, and Swedish trading companies founded later.

The trading companies continued the medieval tradition of importing spices and silks into Europe, but as demand for spices levelled off and as silk was increasingly produced in Italy and Spain, companies added several key goods to their commercial repertoire: porcelain, lacquerware, tea, and cotton cloth. Like spices and silks, the first two goods were luxuries whose cost severely limited their social reach in Europe. Porcelain, which could hold the new hot drinks of tea, chocolate, and coffee without cracking, was produced in Chinese manufactories using technologies that far surpassed European expertise. Already by the fourteenth century, the Chinese porcelain city of Jingdezhen was reputed to be the largest industrial site in the world with over 1,000 kilns that could fire up to 50,000 pieces at a time. Tapping into this source, the European East Indies companies imported over 70 million pieces of porcelain over the course of the seventeenth and eighteenth centuries.[21] These pieces added a touch of exotic elegance to royal palaces, aristocratic châteaux, and high-bourgeois townhouses in Europe. Much the same could be said of Japanese lacquerware, wooden furnishings (cabinets, boxes) coated with resin from sumac trees to add luster to their surface. Imported into

[20] Quoted in Jane Burbank and Frederick Cooper, *Empires in World History: Power and the Politics of Difference* (Princeton, NJ, 2010), 161.
[21] Maxine Berg, "Asian Luxuries and the Making of the European Consumer Revolution," in Maxine Berg and Elizabeth Eger, eds., *Luxury in the Eighteenth Century* (New York, 2003), 236–237.

Europe by the companies and marketed by high-end dealers, lacquer-ware brought the Far East into the parlors and bedrooms of wealthy European consumers.

In the late seventeenth and eighteenth centuries, European trading companies seized on two additional products from Asia – Indian cloth and Chinese tea – whose circulation would far surpass that of imported Asian luxuries both old (spices and silks) and new (porcelain and lac-querware). The success of the trade in cloth and tea is worth noting because economic historians have tended to dismiss Asian imports in this era as insignificant luxuries destined for the privileged few. Yet, the consumption of cloth and tea was far from negligible. It was largely due to the trade in these two popular consumer goods that, by the early 1770s, Asian imports amounted to no less than 11.5 percent of all international imports in Britain, France, and the Netherlands.[22]

Long before and well after the arrival of the first European vessels, India was the greatest textile producer in the world, its renowned cloth gracing markets from the islands of Southeast Asia to Islamic Persia to the Swahili ports of East Africa. It has been estimated that in 1750, the littoral of the Asian subcontinent produced as much as a quarter of the world's textile output, much of it for export. "India clothed the world."[23] The European traders who first approached Indian textile merchants in the early seventeenth century were but marginal figures in this vast market, which already touched many parts of the globe. They did not dream of reorganizing the entire region's system of labor and production, as their counterparts would do in the Americas. Rather, they established fortified trading enclaves on the coast and, with occasional military pressure, tapped into existing commercial structures. In this way, Europeans introduced "armed trading" into the Indian Ocean, a fore-runner of more coercive imperial interventions to come in the nineteenth century.[24]

Although Europeans came late to this global market, they wasted no time building their trade. At first, the VOC and the EIC only purchased Indian cotton fabric in order to exchange it for spices in Southeast Asia,

[22] de Vries, "Connecting Europe and Asia," 92.
[23] Giorgio Riello and Tirthankar Roy, "Introduction," in Giorgio Riello and Tirthankar Roy, eds., *How India Clothed the World: The World of South Asian Textiles, 1500–1800* (Leiden, 2009), 6.
[24] John E. Wills, Jr., "Maritime Asia, 1500–1800: The Interactive Emergence of European Domination," AHR 98 (February 1993), 83–105. The term "armed trading" was coined by K. N. Chaudhuri, *The Trading World of Asia and the English East India Company 1660–1760* (Cambridge, 1978), 110–116. But see Janice E. Thomson, *Mercenaries, Pirates, and Sovereigns: State-Building and Extraterritorial Violence in Early Modern Europe* (Princeton, NJ, 1994), ch. 2.

which the companies in turn sold on European markets. But company officials soon discovered that they could make substantial profits importing the cloth into their home countries and selling it to Europeans or reexporting it to Africa and the Americas. In exchange for silver from Central and South America, for there was little else Europeans could offer Asian merchants who had access to superior and less costly goods, the Dutch, English, and French companies hired Indian brokers to act as their intermediaries and placed large orders for cotton cloth. A cascading series of transactions followed. Brokers retained local merchants, who provided financial advances to artisanal weavers, who used the working capital to buy large quantities of raw materials and to support themselves while completing orders. Long experienced at adapting their products to the particular tastes of far-flung markets, Indian textile artisans were quick to tailor their cloth to European sensibilities. European company ships completed the circle by carrying Indian textiles back to Europe and exporting more silver to Asia.

In the late seventeenth century, what began as a trickle from East to West became a flood, as the import of handwrought Indian piece goods surged past spices to become the main object of company trade. In fashion-conscious Western Europe, a so-called Indian craze took hold of consumers who could not get enough of the fabric (see Figure 2.3). (Admittedly, scholars have shown that the term "craze" overstates the speed with which cotton was adopted, but there is no doubt that cotton was on the rise.) Together, the English and Dutch in the 1680s imported over a million pieces of Indian textiles annually, most of it cotton fabric; the French, headquartered in Pondicherry, brought in an additional 300,000 pieces by the 1730s.[25] Already by 1708, Daniel Defoe could trace the stealthy spread of calico: "it crept into our houses, our closets and bed-chambers; curtains, cushions, chairs and at last the beds themselves were nothing but Calicoes or Indian stuffs. In short, almost everything that used to be made of wool or silk, relating to the dress of women or the furniture of our houses, was supplied by the Indian trade."[26] Although Defoe was prone to polemical exaggeration, the fabric was

[25] Giorgio Riello, "The Globalization of Cotton Textiles: Indian Cottons, Europe, and the Atlantic World," in Giorgio Riello and Prasannan Parthasarathi, eds., *The Spinning World: A Global History of Cotton Textiles, 1200–1850* (Oxford, 2011), 265, table 13.1. For the French company, see Haudrère, *La Compagnie française*, 286–299. Styles, *The Dress of the People*, argues that the rise of cotton was more gradual than historians have suggested, but it was impressive nonetheless.

[26] Quoted in Prasannan Parthasarathi, "Rethinking Wages and Competitiveness in the Eighteenth Century: Britain and South India," *Past & Present* (PP) 158 (February 1998), 79. In fact, demand for cotton only gradually eclipsed that for more durable cloths such as linen. Styles, *The Dress of the People*, ch. 7.

Figure 2.3 Banyan.
Copyright Victoria and Albert Museum. This men's calico banyan produced
between 1750 and 1775 is composed of cotton chinz fabric from the Coromandel
Coast of southeast India, a global textile center. Made for the Western market and
tailored in the Netherlands or England in the style of a Japanese kimono, it was
designed to evoke a generic "orient"

successful enough to alarm European textile manufacturers, who lobbied
to ban its import. As a result, a series of embargoes were instituted across
western Europe, but the bans remained partial: the Dutch Republic
remained free of prohibitions; the French and British continued to reex-
port the cloth; and the British ban allowed certain varieties of Indian
cloth into the home market. Meanwhile, a vigorous contraband trade
developed to provide cloth to consumers in areas with strict domestic
prohibitions, such as France (see Figure 2.4).

Just as the calico bans were beginning to bite, European companies
turned to another Asian commodity that would become enormously
successful. Tea had been grown in China for centuries. When
European trading companies began shipping small quantities of the leaf
back to Europe in the seventeenth century, most elite consumers thought
of it as a rare, high-priced medicine (as they did coffee, tobacco, chocolate, and sugar). However, the tea trade took off after 1713, when China

Figure 2.4 Joseph Gabriel Maria Rossetti, *Manufacture de tissue d'indienne des frères Wetter*, 1764.

Copyright Getty Images. "Indian" cloth being produced in the town of Orange, located in the independent papal state of Comtat Venaissin, which was itself surrounded by French territory. Smuggling from the papal enclave into France was brisk before the French calico prohibition was lifted in 1759. Note the scale of production and the ubiquity of female workers

first allowed European companies direct access to its goods via the port of Canton. Already by 1718, Europeans were importing upward of 2 million pounds a year of the aromatic leaf into Europe, a figure that would climb to no less than 31 million pounds by 1790.[27] The demand for tea rose precipitously as the herb became integral to a cult of polite sociability that swept Europe during the Enlightenment. The rise in demand was met with an unprecedented surge in supply, as production of black tea in southeast China was ramped up in response to orders from European companies in Canton. As the supply rapidly increased, its purchasing price dropped, which in turn led to a fall in retail prices in Britain and the Dutch Republic. Although the British heavily taxed the import, the cheapest varieties of black tea like bohea were smuggled from

[27] Paul Butel, *Histoire du thé* (Paris, 1989), 59.

the European continent into England to offer modest households contraband tea at low prices.[28] As much as two-thirds of the tea consumed in Britain before 1784 was contraband from the Dutch Republic and northern France. Dutch traders also smuggled great quantities of contraband leaf into the British colonies in North America, where taking tea became routine among white colonists.[29]

This helps explain the furious pace at which tea was popularized in Britain, the Dutch Republic, and the North American colonies. As noted in Chapter 1, of all the household goods that were beginning to make their appearance in this period, tea accessories were among the most quickly adopted (see Figure 2.5). Yet, there is evidence that tea consumption rose not only among those who could afford fancy tea services but among the laboring classes as well. Carole Shammas does not hesitate to categorize tea in England as an article of "mass consumption," with annual per capita consumption at perhaps 2 pounds before 1784 and much higher thereafter (when taxes were drastically lowered). White settlers in North America consumed about 0.75 pounds a year.[30] The other country where tea drinking became common was the Dutch Republic. In Amsterdam, about half of the poor households affiliated with the City Orphanage owned at least one article for making tea by the middle of the eighteenth century. When tea kettles or even tea itself was too expensive, the poor could turn to the market in used leaves to make the drink at little cost or simply buy a single cup from one of the city's many petty retailers.[31] If in most of Europe tea consumption was limited to elites, in Britain, the Dutch Republic, and the German port city of Hamburg it reached into the lower echelons of society. In 1743, the merchants of Boulogne were astonished to report that "the taking of tea has spread so universally in England that the people, down to and including sailors and peasants, consume it at all hours of

---

[28] Coffee was even more heavily taxed, which partially explains why tea overtook coffee in Britain from the 1730s. Phil Withington, "Where Was the Coffee in Early Modern England?" *Journal of Modern History* (JMH) 92 (March 2020), 40–75.

[29] Chris Nierstrasz, *Rivalry for Trade in Tea and Textiles: The English and Dutch East India Companies (1700–1800)* (New York, 2015).

[30] Shammas, *The Pre-industrial Consumer in England and America*, 77, 104.

[31] Anne McCants, "Poor Consumers as Global Consumers: The Diffusion of Tea and Coffee Drinking in the Eighteenth century," EHR 61 (2008), 184. See also Bruno Blondé, "Cities in Decline and the Dawn of a Consumer Society: Antwerp in the 17th–18th Centuries," in Bruno Blondé and Natacha Coquery, eds., *Retailers and Consumer Changes in Early Modern Europe: England, France, Italy and the Low Countries* (Tours, 2005), 37–52; and Laura van Aert, "Vendre l'exotique au quotidien: L'implantation urbaine des magasins de produits coloniaux (tabac, thé, café et coton) à Anvers au XVIIIe siècle," *Histoire urbaine* 30 (2011), 41–65.

Figure 2.5 Richard Collins, *A Family of Three at Tea*, 1727.
Copyright Getty Images. The painter of this British family highlights the
elaborate equipment that accompanied tea-taking in affluent households,
including a sugar dish and tongs, a tea canister, a hot-water jug, a spoon
boat with teaspoons, a teapot, porcelain tea bowls, a slop bowl, and the tea
table itself

the day."[32] Although sweetened tea might have given such workers a
temporary boost, it was far less nutritious than traditional beer.

In 1492, the promise of a western sea route to the riches of Asia led to
the accidental "discovery" of the "New World." Although in economic
terms the Americas were first seen as insignificant compared to Asia,
European trade with the Americas would by the eighteenth century
overshadow that between Europe and Asia, the share of Atlantic trade
in total European imports amounting to "at least three times that of the

---

[32] Quoted in Butel, *Histoire du thé*, 84. For social diffusion of English groceries, see Jon
Stobart, *Sugar and Spice: Grocers and Groceries in Provincial England, 1650–1830* (Oxford,
2016), 194–195, 218, 221.

Asian trade."[33] In the two centuries following transatlantic contact, the most important American commodity was silver, which fueled the Asian trade, but the Americas offered a veritable cornucopia of goods, ranging from strange new foods (potatoes, maize, beans, and tomatoes) to furs (to be made into fashionable hats) to exotic woods (such as mahogany). By the middle of the eighteenth century, however, many of the most valuable American commodities – tobacco, sugar, coffee, cacao, and indigo – were cultivated by a brutal system of plantation slavery that would transform the Atlantic world.

Whereas European colonists in Asia tapped into indigenous commercial networks, sometimes by force, their counterparts in the Americas completely reorganized the region's system of production by establishing slave labor camps, "plantations," from Brazil to the Caribbean to southern North America. Plantation slavery wreaked havoc on the environment. Profit-hungry Caribbean planters cleared land and cultivated crops for export like sugarcane, pressing juice from the cane and boiling it in an industrialized process that consumed large swathes of forest. It was not long before whole islands, like Barbados, had been stripped bare. Sugar production gave rise to massive deforestation, which was followed by soil erosion, nutrient depletion, and the extinction of local plant and animal species, leaving a pockmarked landscape ideal for breeding disease-bearing mosquitoes.[34] Driven by escalating European consumer demand, the ecological catastrophe of the Caribbean plantation economy was a taste of things to come, a forerunner of the environmental disasters of climate change and extinctions unleashed by modern industrialization. In both cases, rising levels of consumption propelled large-scale environmental degradation.

As they ravaged the landscape, colonial enslavers ruthlessly exploited the labor of men and women of African descent. Initially, European planters extracted the labor of Native Americans and European indentured servants, but as indigenous people died from European diseases and conflict, and indentured servants became scarcer and more expensive, planters turned to a captive African labor force. While slavery had existed in Africa for centuries, the demand for captives from West and Central Africa intensified as the Iberian empires, followed by the British, French, and other European seaborne powers, established plantations in the Americas. National trading companies and independent merchants

[33] de Vries, "Connecting Europe and Asia," 93.
[34] J. R. McNeill, *Mosquito Empires: Ecology and War in the Greater Caribbean, 1620–1914* (Cambridge, 2010); David Watts, *The West Indies: Patterns of Development, Culture and Environmental Change since 1492* (Cambridge, 1990), 393–443.

carried some 13 million African captives across the Atlantic between the sixteenth and nineteenth centuries in the largest forced migration in human history. Two million men, women, and children died in transit. Roughly half of those who endured the Middle Passage did so in the eighteenth century when the plantation complex in the Americas, particularly in the Caribbean, reached its apogee. Upon arrival, captives were sold by ship captains to planters, who subjected them to backbreaking, often lethal labor to maximize the production of sugar, tobacco, cacao, coffee, and indigo for European (and colonial American) consumption. From the perspective of racist enslavers, the lives of those they subjected to slavery were disposable so long as it was possible to purchase more captives. The violent commodification of enslaved peoples of African descent deepened as European consumption of Atlantic products grew.

The coercion at the heart of the plantation complex raises further questions about the industrious revolution thesis formulated by de Vries. De Vries avoids discussion of American slavery because his argument is predicated on the voluntary expansion of wage labor. And yet, the growth of European consumption depended heavily on a global division of labor that involved, in the Americas, the forced labor of millions of men and women of African descent. Industriousness was not necessarily freely chosen. As an enslaved African in Barbados recounted, "The devil was in the Englishman that he makes everything work; he makes the negro work, he makes the horse work, the ass work, the wood work, the water work and the wind work."[35] The central role of chattel slavery in the rise of European consumption gives the lie to any triumphant account of industriousness. Thus, not only did many Europeans in this period work harder merely to keep their families clothed and fed, as already noted, but, far more disturbing, enslavers forcibly extracted labor from millions of enslaved people of African descent to produce goods in the Americas for European consumption. The brutality of chattel slavery in the Americas cannot be overstated. In Jamaica and Saint-Domingue, for example, enslavers routinely worked the enslaved to death as countless men and women perished after only a few years in the fields. Expecting heavy losses of life from overwork, planters simply acquired more captives from Africa, who they in turn forced to work and die under appalling conditions to keep the plantation machine running.[36] Acknowledging the horrific role of slavery in the

---

[35] Quoted in Thomas Benjamin, *The Atlantic World: Europeans, Africans, Indians and Their Shared History, 1400–1900* (Cambridge, 2009), 403.
[36] Trevor Burnard and John Garrigus, *The Plantation Machine: Atlantic Capitalism in French Saint-Domingue and British Jamaica* (Philadelphia, 2016).

Americas compels us to broaden our conception of the industrious revolution and to reflect on an unequal global division of labor that fueled the eighteenth-century consumer revolution and continues to spur consumer capitalism today.[37]

The American plantation complex vastly increased the supply of consumer goods in Europe. For the first time in history, a global system of production emerged whereby colonists in one hemisphere (the Americas) used labor from another continent (Africa) and crops from still other continents (sugarcane, coffee, indigo, and cotton were all originally from Asia and Africa; only tobacco was indigenous to the Americas) for the benefit of consumers in yet another continent (Europe). As a result of this highly exploitative system of production, a whole range of goods that had barely circulated in Europe before 1650 became widespread over the course of a century and a half. The numbers speak for themselves. By the late eighteenth century, Europeans were annually consuming 13 million pounds of chocolate, 120 million pounds of coffee, 125 million pounds of tobacco, and a whopping half a billion pounds of imported sugar, the latter used to sweeten American coffee and chocolate as well as Chinese tea.[38]

Moreover, the rising production of American slave plantations, combined with heightened competition among planters and falling shipping costs, led to dramatic declines in the price of Atlantic consumer goods over the seventeenth and eighteenth centuries. We have seen how the price of tea dropped, owing to a vast expansion of production in China. A similar decline in prices occurred with respect to American goods. Consider the examples of tobacco and sugar. An ancient Native American staple, tobacco was the first New World grocery to spread throughout colonial America and Europe, and it did so with remarkable speed. With the expansion of production in the Chesapeake (Virginia and Maryland), farm prices plummeted from 40d. (40 pence) a pound in 1618 to 3d. a pound in the 1630s to 2d. in 1660, and less than a penny a pound for the remainder of the century. After 1685, an English tobacco

---

[37] Lemire, *Global Trade and the Transformation of Consumer Cultures*, 63–65, underscores another type of industriousness that did not depend on wage labor: that of Native Americans in the globalized fur trade. For a lucid discussion of capitalism and the global commodification of labor (unfree as well as free), see Andrew B. Liu, *Tea War: A History of Capitalism in China and India* (New Haven, CT, 2020).

[38] Jordan Goodman, "Excitantia: Or, How Enlightenment Europe Took to Soft Drugs," in Jordan Goodman, Paul E. Lovejoy, and Andrew Sherratt, eds., *Consuming Habits: Drugs in History and Anthropology* (London, 1995), 126. For sugar imports, see Robin Blackburn, *The Making of New World Slavery: From the Baroque to the Modern, 1492–1800* (London, 1997), 403. Chocolate remained a high-priced drink for elites, except in Spain where the middling indulged as well.

tax raised the retail price, but the leaf remained relatively inexpensive throughout the next century, in part due to a brisk trade in contraband. Prices on the continent remained low as well. In France, a state monopoly distributed Chesapeake tobacco to every nook and cranny of the kingdom. While the state wished to extract as much revenue as possible from sales of the leaf, the widespread availability of cheap contraband checked state prices and encouraged consumption among the laboring classes.

Sugar, viewed as a spice in the Middle Ages and then used as a sweetener, was first produced in the Middle East and parts of North Africa. After having experimented with sugar plantations in the Atlantic islands of Medeira and São Tomé, the Portuguese established similar plantations in Brazil, which would quickly become the world's greatest producer. In the seventeenth and eighteenth centuries, the Spanish, English, French, and Dutch followed suit in the Caribbean, where sugarcane cultivation overtook that of tobacco, indigo, cotton, and coffee. The production of sugar was an extraordinarily labor-intensive pursuit; at least 60 percent of the 13 million African captives forced to migrate to the Americas worked on sugar plantations. Not only did enslaved men and women cultivate and harvest the cane, toiling in gangs under the close supervision of overseers, but they also processed the harvested cane in semi-industrial mills that crushed the stalks, producing a juice that would be refined into sugar through boiling. This production process led to murderously high death rates, as noted, but the Atlantic slave trade allowed planters to replace and expand their workforce to produce ever larger quantities of the coveted sweetener.

With the plantation complex producing unprecedented volumes of sugar in the Americas, the price of the crystal, once a rare and expensive medicinal luxury, fell precipitously. Over the course of the seventeenth century, as British and French planters in the Caribbean entered the market to compete with Portuguese planters in Brazil, its price in England dropped by half to about half a shilling a pound, only to decline another third by 1750. The great wars of the eighteenth century – the Seven Years' War and the War of American Independence – disrupted supply chains and triggered price spikes, but on the whole, the considerable influx of sugar (and coffee) from the French colony of Saint-Domingue and other Caribbean islands kept prices on the continent low.[39]

---

[39] Ralph Davis, "English Foreign Trade, 1660–1700," EHR 7 (1954), 150–166; Sydney Mintz, *Sweetness and Power: The Place of Sugar in Modern History* (New York, 1985); Shammas, *The Pre-industrial Consumer in England and America*, 93–102; Emma Spary, *Eating the Enlightenment: Food and the Sciences in Paris, 1670–1760* (Chicago, 2012), 88–91.

The large supply and low prices of slave-produced goods opened "vast new sources of demand ... which introduced the middle classes and the poor to novel habits of consumption."[40] These words, written by Ralph Davis long before the historiographical turn to consumption, have been confirmed by recent scholarship. Psychoactive Atlantic commodities like tobacco, sugar, and coffee – and Chinese tea (also taken with Caribbean sugar) – were among the most widely consumed nonsubsistence goods of the eighteenth century. As with tea, Shammas categorizes tobacco, sugar, and coffee as "objects of mass consumption," meaning that 25 percent of the adult population may have used them at least once daily.[41] Elites may have snorted tobacco snuff from precious silver boxes, but sailors, soldiers, artisans, and peasants also puffed the leaf through cheap ceramic pipes. Laborers in Britain drank sugary tea on a regular basis, raising the annual consumption of sugar to twenty pounds a head by 1800, just as their counterparts on the continent sipped sweetened coffee (or chocolate in Spain).[42] Street sellers in Austrian cities sold a cup of coffee with a crescent roll for only one kreuzer.[43]

The trade in global commodities extended beyond Europe's port towns to suffuse much of the continent. The Asian goods imported by national trading companies were either sold at port auctions and then distributed to inland retailers or reexported to other European countries, colonies in the Americas, or the African coast. Goods from the Americas were likewise widely redistributed once they entered European ports. The merchants of Bordeaux reexported large quantities of Caribbean sugar and coffee to Hamburg, a European center of sugar refining that supplied northern Germany, central Europe, and Scandinavia. Farm hands in Westphalia, Hesse, and Saxony drank coffee on a daily basis.[44] Urban and rural Danes sipped sweetened tea and coffee and smoked tobacco.[45] Dutch traders sold imported Chesapeake tobacco to processors in Holland and Alsace, where the leaf was mixed with lesser-quality

[40] Davis, "English Foreign Trade," 151.
[41] Shammas, *The Pre-industrial Consumer in England and America*, 93–105. Maud Villeret, *Le goût de l'or blanc: Le sucre en France au xviiie siècle* (Rennes, 2017), demonstrates the growth of sugar consumption in France but does not characterize it as mass consumption.
[42] Benjamin, *The Atlantic World*, 417.
[43] Michael North, *"Material Delight and the Joy of Living": Cultural Consumption in the Age of Enlightenment in Germany*, trans. Pamela Selwyn (New York, 2016), 155. De Zwartt and van Zanden, *The Origins of Globalisation*, 248–249, also suggest that the decline in prices of overseas goods expanded their social circulation in Europe.
[44] North, *"Material Delight and the Joy of Living,"* 159.
[45] Mikkel Venbork Pedersen, "Filtering Impressions: Encounters with Fashionable Goods in Danish Everyday Life in the Eighteenth Century," in Evelyn Welch, ed., *Fashioning the Early Modern* (Oxford, 2017), 321–348.

homegrown tobacco to supply the German lands, Scandinavia, Switzerland, Savoy, and (illegally) France. Global commodities deeply penetrated the continent of Europe, stretching from port towns and their hinterlands to large capitals, provincial towns, and, to a much lesser but still visible extent, rural villages.[46]

Import Substitution

Global trade not only introduced European consumers to new kinds of goods. It also stimulated consumption by inspiring innovation among European producers through a process economists call import substitution. Import substitution refers to the replacement of foreign imported goods with domestically produced substitutes. In the twentieth century, import substitution was common in the Global South where postcolonial nations instituted heavy tariffs to protect nascent domestic industries from competition from industrialized countries in the Global North. Tariffs encouraged citizens of developing countries to produce goods that had once been imported, thereby boosting domestic industry and enabling countries in the Global South to gain a degree of national economic independence. Under very different circumstances in the seventeenth and eighteenth centuries, circumstances in which Europeans had enormous difficulty competing with superior Asian producers, protectionist policies in Europe spurred similar processes of import substitution, encouraging European producers to make imitations of Asian goods. European facsimiles were often significantly lower in price and of lesser quality – today we would call them knock-offs.

To some degree, we have seen import substitution at work in the case of colonial groceries. Colonial planters in the Americas cultivated Asian and Middle Eastern crops (coffee, sugar, and cotton), which were imported into Europe. American tobacco was transplanted to Europe itself, though in this case the European-grown commodity had to compete with a colonial American one. However, the process of import substitution was much clearer in the case of manufactured wares such as ceramics and textiles.[47] In the seventeenth-century, European East Indian companies began to import Chinese porcelain, introducing a

---

[46] See, for example, Michael Kwass, *Contraband: Louis Mandrin and the Making of a Global Underground* (Cambridge, MA, 2014); James Livesey, *Provincializing Global History: Money, Ideas, and Things in the Languedoc, 1680–1830* (New Haven, CT, 2020); Emma Rothschild, "Isolation and Economic Life in Eighteenth-Century France," AHR 119 (October 2014), 1055–1082.

[47] See, notably, Maxine Berg, *Luxury and Pleasure in Eighteenth-Century Britain* (Oxford, 2005).

product that competed favorably with the pewter dishes, plates, and goblets common in middling and elite households. One response to the influx of Chinese porcelain was to tax it and create state-sponsored porcelain works, such as those established in Sèvres, Vienna, and Florence. However, the porcelain produced by such works was very expensive and did not circulate far beyond the aristocracy. The more successful substitute for imported Chinese porcelain was European-made earthenware. Artisans in Delft and other towns in the Netherlands developed the craft of tin-glazed pottery, which would come to be known as Delftware. This blue-and-white ceramic was a hit throughout northwestern Europe and soon faced competition from British producers like Josiah Wedgwood, who in the middle of the eighteenth century devised his own fashionable imitation of Chinese porcelain, known as creamware. These new ceramics – Delftware, creamware, and other earthenware products – became so popular that they began to replace the hardy pewter dishes of the past (which had themselves replaced wood). Middling consumers came to prefer fragile ceramic dishes and plates to their durable metallic predecessors. Although rich and poor households had long appreciated the refundability of objects made of pewter (and silver), for such metallic objects stored value and could easily be sold for cash or credit, fashionability began to take precedence over refundability. Even gold and silver jewelry was increasingly valued for its elegance and workmanship rather than its intrinsic value.[48]

A similar story unfolded with respect to Indian cotton, which, like linen, gradually but steadily replaced the heavy woolen cloth of old. As we have seen, the successful introduction into Europe of cottons from India gave rise to various prohibitions against the import, production, and use of the cloth. However, because most prohibitions were limited in scale, forbidding imports but allowing nascent national industries to develop, calico manufactories sprouted in Marseille, London, Amsterdam, and Geneva, the production from which grew to supplant imports by the end of the century. In Britain, calico production became quite advanced as innovative manufacturers developed new technologies, principally the use of copper plates (rather than wood-blocks) for printing color designs on cloth. The new British-made calicos, like the Indian imports before them, were marketed in both Britain and its colonies. In France, after the lifting in 1759 of a comprehensive ban on both the domestic production and importation of "Indian" cloth, calico printing workshops multiplied, the most famous of which was established

---

[48] Helen Clifford, "A Commerce with Things: The Value of Precious Metalwork in Early Modern England," in Berg and Clifford, eds. *Consumers and Luxury*, 147–168.

by the entrepreneur Christophe-Phillippe Oberkampf in Jouy, southwest of Paris. Calico manufactories, which historians have called "proto-factories" because they employed such large and disciplined workforces, also appeared in Russia, the Hapsburg states, and Catalonia (see Figure 2.4). In Barcelona, calico manufacturers reached beyond local and metropolitan markets to supply Spanish colonies in the Americas. From the port of Veracruz, a point of entry into Spanish America, colorful calico from Barcelona spread to Mexico, the Caribbean, Argentina, and Uruguay.[49]

Japanese and Chinese lacquerware also inspired imitations in Europe. As with Chinese porcelain and Indian cloth, European knock-offs of finely varnished Asian furniture and decorative objects widened the market. While aristocrats and wealthy bourgeois continued to appreciate authentic Japanese lacquerware, they and many others became increasingly interested in glossy but less expensive homemade substitutes. In Paris, the Martin brothers gained an international reputation for the skill and artistry with which they applied their special "Martin varnish" to coach panels, screens, snuffboxes, cabinets, writing tables, chests of drawers, and chairs. The success of their enterprise, like that of Oberkampf's calico works, lay in "their capacity to combine high-cost, high quality products with a range of very much lower-priced articles produced and sold in more extensive markets."[50] Whether consumers were in the market for a modest snuffbox or a grand coach, they could partake of a European-produced varnish that evoked Asian exoticism and luxury.

Modern Materiality

As the transition from wool to cotton and linen suggests, import substitution was part of a broader shift from the consumption of expensive, high-quality, durable materials that stored value over long periods of time to cheaper, more fragile, and more fashionable semidurables that were rapidly replaced. Indeed, in the case of textiles, the process had begun earlier, before the introduction of Indian cloth, when lighter and less expensive woolens called "new draperies" replaced the heavy woolen cloth of old. The introduction of cotton dramatically accelerated this

[49] J. K. J. Thomson, *A Distinctive Industrialization: Cotton in Barcelona 1728–1832* (Cambridge, 1992); Marta Vicente, *Clothing the Spanish Empire: Families and the Calico Trade in the Early Modern Atlantic World* (New York, 2006). Spanish America also imported many products directly from Asia, such as Japanese lacquerware, Chinese porcelain and silk, and Southeast Asian spices.

[50] Michael Sonenscher, *Work and Wages: Natural Law, Politics and the Eighteenth-Century French Trades* (Cambridge, 1989), 230.

process. As Spaniard F. Romà y Rosell noted in 1768, "people no longer concern themselves with buying solid and heavy clothes that they pass down to their great-grandson ... They like light clothes, the low price of which makes the pleasure of following annually changing fashion more accessible."[51] In an age without savings banks, families continued to buy expensive, value-storing, durable, and semidurable goods, such as silver jewelry, pocket watches, pewter dishes, and clothing, which in a pinch could be sold, exchanged, or pawned for cash. But it is clear that a transition from refundable durables toward lighter materials that required more frequent replacement was underway, a trend that would culminate in the twentieth century with the invention of disposable plastics and the concept of built-in obsolescence. The virtual disposability of the early modern clay tobacco pipe was a sign of things to come.

Cotton textiles illustrate this transformation well but other examples abound. Wealthier households supplanted silver and pewter goblets with fragile drinking glasses. Durable tapestries, which had decorated great halls since the Middle Ages, were replaced by stylish wallpaper. Lighter furniture (some of which was now made with tropical hardwood) took the place of heavier oak predecessors. Solid brass and silver candlesticks gave way to hollowed out facsimiles. Mixed silk replaced pure silk. Inexpensive ephemeral books and pamphlets overtook heavy tomes. Faux jewelry and plated silver became as popular as the real thing. As a French almanac declared,

The pearls manufactured in Paris are so ingeniously made that they display all the shine and richness of fine (natural) pearls; they are highly prized and one has no hesitation in including them in the category of jewels or in using them in the most elegant toilettes. Pearls are made in Paris that imitate natural ones so well and are at such a good price, that most women think themselves able to do without fine ones.[52]

The shift from durable to semidurable products, from high-priced luxury to moderately priced semiluxury, from "real" to imitation, and

[51] Quoted in Claverías, "L'inégalité comme norme," 35.
[52] Quoted in Natacha Coquery, "Language of Success: Marketing and Distributing Semi-Luxury Goods in Eighteenth-Century Paris," *Journal of Design History* (JDH) 17 (2004), 81. In Paris, even the materials from which buildings were constructed became cheaper. Allan Potofsky, *Constructing Paris in the Age of Revolution* (Basingstoke, 2009), 11, 23–24. In 1788, J. Sempere Gurainos noted the changing materiality of furniture: "if furniture was more costly [in the previous age], it also lasted longer, and after having served for many years one was always able to use the materials from which it was fabricated; which does not happen with wallpaper, tables, sofas and other furnishings that are in fashion today" (Claverías, "L'inégalité comme norme," 35).

from refundability to fashionability allowed consumers to buy more goods. Although middling households in the eighteenth century do not appear to have spent more on goods as a proportion of their total income than they had previously, they were nevertheless able to accumulate more things, in part because the prices of certain newly fashionable products were declining. The shift toward modern materiality also encouraged faster replacement rates and accelerated fashion-cycles as consumers sought to supplant damaged, worn-out, or simply outmoded articles with new ones. Small wonder the adjective "new" began to appear more frequently in after-death inventories in the seventeenth and eighteenth centuries.[53]

The rise of consumption between 1650 and 1800 cannot be attributed to "Schumpeterian growth" – that is, growth propelled by radical technological innovation that revolutionizes the economy by completely destroying one system of production, exchange, and consumption and replacing it with another. As we have seen, consumption over the course of this period expanded gradually thanks to relatively mundane processes such as agricultural specialization, the spread of proto-industry, and the development of intra-European production and commerce – "Smithian growth" in other words. The most dramatic change occurred in the area of overseas trade as state-sponsored companies and independent merchants established new circuits of global commerce that, for the first time in history, directly linked the continents of Europe, Asia, Africa, and the Americas. Such overseas trade intensified in the late seventeenth and eighteenth centuries when Dutch, English, French, and other European trading companies began to import new goods from Asia, which were consumed on a much larger scale than the luxury goods they had previously traded.

More important still, the emergence of the plantation complex in the Americas, based on the unprecedented forced migration and brutal enslavement of millions of men, women, and children of African descent, vastly increased the influx of low-priced imported consumer goods into Europe. Although not fully explored in early work on consumption, this profoundly troubling dimension of Atlantic history is now seen as central to the consumer revolution. Indeed, if any form of production calls to mind McKendrick's original theory that the consumer revolution was the analogue to a revolution in production, "the necessary convulsion on the demand side of the equation to match the convulsion on the supply

---

[53] Blondé, "Cities in Decline and the Dawn of a Consumer Society"; Mark Overton, Jane Whittle, Darron Dean, and Andrew Hann, *Production and Consumption in English Households, 1600–1750* (New York, 2012), 114–115.

side," it was the semi-industrialized slave labor camp that proliferated in the Americas (especially in the Caribbean) and not the European factory, which was only just beginning to emerge in the late eighteenth century.[54]

The growth of world trade and the global division of labor that accompanied it in the seventeenth and especially eighteenth centuries fundamentally changed practices of consumption in Europe and its colonies. European consumers of varying social status altered their diets and modes of sociability as they incorporated into their daily lives Chinese tea and porcelain and American coffee, chocolate, and sugar. Another psychoactive import, American tobacco, was wildly successful among pipe-smoking laborers and snuff-taking elites. Meanwhile, the introduction of Indian cotton changed the way people dressed, adding lightweight and magnificently colorful cotton clothing to their wardrobes. Demand for cotton textiles, combined with protectionist prohibitions on Asian imports, gave rise to the production of cotton cloth in Europe, which would become the leading sector of the Industrial Revolution in the nineteenth century. Such global goods were generally available in high- and low-end markets, putting them within reach of ordinary consumers in the middling and even laboring classes. The following chapters will consider how these and other goods were advertised and marketed, what they meant to the people who made, sold, and consumed them, and how their consumption altered the society, culture, and politics of the age.

---

[54] McKendrick, Brewer, Plumb, *The Birth of Consumer Society*, 9. Acknowledging the loss of life and suffering of enslaved people of African descent in the Americas as well as the tragic experiences of many other peoples vulnerable to European colonization, de Zwart and van Zanden, *The Origins of Globalisation*, 278, conclude that the "net effect of globalization on global well-being … was strongly negative."

3   Going Shopping

> In the city [of Paris] it is most striking to see the quays, bridges, intersections, public squares, street corners, and the length of streets clogged with mobile stalls, shops, stands, to see even grocery and hardware stores protruding into the streets.[1]

Retail was an essential feature of the consumer revolution. Thus far, we have looked at the kinds of goods consumers acquired and the trade networks through which such goods pulsed. It is now time to consider how goods were marketed to consumers and how consumers responded. From 1650 to 1800, points of contact between retailers and consumers multiplied as more and more shops opened and as merchants and retailers experimented with ways to display and advertise their merchandise. In fact, some economic historians argue that a dynamic "retail revolution" fueled the growth in consumption "by lowering the transaction costs of bringing new market wares to wider strata of poorer customers."[2] Of course, as we have seen, using the term "revolution" to describe a process that took decades to unfold is problematic, but it is clear that retailers of luxury and semiluxury goods proliferated in this period and that many of them employed new techniques to draw the attention of consumers. As consumers responded to the marketing aimed at them, an evolving dialogue between buyers and sellers stimulated supply and demand.

Retail Revolution?

Histories of retail tend to focus on either the nineteenth century, when department stores featuring monumental architecture, fixed prices, and legions of salaried personnel were founded, or the twentieth century, when chain stores like Wal-Mart enabled mass consumption. That both

---

[1] Louis-Sébastien Mercier, *Le Nouveau Paris* (Paris, nd), V: 236.
[2] Danielle van den Heuvel and Sheilagh Ogilvie, "Retail Development in the Consumer Revolution: The Netherlands, c. 1670–c. 1815," *Explorations in Economic History* 50 (January 2013), 69.

types of brick-and-mortar stores are now threatened by online behemoths like Amazon suggests that retail markets exist in a constant state of flux. Indeed, retail existed long before the appearance of the department store. As the first generation of consumption studies emphasized, shops flourished in the eighteenth century as retailers experimented with new forms of advertising and shopping for fashionable goods became a leisure activity for the affluent. For McKendrick and his cohort, innovative retail was one of the engines that drove the consumer revolution.[3]

Today, historians stress that the history of the retail shop, like that of consumption more generally, goes back centuries and was anything but linear. During the Italian Renaissance, patricians in thriving commercial cities like Venice could buy local and foreign goods at any number of shops. Even small Italian towns like Poppi in Tuscany, with a population of 1,450, boasted multiple grocery stores, bakeries, butcher shops, and drugstores in addition to a mercer's shop, a barber, a tailor, and a shoemaker.[4] The shop was no more an innovation of the eighteenth century than it was of the nineteenth or twentieth.

Further, historians have stressed that early modern men and women bought goods from a variety of retail sites, not just shops. Even as permanent shops proliferated in the eighteenth century, they had to compete with a well-established system of fairs, markets, and peddling. Often international in scale, fairs were periodic events at which merchants sold wholesale to other merchants and hawked textiles and other goods directly to customers. Some fairs took place in big cities like Frankfurt and Leipzig while others assembled in rural villages in which traders sold livestock, agricultural produce, and finished goods. Like fairs, markets were common in towns across Europe and colonial America. Once or twice a week on appointed days, traders, farmers, and artisans brought their goods to specifically designated urban marketplaces and set up stalls to sell various items, notably food products such as bread, meat, poultry, fish, dairy, and vegetables. Most townspeople went to markets regularly to buy provisions for the household. For the poor, markets were particularly important because laborers could buy small amounts of basic goods at relatively low prices.

Peddlers, smugglers, and street sellers were also a lively presence in early modern towns and villages. Peddlers and smugglers, many of whom hailed from Alpine villages, traveled far and wide to cart goods from town

[3] Neil McKendrick, John Brewer, and J. H. Plumb, *The Birth of a Consumer Society: The Commercialization of Eighteenth-Century England* (Bloomington, IN, 1982).

[4] Evelyn Welch, *Shopping in the Renaissance: Consumer Cultures in Italy, 1400–1600* (New Haven, CT, 2005), 9.

to countryside. They might hawk their wares in village squares (to the consternation of sedentary local retailers), sell them out of taverns and inns, or go from farmhouse to farmhouse in search of customers. Some itinerant traders were well-established merchants who could tap into extensive family trade and credit networks to earn a respectable living; others were destitute migrants who, with a pack of cloth, buttons, ribbons, or tobacco on their backs, aroused suspicions of criminality; still others moved precariously between these two poles. Regardless of the scale of their enterprise, peddlers served as key intermediaries between towns and countryside, venturing into remote villages where there were few regular shops. Many of them violated fiscal and commercial laws while practicing their trade, but consumers welcomed them just the same.[5]

Meanwhile, every major burg had an abundance of street sellers who cried out to passersby as they carried baskets, pushed carts, and set up makeshift tables on busy corners. Street sellers, who were often women from the poorest levels of urban society, were part of a vital low-end market in all manner of clothing, food, books, furniture, and jewelry, much of which, including leftovers from well-stocked kitchens, was secondhand, and some of which was stolen. Indeed, fashion among the middling and poor often lagged behind the wealthy because the nobility and the bourgeoisie sold outmoded goods to retailers, who in turn peddled them at a discount to less affluent customers. This kind of resale, which dramatically expanded the circulation of goods, allowed secondhand buyers, who were often (but not always) of lesser social status than firsthand owners, to gain access, however belated, to the world of fashion. Further, although municipal laws and guild regulations attempted to protect licensed market sellers and permanent shopkeepers from interloping peddlers and street dealers, many itinerant traders practiced their craft illicitly, pushing retail markets beyond their officially sanctioned boundaries to deliver inexpensive goods to the laboring classes. Occasionally, unlicensed street dealers like a certain Mrs. Buijs, who sold tea door-to-door through the streets of the Dutch city of Arnhem, were arrested, but most were nimble enough to evade municipal authorities.[6] Extralegal traders – peddlers, smugglers, street dealers,

---

[5] Laurence Fontaine, *History of Pedlars in Europe*, trans. Vicki Whittaker (Durham, NC, 1996).

[6] Danielle van den Heuvel, "Policing Peddlers: The Prosecution of Illegal Street Trade in Eighteenth-Century Dutch Towns," *Historical Journal* (HJ) 58 (June 2015), 367–392. See also Cissie Fairchilds, "The Production and Marketing of Populuxe Goods in Eighteenth-Century Paris," in John Brewer and Roy Porter, eds., *Consumption and the World of Goods* (London, 1993), 228–248; Laurence Fontaine, ed., *Alternative Exchanges: Second-Hand Circulations from the Sixteenth Century to the Present* (New York, 2008);

and pawnbrokers (who sold used and stolen clothing that had been hocked for credit) – provided the laboring poor with a wide array of relatively inexpensive goods. The same shadowy retail markets in the Americas allowed the enslaved and other laborers to acquire clothing and merchandise that might have otherwise been out of reach.

Even as older forms of retail such as fairs, markets, and peddling persisted, the number of permanent shops rose dramatically in European cities and towns over the course of the seventeenth and, especially, eighteenth centuries. The Netherlands may have been "the first economy to experience an explosive transformation in retailing" but the same trend would soon be apparent in major commercial centers across Europe, from western Europe (London, Paris, and Madrid) to central Europe (Hamburg, Frankfurt, and Vienna) to the Mediterranean coast (Rome, Naples, Barcelona, Cadiz, and Seville).[7] In some areas, the density of shops became surprisingly high, even higher than it is today. There was one shop for every forty-three people in England and Wales in the middle of the eighteenth century.[8] Even cities that were stagnant (like Venice) or in decline (like Antwerp) had more mercer's shops than ever before – one for every twenty-six people in Antwerp – though the density of shops in central Europe and Scandinavia was much lower than in western Europe.[9] Retail also extended deeper into the countryside where multitasking townspeople and villagers maintained small businesses on the side.[10] In France, luxury and semiluxury retail trades in watches,

---

Michael Kwass, *Contraband: Louis Mandrin and the Making of a Global Underground* (Cambridge, MA, 2014); Beverly Lemire, "Peddling Fashion: Salesmen, Pawnbrokers, Taylors, Thieves and the Second-Hand Clothes Trade in England, c. 1700–1800," *Textile History* 22 (1991), 67–82; Daniel Roche, *The Culture of Clothing: Dress and Fashion in the Ancien Regime*, trans. Jean Birrell (Cambridge, 1996).

[7] Van den Heuvel and Ogilvie, "Retail Development in the Consumer Revolution," 69–87. It is now clear that the growth of shops was not limited to northwestern Europe. For Spain, see Daniel Muñoz Navarro, ed., *Comprar, vender y consumir. Nuevas aportaciones a la historia del consumo en la España moderna* (València, 2011); L. Torra, "Las botigues de teles de Barcelona: aportación al studio de la oferta de tejidos y crédito al consomo (1650–1800)," *Revista de Historia Económica* 21 (2003), 89–105.

[8] Hoh-Cheung Mui and Lorna H. Mui, *Shops and Shopkeeping in Eighteenth-Century England* (Montreal, 1989), 40.

[9] Patricia Allerston, "Meeting Demand: Retailing Strategies in Early Modern Venice" in Bruno Blondé and Natacha Coquery, eds., *Retailers and Consumer Changes in Early Modern Europe: England, France, Italy and the Low Countries* (Tours, 2005), 169–188; L. van Aert and I. van Damme, "Retail Dynamics of a City in Crisis: The Mercer Guild in Pre-Industrial Antwerp," in Blondé and Coquery, eds., *Retailers and Consumer Changes in Early Modern Europe*, 150.

[10] Ian Mitchell, *Tradition and Innovation in English Retailing, 1700 to 1850* (London, 2016), 78–79; Sheilagh Ogilvie, "Consumption, Social Capital, and the 'Industrious Revolution' in Early Modern Germany," JEH 70 (June 2010), 287–325; Jon Stobart, *Sugar and Spice: Grocers and Groceries in Provincial England, 1650–1830* (Oxford, 2016).

wigs, furniture, books, earthenware, colonial groceries, tobacco, prepared foods, and textiles sprouted in small and middling towns alongside
older professions. In the booming port town of Nantes, the number of
grocers doubled over the eighteenth century, while that of limonadiers
(sellers of coffee and other drinks) increased sixfold, though cafés
remained clustered in the wealthier parts of town.[11] Female producers
and sellers played a key role in the expansion of many of these trades.
While historians have long emphasized that women constituted a driving
force behind the growth of demand, many scholars now suggest that
women may have had an equally transformative effect on the supply side
of the equation as shopkeepers in the lively retail sector.[12]

Napoleon's dismissive (and probably apocryphal) quip that Britain was
"a nation of shopkeepers" could have easily been applied to any number
of other European nations, including his own. It also applied to colonies
in the Americas. Shops multiplied in bustling ports as goods from
Europe reached towns from Boston to Philadelphia, Montreal to New
Orleans, Kingston to Cap français, and Havana to Buenos Aires. Even
backcountry Virginians bought imported tea, handkerchiefs, mirrors,
and china as well as everyday necessities from local shops.[13] Retail
gradually spread into the countryside on both sides of the Atlantic.

Many shops were small affairs run by producer-retailers who sold the
products that they made. For innumerable tailors, seamstresses, shoe-
makers, cabinetmakers, watchmakers, silversmiths, or bakers, shops were
scarcely more than workshops, storage rooms, or the front room of an
otherwise residential home. However, producer-retailers in the luxury
and semiluxury trades increasingly strove to enhance the appeal of their
shops, as did a growing breed of retailer who, rather than making the
goods they sold, bought them from wholesalers and marketed them
in interior spaces designed to draw well-heeled customers. High-end
shops specializing in fashionable textiles and clothing, porcelain and

[11] Maud Villeret, *Le goût de l'or blanc: Le sucre en France au xviiie siècle* (Rennes, 2017),
299–300.
[12] Monica Chojnacka, *Working Women of Early Modern Venice* (Baltimore, 2001); James
Collins, "Women and the Birth of Modern Consumer Capitalism," in Daryl Hafter and
Nina Kushner, eds., *Women and Work in Eighteenth-Century France* (Baton Rouge, LA,
2015), 152–176; Clare Haru Crowston, *Fabricating Women: The Seamstresses of Old
Regime France, 1675–1791* (Durham, NC, 2001); Clare Haru Crowston, *Credit,
Fashion, Sex: Economies of Regard in Old Regime France* (Durham, NC, 2013);
Alexandra Shepard, *Accounting for Oneself: Worth, Status, and the Social Order in Early
Modern England* (Oxford, 2015). But see Sheilagh Ogilvie, *A Bitter Living: Women,
Markets, and Social Capital in Early Modern Germany* (Oxford, 2003), which stresses
the legal and social barriers to German women's participation in markets.
[13] Ann Smart Martin, *Buying into the World of Goods: Early Consumers in Backcountry
Virginia* (Baltimore, 2008).

earthenware, metal toys and trinkets, and colonial groceries took off, especially in wealthy urban neighborhoods and in areas near theaters and promenades where streets were increasingly paved and lit with oil lamps or candles in glass-paned lanterns.

This trend began early in the seventeenth century when the equivalent of today's luxury shopping malls were first constructed. At the Palais de Justice in the center of Paris, a complex of hundreds of arcaded shops offered elite customers lace, gloves, jewelry, and other fine products. According to a Dutch travel writer, "the Palais is the center and essence of all the beautiful clothing shops. One is amazed at the extraordinary abundance of precious commodities of all sorts enclosed here. The hardest part is deciding in which boutique to make one's purchases."[14] Similar luxury malls appeared in seventeenth-century London, such as the New Exchange located in the aristocratic West End, which boasted a hundred shops lining two floors. In an environment that was open to the public, yet, thanks to a covered inner court, protected from the dirt and clutter of the street, men and women could stroll, talk, socialize, gossip, and flirt as they browsed fine textiles, accessories, porcelain, perfume, and books.

Shop design further developed in the eighteenth century. While most shops continued to sell basic goods over rough-hewn counters or through open street-windows, many luxury and semiluxury shops adopted new strategies to lure well-off customers into their establishments (see Figure 3.1). Shopkeepers enhanced the façade of their shops by attaching fascia boards, hanging signs, and glazing windows behind which they now displayed goods, often a single article behind each pane, to encourage what we now call window-shopping. The most ambitious shopkeepers remodeled their interiors to look like the fancy rooms found in their respectable clients' homes. They relegated work areas to back rooms; appointed walls with cornices and moldings; divided space with pillars, arches, and screens; improved lighting by adding lamps, candlesticks, and sconces; hung mirrors and pictures on the wall; installed shelves, drawers, hooks, and glass cases to display goods (in keeping with window displays in the front); and provided customers with upholstered chairs to ensure a comfortable and sociable experience. Introduced piecemeal, these new features aimed to sustain the reputation of the shopkeeper and to establish the shop as a place of refined leisure. They also enhanced

---

[14] Quoted in Jennifer Jones, *Sexing la Mode: Gender, Fashion, and Commercial Culture in Old Regime France* (Oxford, 2004), 152. Nicolas Lyon-Caen, "Les marchands du temple. Les boutiques du Palais de justice de Paris aux xvie–xviiie siècles," *Revue historique*, 674 (2015), 323–352.

Figure 3.1 Shop of "La Marchande de modes" from the *Encyclopédie*
Gravure, 1777.
The George Peabody Library, The Sheridan Libraries, Johns Hopkins
University. An engraving of a finely appointed fashion merchant's shop, in which
the shopkeepers and customers are all women. The *Encyclopédie* devoted many
articles to the production and commercialization of consumer goods

the appeal of the merchandise on offer to create what Natacha Coquery
calls a "culture of consumption."[15] As Sophie van la Roche, a foreign
visitor to eighteenth-century London, noted in her diary, "Behind the
great glass windows absolutely everything one can think of is neatly,
attractively displayed, in such abundance of choice as almost to make
one greedy."[16] In an age before commercial brands, when goods were yet
to be standardized and quality varied enormously, the physical environment of the shop was a crucial marketing tool. A smart-looking shop
signaled the trustworthiness of the shopkeeper and the quality of his or
her goods.

Few mastered the shop as a marketing tool quite like Josiah
Wedgwood. A successful pottery manufacturer, Wedgwood set up
several large finely appointed showrooms in London and other cities to
put his wares on display. In heavily publicized exhibitions, he laid out

[15] Natacha Coquery, *Tenir Boutique à Paris au XVIIIe siècle* (Paris, 2011), 24.
[16] Quoted in Nancy Cox, *The Complete Tradesman: A Study of Retailing, 1550–1820* (New
York, 2000), 12.

newly designed sets of tableware, including china that had been ordered by the queen herself, for all to see. In 1774, he exhibited the Russian service he made for Catherine the Great, the display of which he predicted, "would bring an immence (sic) number of People of Fashion into our Rooms – would fully complete our notoriety to the whole Island & help us greatly, no doubt, in the sale of our goods, both useful and ornamental."[17] He was right. Aristocrats and other fashionable elites thronged the showroom to see the latest designs in tableware.

An industrialist rather than a shopkeeper, Wedgwood was something of an exception. A more typical example of high-end shop design might be Martha Braithwaite's goldsmith's shop, which had glass-fronted cupboards, nests of drawers, show boards, and three glass cases with oak drawers lined with velvet.[18] Across the Channel, Parisian luxury retailers also created elaborate shops. Mercer Charles Raymond Granchez owned a shop near the Pont Neuf called Le Petit Dunkerque, named after the port through which many English goods entered France. True to the mercers' slogan "makers of nothing, sellers of everything," Granchez sold a wide variety of furniture (tea tables, chests of drawers), pottery (teapots, vases, punch bowls), decorative household goods (candlesticks, clocks), jewelry (necklaces, watches), and accessories and novelties (snuffboxes, pinchbeck buttons, shoe buckles, inkstands, assorted containers for razors and scissors). But what was truly extraordinary about Le Petit Dunkerque was its brilliant interior – the ceiling, back wall, and counter were composed of hundreds of mirrors that reflected the shiny objects on display. Heated by a stove to keep customers warm in winter and lit up with lanterns in the evening, the shop was adorned with mahogany columns and display cabinets. After spending "many hours" at Le Petit Dunkerque, Baroness d'Oberkirch exclaimed, "nothing is as pretty and brilliant as this boutique, filled with jewelry and golden trinkets."[19] A poet describing his sublime experience in the mirrored shop wrote, "I saw myself in the Heavens" without ever having to leave earth. Granchez was selling the *experience* of the shop as much of the goods themselves, which is why many of the items on display bore an inscription of the shop's name. The shop was the brand.

The proliferation and refurbishing of luxury and semiluxury boutiques helped turn shopping into a leisure activity for elites and the middling

[17] Quoted in McKendrick, Brewer, and Plumb, *The Birth of a Consumer Society*, 121.
[18] Claire Walsh, "Shop Design and the Display of Goods in Eighteenth-Century London," JDH 8 (1995), 162.
[19] Quoted in Coquery, *Tenir Boutique à Paris au XVIIIe siècle*, 208. See also Carolyn Sargentson, *Merchants and Luxury Markets: The Marchands Merciers of Eighteenth-Century Paris* (London, 1996).

classes. Although the traditional means of marketing luxury goods, by which producers and retailers visited important clients in the latter's homes, did not disappear, the spread of fancy shops in such affluent neighborhoods as the West End in London and the faubourgs St-Germain and St-Honoré in Paris attracted clients to the marketplace and encouraged them to engage in shopping as a new form of sociable recreation. It is no coincidence that the act of shopping as a leisure activity began to make its appearance in diaries in the seventeenth and eighteenth centuries. The obsessive chronicler Samuel Pepys recorded a visit to the New Exchange on 10 April 1663, "[I] met my wife and walked down to the New Exchange; there laid out 10s upon pendants and painted leather gloves very pretty and all the mode."[20]

Coined in the eighteenth century, the word "shopping" began to appear in diaries as well. The German tourist Johanna Schopenhauer described how she and friends "set off shopping" in London. "This means going into at least twenty shops, having a thousand things shown to us which we do not wish to buy, in fact turning the whole shop upside down and, in the end, perhaps leaving without purchasing anything."[21] She was joking about the fact that shopping was sometimes an activity unto itself, independent of the functional goal of acquiring goods. (Of course, as retailers understood, all that time visiting shops ultimately encouraged customers to make purchases.) Schopenhauer's observation also reveals how shopping became linked to tourism, an association that was particularly strong in Paris where elite tourists visited the city's renowned boutiques just as they did its famous salons and cabinets of curiosities. City guidebooks now listed commercial addresses to visit in addition to public buildings and landmarks. The same Baroness d'Oberkirch who shopped until she dropped at Le Petit Dunkerque also "went to the shop of a cabinetmaker called Éricourt, who made marvelous furniture. He showed us all sorts [of furniture]. I spent more than two hours there."[22]

The diary entries of Pepys, Schopenhauer, and d'Oberkirch all raise the question of gender. Were women more inclined to shop than men? How did gender shape the interactions between shopkeepers and customers? Unfortunately, there is no clear historiographical consensus on these matters. Some historians argue that women became associated with shopping in the eighteenth century, while others suggest that men

---

[20] Linda Levy Peck, *Consuming Splendor: Society and Culture in Seventeenth-Century England* (Cambridge, 2005), 42–61 (Pepys on 60).
[21] Quoted in Cox, *The Complete Tradesman*, 143.
[22] Quoted in Coquery, *Tenir Boutique à Paris au XVIIIe siècle*, 208.

enthusiastically participated in shopping as well. One way to parse this debate is to consider the different kinds of primary sources that historians use. Those who examine representations of women in print (novels, pamphlets, fashion journals, and satirical engravings) have found an abundance of evidence suggesting that shopping was heavily gendered. The caricature "Miseries of Human Life, During the Endless Time That You Are Kept Waiting in a Carriage" (c. 1808) depicts two Englishmen waiting impatiently outside a shop as their frivolous wives linger inside admiring fashionable cloth. As Jennifer Jones has shown, many French cultural critics in the late eighteenth century characterized the excessive desire to consume as a distinctly feminine trait. Hence, men who paid too much attention to fashion were often characterized as effeminate dandies who were obsessed with clothing and accessories. Meanwhile, writers and cartoonists depicted the shop as a sexually dangerous environment in which male customers flirted with pretty young shop girls. For real men (not dandies), it was supposedly shop women (not goods) that stoked desire (see Figure 3.2).[23]

However, such representations did not always reflect the complexity of actual practices. It is certainly true that women played an important role in the retail sector. Van de Heuvel and Ogilvie, and Fontaine argue that many women of the laboring classes in the Netherlands, England, and France were able to carve out a degree of autonomy by running small retail businesses as subsidiary occupations.[24] By engaging in retail on the side, often beyond the reach of urban guilds, women gained access to cash income and, with it, a bit of independence from their husbands in an otherwise heavily patriarchal society.[25] Higher up the retail chain, women ran fashion shops, offering expertise and advice on clothing, accessories, and hairstyles. In Paris, fashion merchant Rose Bertin out-fitted aristocrats and wealthy bourgeois from all over Europe and America; she personally helped Queen Marie Antoinette define a distinctive style that set the standard at court and in the city.[26] On the other side of the shop counter, married women were regular customers because they were largely responsible for the day-to-day running of their

---

[23] Jones, *Sexing la Mode*; Elizabeth Kowaleski-Wallace, *Consuming Subjects: Women, Shopping, and Business in the Eighteenth Century* (New York, 1997); John Styles and Amanda Vickery, eds., *Gender, Taste, and Material Culture in Britain and North America, 1700–1830* (New Haven, CT, 2006).

[24] Van den Heuvel and Ogilvie, "Retail Development in the Consumer Revolution"; Laurence Fontaine, *Le Marché: Histoire et usages d'une conquête sociale* (Paris, 2014).

[25] In much more difficult circumstances, some enslaved people in the Americas also gained a measure of autonomy by trading in local markets on the margins of the plantation economy.

[26] Crowston, *Credit, Fashion, Sex*; Caroline Weber, *Queen of Fashion* (New York, 2006).

A MORNING RAMBLE, or The MILLINERS SHOP.

Figure 3.2 *A Morning Ramble, or The Milliners Shop*, 1782.
The Lewis Walpole Library, Yale University. Male customers flirt with female
shopkeepers in this satirical image of a milliner's shop. Behind the man offering a
masquerade ticket to one of the shop women sit boxes of trifles fancifully labeled
"Feathers," "Love," "Coxcomb," and "Mode"

households, which included buying basic provisions from local retailers. (In wealthier households, servants did the daily shopping.) Historians have long assumed that beyond such quotidian purchases, married women were unable to buy much from shops because they could not contract debt. The laws of coverture, by which the legal existence of wives inhered in that of their husbands, entitled the latter to ownership of all of the household's movable property and implied that married women could not, in their own name, buy any goods on credit beyond daily necessities. In principle, this legal regime sharply limited women's autonomy as consumers because many retail transactions involved shop credit. But a wave of recent research suggests that coverture was widely ignored by shopkeepers in eighteenth-century western Europe and in colonial America, allowing married women to contract store credit and acquire all sorts of things in their own names.[27] This is an important finding, as it accords with historical accounts that portray women in this period as substantial drivers of consumption.

Men, however, did not neglect the world of retail. On the contrary, not only were the majority of shopkeepers men but married men regularly purchased goods such as furniture, clothing, food, home furnishings, and books.[28] They entered shops as routinely and avidly as women. Popular representations to the contrary, acquisitiveness was hardly an exclusively feminine characteristic. Recall Lord Chesterfield's warning to his son that many men have been destroyed by their fervor for snuffboxes, watches, canes, and the like.[29] Men may have flirted with shop girls but they were also interested in buying the goods that shops were offering. Thus, literary representations of women as especially crazed shoppers must be set alongside evidence of actual shopping practices to gain a more nuanced picture of the ways in which gender operated in the world of retail.

[27] Crowston, *Credit, Fashion, Sex*, ch. 7; Margot Finn, "Women, Consumption and Coverture in England, c. 1760–1860," HJ 39 (September 1996), 703–722; Julie Hardwick, *Family Business: Litigation and the Political Economies of Daily Life in Early Modern France* (Oxford, 2009); Ellen Hartigan-O'Connor, "Collaborative Consumption and the Politics of Choice in Early American Port Cities," in Styles and Vickery, eds., *Gender, Taste, and Material Culture in Britain and North America, 1700–1830*, 125–149; Peck, *Consuming Splendor*, 21.

[28] Margot Finn, "Men's Things: Masculine Possession in the Consumer Revolution," *Social History* 25 (2000), 133–155; Michael Kwass, "Big Hair: A Wig History of Consumption in Eighteenth-Century France," AHR 111 (June 2006), 631–659; Amanda Vickery, "His and Hers: Gender, Consumption, and Household Accounting in Eighteenth-Century England," in Lyndal Roper and Ruth Harris, eds., *The Art of Survival: Essays in Honor of Olwen Hufton* (Oxford, 2006), 12–38.

[29] Styles and Vickery, *Gender, Taste, and Material Culture in Britain and North America, 1700–1830*, 5.

If the rising number and changing designs of shops were essential to the growth of consumption, so was the growing role of shop credit. Credit, the use of which can be traced back to antiquity, became ubiquitous in the early modern period. Governments drew on it to field mighty armies and merchants to outfit globe-trotting ships, but local shopkeepers and petty traders (often women) also extended more and more credit to customers. Consumption and credit rose together in the seventeenth and eighteenth centuries. Long before the invention of the credit card, shop credit boosted the purchasing power of consumers. Although the precise evolution of shop credit remains to be charted, historians have found that in commercialized areas of Europe and the Americas, many goods could be bought wholly or partially on credit by the eighteenth century.

In England, the pervasive use of store credit dates to the late sixteenth and early seventeenth centuries when, due to a scarcity of gold and silver, retailers increasingly accommodated consumers with credit.[30] The same dependency on credit shaped French commercial expansion. In Paris, bakers and other food sellers often acted as neighborhood bankers, allowing the "deserving" poor to eat before demanding that they settle up. If small bits of shop credit were not enough, the laboring poor could pawn clothing and hardware for cash in the hope of buying the items back in better times.[31]

Retailers were particularly accommodating of their middling and elite clients. High-ranking nobles who bought luxury goods on credit were notoriously slow to pay their bills, as the records of a late eighteenth-century Parisian jeweler named Aubourg show. Only 14 percent of his sales were immediately paid for in cash, whereas the rest were made on credit with the assumption that customers would settle their debts after a fixed number of days or months. It took three and a half months for the chevalier Dorat to pay Aubourg the 150 livres he owed for a cane with a golden handle.[32] The marquise de Bercy made her purveyors wait longer, up to three years in certain cases.[33] Although most nobles were wealthy enough to pay for such goods at the moment of sale, they exploited their power over retailers to delay payment, knowing that the latter had little recourse against such tardiness. Rather than risk alienating their customers by litigating, shopkeepers thought it wiser to cultivate

---

[30] Craig Muldrew, *An Economy of Obligation: The Culture of Credit and Social Relations in Early Modern England* (New York, 1998).
[31] Steven L. Kaplan, *The Bakers of Paris and the Bread Question, 1700–1775* (Durham, NC, 1996).
[32] Coquery, *Tenir Boutique à Paris au XVIIIe siècle*, 201–205.
[33] Crowston, *Credit, Fashion, Sex*, 175.

ties with men and women of quality, who were, after all, walking advertisements for the shops that they frequented. Accordingly, shopkeepers did not explicitly charge interest on the credit that they advanced, but they did set high prices, implicitly including interest charges in the cost of their merchandise.

Extremely fragile insofar as it rested overwhelmingly on personal trust, the system of credit was all the more precarious since shopkeepers tended to purchase their own stock on credit from wholesalers. Caught between what they owed their wholesalers and what their customers owed them, retailers attempted to build favorable reputations that would keep wholesalers at bay as they applied pressure on their own customers. But sudden demands by wholesalers to settle a debt, combined with an inability to persuade their own customers to pay up, led many a retailer to bankruptcy, which was a built-in feature of the dangerously volatile credit system.

We have already noted how high-end goods and their low-end versions enjoyed wide circulation in this period. Sometimes, high and low versions passed through different retail markets – for example, coffee was sold in both high-end coffee shops and by itinerant peddlers hawking used grounds – but many shops sold goods of varying quality under the same roof to attract a broad swathe of customers.[34] Wedgwood himself spoke of the opportunity to sell his vases to "the Middling Class of People" at a "reduced price" after "the Great People" had purchased them at a "great price."[35] Less famous retailers followed similar principles. The Parisian haberdasher du Bail advertised both "fine and false" jewelry ("the beautiful as well as the everyday"), "fine and ordinary" sponges, and "beautiful and ordinary" whistles. In this case, too, luxury goods and cheap imitations of them (classified as "semi-luxe" or "populuxe" by historians) were on sale in the very same shop.[36] In Paris, tables for sale at the same shop ranged in price from 2 to 240 pounds, candlesticks from 4 to 200 pounds, allowing skilled craftsmen and lower-level professionals to buy into the world of goods on a modest scale. The same can be said for cosmetics, which were sold on a scale of quality and cost from 3 to 24 pounds.[37] Even exclusive shops that sold luxury items for

---

[34] Stobart, *Sugar and Spice*, 219–221.

[35] Quoted in Robin Reilly, *Wedgwood* (New York, 1989), I: 361.

[36] Natacha Coquery, "Language of Success: Marketing and Distributing Semi-luxury Goods in Eighteenth-Century Paris," JDH 17 (2004), 82, 86; Cissie Fairchilds, "The Production and Marketing of Populuxe Goods in Eighteenth-Century Paris," in John Brewer and Roy Porter, eds., *Consumption and the World of Goods* (London, 1993), 228–248.

[37] Catherine Lanoë, *Le Poudre et le fard: Une histoire des cosmétiques de la Renaissance aux Lumières* (Seyssel, 2008), 323. For grocers and confectioners, Villeret, *Le goût de l'or blanc*, 333.

hundreds, or thousands, of pounds were sure to sell a multitude of knickknacks at affordable prices. At a time when better-paid laborers earned 2 pounds a day, the Parisian tapestry-maker Law sold elaborate beds for 1,000 pounds alongside hourglasses, inkwells, reading chairs, music stands, board games, and mirrors for 2 pounds or less.[38] Such a shop was well within reach of the middling classes even as it excluded the laboring poor.

Advertising

In the eighteenth century, marketing occurred mainly at the site of the shop through signs, façades, window displays, interior design, and face-to-face encounters between shopkeepers and customers. However, tradespeople and retailers increasingly turned to print advertising to boost demand for their products. McKendrick, Brewer, and Plumb argued that like modern consumption itself, modern print advertising originated not in the mid-nineteenth century, as historians had long claimed, but rather in the eighteenth century.[39] Although their book focused almost exclusively on newspaper advertisements, current research suggests that the newspaper was only one of several advertising outlets in this era. Retailers also diffused words and images through trade cards, handbills, catalogues, almanacs, and the fashion press. Further, we now know that the use of print advertising was not unique to England. Tradespeople and retailers employed similar methods of marketing in towns across Europe and colonial America.

The most widespread form of advertisement was not the newspaper announcement but the trade card and handbill.[40] Merchants, artisans, and shopkeepers distributed hundreds of thousands of trade cards, precursors of today's business cards, to customers every year in England alone. Handbills were commonly printed on invoices. Distributed after sales had been completed, both kinds of ephemeral texts encouraged return business by reminding customers of the appeal of a particular shop. To this end, such advertisements – unlike newspaper ads of the day – often used imagery. Some images publicized the shop itself, depicting elaborate façades or welcoming interior scenes. Others promoted the goods on offer, highlighting their abundance, quality, variety,

---

[38] Coquery, *Tenir Boutique à Paris au XVIIIe siècle*, 291.
[39] McKendrick, Brewer, and Plumb, *The Birth of a Consumer Society*.
[40] Maxine Berg and Helen Clifford, "Selling Consumption in the Eighteenth Century: Advertising and the Trade Card in Britain and France," *Cultural and Social History* 4 (2007), 145–170.

novelty, and low price. Sometimes reinforced by long lists of merchandise, cornucopian images attempted to stir the imagination of
consumers. Luxury retailers also used cards to call attention to the royal
or aristocratic patronage that they received. Londoner J. A. Carter
boasted that he was "Hatter to the Their Royal Highnesses the Princes
of Wales, Prince Frederick and Prince Wilh. Henry." The Parisian
candy-maker Ravoise proclaimed himself "Confectioner of the Queen
for the court sweets."[41] Finally, some shopkeepers telegraphed the foreign and exotic (usually Asian) provenance of their goods.[42] The elaborate trade card for Gersaint's Parisian shop À la Pagode, designed by
painter François Boucher, depicted such "curious and foreign" merchandise as Japanese lacquered cabinets, Chinese porcelain tea sets,
pagodes, gem stones, and shells (see Figure 3.3). Trade cards for British
tobacco dealers featured exotic African and Native American figures
whose depiction as inferior to dominant European merchants and colonists demarcated a clear racial hierarchy (see Figures 3.4 and 3.5).

If trade cards and handbills circulated locally among customers, newspapers, which were part of a thriving periodical press in this period,
flowed beyond a given neighborhood or town, offering retailers an
opportunity to reach a larger audience of potential customers. Not as
many retailers took advantage of this opportunity as had exploited trade
cards and handbills, but those who did, such as sellers of books, medicinal goods, and beauty products, were able to reach a wider public. In
the Dutch Republic, where newspaper advertisements first appeared,
book advertisements composed a large portion of copy early on. In
England, where weekly papers printed around fifty advertisements an
issue, medicinal remedies were common. The manufacturer of Daffy's
Elixir built a nationwide brand by placing inserts in papers across the
country.[43]

In France, too, advertisements filled Parisian and provincial newspapers. It is no coincidence that weekly advertisers promoted many of
the same goods that were on the rise in after-death inventories: fashionable clothing, personal accessories, furniture, and household furnishings.

[41] Natacha Coquery, "French Court Society and Advertising Art: The Reputation of
Parisian Merchants at the End of the Eighteenth Century," in C. Wischerman and
E. Shore, eds., *Advertising and the European City. Historical Perspectives* (Aldershot,
2000), 107.
[42] Natacha Coquery, "Selling India and China in Eighteenth-Century Paris," in Maxine
Berg, Felicia Gottmann, Hanna Hodacs, and Chris Nierstrasz, eds., *Goods from the East,
1600–1800: Trading Eurasia* (Houndmills, 2015), ch. 15.
[43] R. B. Walker, "Advertising in London Newspapers, 1650–1750," *Business History* 15
(1975), 112–130.

Figure 3.3 Gersaint's trading card for À la Pagode. Bibliothèque
nationale de France. Gersaint's shop on the Notre Dame Bridge had
been immortalized by Jean-Antoine Watteau's 1720 painting, *Enseigne
de Gersaint*, which showed a worker packing away a portrait of the
recently deceased Louis XIV. Boucher's trading card emphasizes that
the inventory of the shop was expanding beyond paintings to assorted
luxury goods, including many imports from Asia.

Figure 3.4 Tobacco wrapper or trade card, c. 1700–1799.
Copyright Museum of London. This image refers to John Smith's *The Generall Historie*, which recounts how the British captain captured "the Virginia Indian King of Paspanegh" after nearly strangling him to death. The wrapper or card demonstrates the authenticity and quality of Gaitskell's tobacco by linking it to stories of colonial domination

Figure 3.5 Tobacco dealer's trade card.
New York Public Library. A pipe-smoking colonial American planter/merchant leans back and puts his foot up on a hogshead as he watches enslaved black men cultivate tobacco for export to Britain. The card associates tobacco with white supremacy, wealth, and leisure

But, like English papers, they seemed to specialize in advertisements for proprietary medicines, remedies, and cosmetics. In Montpellier, the apothecary Carquet advertised a special purgative liqueur endorsed by a prominent medical professor that would cure whatever ailed you.[44] Parisian cosmetics-maker Joseph Collin, who touted a patent from the Academy of Sciences and the patronage of the empress of Russia, advertised a vegetable-based rouge that did not contain the harmful chemicals found in competing brands. Antoine Maille of mustard fame claimed that that his vinegar rouge "was a singular and useful discovery... that gives the skin the most beautiful tone, the color of the rose, the complexion of youth."[45] The *Affiches de Lyon* tempted readers with medicinal

[44] Colin Jones, "The Great Chain of Buying: Medical Advertisement, the Bourgeois Public Sphere, and the Origins of the French Revolution," AHR 101 (February 1996), 33.
[45] Quoted in Morag Martin, *Selling Beauty: Cosmetics, Commerce, and French Society, 1750–1830* (Baltimore, 2009), 68.

coffee from Yemen and Martinique.[46] Aimed at elites and the middling classes, such advertisements helped stimulate a vigorous trade in health and beauty products.

Advertisements also appeared in a new type of periodical, the fashion journal. Since the Renaissance, knowledge of court fashion had spread outward from Italian towns (and then Paris) to foreign capitals across Europe by way of fashion dolls, elaborate life-size mannequins dressed in the latest styles. In the late seventeenth and eighteenth centuries, print overtook the expensive fashion doll to become the main vehicle for the spread of high fashion. Fashion plates and then periodicals such as the *Mercure Galant* and *Journal des Dames* commented on interior decoration and women's and men's clothing, accessories, and hairstyles, before the first true French fashion magazines, the *Courrier de la mode* (1768–1770) and the *Cabinet des Modes* (1785–1793) appeared in the late eighteenth century. Promoting the French fashion industry through a mix of articles, advertisements, and images, the *Cabinet des Modes* provided detailed illustrations of what men and women wore while strolling through the Tuileries or along the Champs-Elysées. The magazine circulated through Europe, spawning imitations such as the German-language *Journal des Luxus und der Moden* (1786–1827) printed in Weimar, which familiarized aristocratic and bourgeois readers with juicy details about the latest fashions in London and Paris and the ways in which Germans appropriated them. One report noted how English and French fashion became gendered in the northern region of Mecklenburg: "The inhabitants of Mecklenburg are like other Germans; they imitate both the English and the French, though with one important difference. The men arrange their clothes, their households, their carriages, and gardens in the English style, while elegant ladies still follow the lead of Parisian fashion dealers, who send their outdated goods to the North."[47] Fashion knowledge about who consumed what and how was now itself commodified through the commercial press.

Producer–Consumer Dialogue

Aware of the dynamic retail sector, historians today emphasize the reciprocal relationship between supply and demand. Mediated by merchants and retailers, new channels of dialogue opened between producers and

---

[46] Julie Hardwick, "Fractured Domesticity in the Old Regime: Families and Global Goods in Eighteenth-Century France," AHR 124 (October 2019), 1271.

[47] Quoted in Michael North, *"Material Delight and the Joy of Living": Cultural Consumption in the Age of Enlightenment in Germany*, trans. Pamela Selwyn (New York, 2008), 48.

consumers in the seventeenth and eighteenth centuries. Not only were there more points of contact between retailers and customers than ever before but more information flowed between them. As consumers learned about the world of goods, retailers, merchants, and producers gauged and shaped consumer tastes. The information exchanged in this accelerating dialogue created feedback loops between producers and consumers that often (though not always) stimulated supply and demand. Thus, demand was neither a direct emanation of primordial human needs nor an automatic response to commercial manipulation. It was a social and cultural phenomenon that developed through communication systems mediated by "information brokers" of all types.[48]

Consider how this worked on three different geographic scales. In long-distance trade between Europe and Asia, East India companies learned how to generate demand for overseas goods by accounting for the tastes of European consumers. The success of the British East India Company was anything but foreordained. In its early days, it had a difficult time selling Indian cloth, but company agents discovered that by modifying the design of the fabric, they could improve sales in the home market. With the help of highly skilled Indian producers who were accustomed to adapting the size, shape, color, and imagery of cloth to the specific demands of distant markets, agents experimented with new designs to make foreign textiles more appealing to British consumers. As early as 1643, the directors of the company, faced with sluggish demand, instructed agents to alter the color scheme of Indian cloth. Whereas Indian painters and printers tended to place white patterns on colored backgrounds, agents asked producers to invert this design and place colored patterns on white backgrounds, an innovation that made the cloth more attractive in the home market and boosted demand.[49] Soon directors were sending sample patterns to Indian textile workers, who freely elaborated on them to produce hybrid products that blended Asian and European motifs. The French Indies Company produced similar hybrids, domesticating the exotic by inserting for instance familiar images from the fables of Jean de La Fontaine in otherwise "Indian" cloth.[50] The same method of accounting for tastes manifested itself in the porcelain market where company traders and Chinese producers adapted

[48] Crowston, *Credit, Fashion, Sex*, 139. See also Jean-Yves Grenier, *L'économie d'Ancien Régime* (Paris, 1996), chs. 11, 14.
[49] John Irwin and Katherine Brett, *Origins of Chinz* (London, 1970), 4–5. John Styles, "Product Innovation in Early Modern London," PP 168 (August 2000), 124–169.
[50] For the English case, see Beverly Lemire, "Domesticating the Exotic: Floral Culture and the East India Calico Trade with England, c. 1600–1800," *Textile: Cloth and Culture* 1 (2003), 64–85.

to the European market. Across the globe, merchants strove to take the measure of consumer tastes and tailor their products accordingly. In the end, overseas trading companies were selling objects that were hybrid constructs of the market, seeming to represent the lives and values of the East but fabricated by Asian producers to meet Western preconceptions of Eastern art.[51]

Dialogue between producers and consumers also intensified within Europe. The success of the renowned Lyon silk industry rested on its ability to respond to changing consumer tastes in Paris and then to market fashionable new designs across the continent. To stay on top of Paris fashion, silk merchants annually sent professional designers to the capital to observe the latest trends. For inspiration, designers visited production sites like the Gobelins tapestry works and Sèvre porcelain manufactory, promenaded through the gardens of Versailles, attended Parisian theaters, perused fashionable shops along the Rue St Honoré, and went to church in elite neighborhoods. Having taken in the latest Parisian trends, designers would create new lines of silks and send their work back to Lyon. This designer-mediated conversation between producer and consumer allowed the Lyon silk industry to maintain the upper hand over its rivals, whose designs remained perpetually behind the times. Similarly, in the realm of pottery manufacturing, Wedgwood was highly attentive to his customers' wishes. When his brother urged him not to respond to the "whims" of his clients, he replied that his manufactory had established its "character for Universality" by "taking up hints given by customers and bringing them to perfection."[52] As economic historian Carlo Poni concluded, the most successful firms of the age "engaged in a dialogue with the taste of consumers, who became increasingly refined and demanding, in turn influencing the strategies of the producers."[53]

---

[51] European exporters also endeavored to account for distant localized tastes. After developing the skills to make cotton cloth in the manner of Indian producers, the merchants of Barcelona prompted King Charles III to ask officials in America to report on the "whims" of colonial consumers and the "means to satisfy them." Quoted in Marta Vicente, *Clothing the Spanish Empire: Families and the Calico Trade in the Early Modern Atlantic World* (New York, 2006), 81. For a similar dynamic in the Atlantic wine market, see David Hancock, *Oceans of Wine: Madeira and the Emergence of American Trade and Taste* (New Haven, CT, 2009). For slave-ship outfitters gathering information about consumer demand on the African coast, see Anne Elizabeth Ruderman, "Supplying the Slave Trade: How Europeans Met African Demand for European Manufactured Products, Commodities and Re-exports, 1670–1790" (Dissertation, Yale University, 2016).

[52] Josiah Wedgwood Jr. to Thomas Wedgwood, ca. 1790, *Correspondence of Josiah Wedgwood, 1781–1794* (Manchester, 1906), 117.

[53] Carlo Poni, "Fashion as Flexible Production: The Strategies of the Lyons Silk Merchants in the Eighteenth Century," in Charles Sabel and Jonathan Zeitlin, eds.,

This type of dialogue unfolded in miniature form in shops across Europe. As we've seen, window displays, handbills, and print advertisements diffused information about goods, but perhaps more important was the oral advice sellers provided individual customers about what they should buy. Indeed, the advice of producers, merchants, shopkeepers, and peddlers was invaluable for customers eager to exhibit good taste. One R. Campbell relied on his upholsterer for good "judgment ... on the choice of goods" and "taste in the fashions."[54] In Paris, architects increasingly acted as interior decorators for elite households, while "fashion merchants" provided counsel on clothing and accessories for fashion-conscious clients.[55] The marquise de Bercy consulted regularly with merchants and seamstresses as she went about assembling her many outfits, but it fell to the fashion merchants in particular "to guide her through the creation of a complete outfit, from headpiece to gloves, jewelry, and neckerchiefs, all made or chosen to match her dress and its embellishments."[56] Shops encouraged conversations that diffused fashion knowledge and boosted demand.

Historians today no longer explain the growth of eighteenth-century consumption in terms of autonomously developing supply (early industrialization) or autonomously developing demand (consumerism). Instead, they emphasize how supply and demand intersected in ways that ultimately stimulated both. To be sure, the intensity of the dialogue between producers and consumers that took place at that intersection pales in comparison with that of today when online consumers – willingly

World of Possibilities: Flexibility and Mass Production in Western Industrialization (Cambridge, 1977), 37–74. See also Lesley Miller, "Paris–Lyon–Paris: Dialogue in the Design and Distribution of Patterned Silks in the Eighteenth Century," in Robert Fox and Anthony Turner, eds., *Luxury Trades and Consumerism in Ancien Régime Paris* (Farnham, 1998), 139–167; William Sewell, "The Empire of Fashion and the Rise of Capitalism in Eighteenth-Century France," PP 206 (February 2010), 91–94; Vicente, *Clothing the Spanish Empire*, 81. For Wedgwood's plans to market wares according to perceived national tastes in Europe, see Ashli White, *Revolutionary Things* (New Haven, CT, forthcoming). For the importance of such dialogue in the book trade, see Robert Darnton, Keynote Address at "Fighting Words: Polemical Literature in the Age of Democratic Revolutions," Princeton University, April 15, 2016; Andrew Pettegree, *The Invention of News: How the World Came to Know About Itself* (New Haven, CT, 2014), 311.

[54] Quoted in Clive Edwards, "The Upholsterer and the Retailing of Domestic Furniture, 1600–1800," in Blondé and Coquery, eds., *Retailers and Consumer Changes in Early Modern Europe*, 63.

[55] Basile Baudez, "Architects and Interior Decoration in the Age of Gouthière," lecture at the Frick Collection, February 8, 2017.

[56] Crowston, *Credit, Fashion, Sex*, 174. For a colonial example, see Sarah Templier, "The Power of Consumer Desire: The Trade and Consumption of Textiles and Clothing in French and British North America, 1713–1760" (PhD dissertation, Johns Hopkins University, 2020), ch. 4.

or unwillingly, knowingly or unknowingly – provide corporations with massive amounts of personal data that corporations turn around and sell for a profit or use for their own finely targeted advertising. The exchange of information between producers and consumers in the seventeenth and eighteenth centuries was far less comprehensive (and, arguably, far less intrusive), but it did nonetheless create new reciprocal links between supply and demand. On the supply side, as more and more shops opened in towns throughout Europe and its far-flung empires, producers, merchants, and retailers reached out to potential customers by enhancing the physical space of the shops, consulting with clients, distributing printed trade cards and handbills, and advertising in newspapers and fashion journals. Peddlers, smugglers, and street sellers engaged consumers in less wealthy neighborhoods and villages. On the demand side, consumers expressed their preferences by talking to shopkeepers about their merchandise, buying certain goods and not others, and enthusiastically pursuing particular trends in fashion. Such signals did not escape the notice of traders, many of whom adapted to changing tastes and marketed their goods accordingly. The development of such robust communication between producers and consumers, and the increased circulation of information about taste that resulted from it, spurred rising levels of consumption.

4   The Cultural Meanings of Consumption

> Clothes came as sluggishly as food ... I made shift, however, with a little over-work, and a little credit, to raise a genteel suit of clothes, fully adequate to the sphere in which I moved. The girls eyed me with some attention; nay, I eyed myself as much as any of them.[1]

European consumption grew gradually but unmistakably between 1650 and 1800, thanks in part to changes in labor, production, trade, and marketing. The fact that more and more people were consuming an ever wider array of goods, however, raises a number of questions about motivation and meaning. Why did women and men want more stuff? Why did they pursue particular kinds of goods? What did such goods come to mean to those who produced, marketed, purchased, and used them? And to what extent did the growth of consumption reflect or contribute to a broader evolution in cultural values? If, as cultural theorists suggest, there is no innate universal propensity to consume beyond the strictest biological minimum (and humans have chosen to forgo that on occasion), then it is important to explore the cultural contexts in which meanings are forged and desires take shape. Questions of meaning are notoriously difficult to answer, but historians have borrowed conceptual tools from sociologists and anthropologists to discern the significance of the expanding world of goods.

Social Emulation?

When Neil McKendrick first articulated the thesis that a "consumer revolution" swept England in the eighteenth century, he explained the motivation to consume in terms of social emulation. Although the rich "led the way" in spending, they were eagerly followed by the rest of society.

---

[1] Quoted in John Styles, *The Dress of the People: Everyday Fashion in Eighteenth-Century England* (New Haven, CT, 2007), 1.

In imitation of the rich the middle ranks spent more frenziedly than ever before, and in imitation of them the rest of society joined in as best they might – and that best was unprecedented in the importance of its impact on demand. Spurred on by social emulation and class competition, men and women surrendered eagerly to the pursuit of novelty, the hypnotic effects of fashion, and the enticements of persuasive commercial propaganda. As a result many objects, once the prized possessions of the rich, reached further and further down the social scale.[2]

McKendrick made this claim with the implicit support of a number of important sociologists. At the turn of the twentieth century, Thorstein Veblen, known today for his theory of "conspicuous consumption," argued that in modern societies where the boundaries between social classes are not perfectly clear, the upper class sets the standard of consumption for subordinate classes, which strive to imitate that standard in the pursuit of status.

The norm of reputability imposed by the upper class extends its coercive influence with but slight hindrance down through the social structure to the lowest strata. The result is that members of each stratum accept as their ideal of decency the scheme of life in vogue in the next higher stratum, and bend their energies to live up to that ideal.[3]

We can hear echoes of Veblen in McKendrick when he describes England's social structure as particularly fluid and therefore ripe for class competition, social emulation, and the rapid downward diffusion of new consumer desires.

In 1904, German sociologist Georg Simmel added a twist to Veblen's theory of cultural trickle-down. In what would become a classic article on fashion, Simmel argued that as soon as the lower classes begin to "copy" the style of the upper classes, the upper classes "turn away from this style and adopt a new one, which in its turn differentiates them from the masses; and thus the game goes merrily on."[4] The contest accelerates, he went on to say in a statement that McKendrick again echoes, in periods of upward social mobility when social classes approach one another.

Such theories of consumption and its downward diffusion have left a deep imprint on discussions of court society and the expansion of courtly consumption in eighteenth-century Europe. Borrowing directly from Veblen, sociologist Norbert Elias claimed that conspicuous consumption was "an indispensable instrument" at the royal court, where the struggle for status was particularly intense. But courtly values and forms of

[2] Neil McKendrick, John Brewer, and J. H. Plumb, *The Birth of a Consumer Society: The Commercialization of Eighteenth-Century England* (Bloomington, IN, 1982), 10–11.
[3] Thorstein Veblen, *The Theory of the Leisure Class* (1899; New York, 1975), 84.
[4] Georg Simmel, "Fashion," *American Journal of Sociology* 62 (1957), 545.

consumption "constantly percolated downwards" to inferior groups who sought to imitate their superiors.[5] Hence, by the middle of the eighteenth century, objects invented at court to display aristocratic civility had spread to the lower orders. For example, the fork, once a novelty limited to the continent's most exclusive royal courts, was soon used by the bourgeoisie and even ordinary townspeople.

It is hardly surprising that McKendrick and others have sought to explain the growth of consumption in terms of social emulation because many eighteenth-century commentators explained it in precisely the same way. Any historian familiar with Veblen, Simmel, and Elias could not help but be struck by the following passage written by eighteenth-century novelist Henry Fielding:

> Thus while the Nobleman will emulate the Grandeur of a Prince; and the Gentleman will aspire to the proper State of the Nobleman; the Tradesman steps from behind his Counter into the vacant Place of the Gentleman, Nor doth the Confusion end here: It reaches the very Dregs of the People, who [aspire] still to a Degree beyond that which belongs to them.[6]

Fielding was typical of writers of his age who decried the spread of "luxury" beyond the boundaries of a narrow elite. Such diffusion, they warned, erased age-old marks of distinction and threw the social hierarchy into chaos and confusion. The marquis de Mirabeau claimed to have mistaken his blacksmith for a gentleman when the artisan appeared before him in his Sunday best and powdered wig. "Will such a lord deign to dance in the streets?" the marquis jested sarcastically.[7] A similar condemnation of social confusion was articulated by an anonymous bourgeois from Montpellier, for whom nothing was "more impertinent than to see a cook or valet don an outfit trimmed with braid or lace, strap on a sword, and insinuate himself among the finest company."[8] Such socially conservative moralizing often turned against women. "Dressed in light or printed cottons," fumed Jacob-Nicolas Moreau, women of the lower classes "think themselves ... superior to their social condition because ladies of quality too wear calicoes."[9] Plenty of statements by

---

[5] Norbert Elias, *The Court Society*, trans. Edmund Jephcott (New York, 1983), 56 n.30, 63–65; Norbert Elias, *The Civilizing Process: The History of Manners*, trans. Edmund Jephcott (Oxford, 2000), 386–387, 422–436.

[6] Henry Fielding, *Enquiry into the Causes of the Late Increase in Robbers* (London, 1751), 6.

[7] Marquis de Mirabeau, *L'Ami des hommes* (Avignon, 1756), I: pt. 1, 152.

[8] Quoted in John Shovlin, "The Cultural Politics of Luxury in Eighteenth-Century France," *French Historical Studies* (FHS) 23 (2000), 587.

[9] Quoted in Giorgio Riello, *Cotton: The Fabric That Made the Modern World* (Cambridge, 2013), 133.

contemporary observers lent support to McKendrick's concept of emulation.

Despite evidence from eighteenth-century prescriptive literature, however, historians have grown skeptical of the emulation thesis. Certainly, the display of luxury goods projected status and power. Many types of food, clothing, furniture, and accessories functioned as what economists call "positional goods," products that situated consumers in the social order. But the emulation thesis has been widely criticized for failing to account for the complicated process by which consumer taste was formed in this period. Lorna Weatherill first cracked the edifice of the thesis when she discovered that consumption patterns in England between 1660 and 1760 did not always match the social hierarchy.[10] According to her data, professionals and merchants had more decorative goods (mirrors, china, pictures) than higher-status English gentry, just as urban tradesmen possessed more stuff (forks and knives, china, furniture, window curtains) than higher-status rural yeomen. As a critic noted disapprovingly of English shopkeepers, "Do they not, in general, enjoy a much greater share of the conveniences and superfluities of life, than landholders of far superior property?"[11] The same pattern emerged on the continent where urban merchants often cultivated more refined habits of consumption than higher-status rural nobles.[12] Traders in colonial ports like Pondicherry were also known to consume disproportionately large quantities of global luxuries.

The consumption hierarchy did not always mirror the social hierarchy. Men and women who lived in urban areas and participated in commerce – or who produced fashion goods themselves[13] – tended to acquire more things and a wider variety of them than their immediate social superiors. They did not slavishly copy social groups above them; in fact, there are cases in which fashions trickled up the hierarchy rather than down. Nor did patterns of consumption always reflect the wealth of consumers. On the whole, affluent families consumed more than poor ones, but wealth does not explain everything. Overton et al. found that

---

[10] Lorna Weatherill, *Consumer Behaviour and Material Culture in Britain, 1660–1760* (London, 1988); see also Mark Overton et al., *Production and Consumption in English Households, 1600–1750* (New York, 2012).

[11] Quoted in Ian Mitchell, *Tradition and Innovation in English Retailing, 1700 to 1850* (London, 2016), 91.

[12] Philippe Meyzie, *L'Alimentation en Europe à l'époque moderne* (Paris, 2010), 167. For the Netherlands, see Anne McCants, "Becoming Consumers: Asiatic Goods in Migrant and Native-Born Middling Households in 18th-Century Amsterdam" in Maxine Berg, ed., *Goods from the East, 1600–1800: Trading Eurasia* (Houndmills, 2015), ch. 13.

[13] Clare Haru Crowston, *Fabricating Women: The Seamstresses of Old Regime France, 1675–1791* (Durham, NC, 2001).

the acquisition of certain goods, such as window curtains, saucepans, and tea and coffee equipment, did not closely correlate to wealth. Location (urban versus rural) and occupation (service, retail, and maritime versus agriculture) had more to do with consumer behavior than did wealth alone.[14]

The critique of social emulation should not be taken to imply that consumption had no social ramifications at all. It certainly did, but the relationship between consumption and social status seems to have been changing. In the Middle Ages, the link between appearance and status was relatively direct. Material symbols did not merely reflect social identity but contributed to its very constitution; in a literal sense, kings, clergy, officeholders, guild masters, and others were, to some extent, the clothes they wore. However, the rise of commerce over the course of the early modern period threatened to disrupt the strict relationship between materiality and identity. The profusion of goods made consumption a less reliable indicator of status, imperiling the legibility of the social order. Between 1300 and 1600, national and local rulers responded to this cultural challenge by promulgating sumptuary legislation, which sought to fix in law the relationship between consumption and status.[15] But sumptuary law failed to resolve the crisis as it proved impossible to control the hierarchy of appearances through legislation. Another response was to perfect what Jean-Yves Grenier has called "an economy of identification" in which goods were subject to hierarchical taxonomies of quality. Ideally, the highest quality goods were to be consumed by the most highly ranked individuals. Yet, the social mobility of the period, not to mention the production of merchandise that imitated quality goods, made such an economy difficult to maintain in practice.[16] As the expansion of the world of goods accelerated in the seventeenth and eighteenth centuries, I would argue, an alternative model of social distinction emerged in which the relationship between consumption and status was mediated by a set of rapidly developing consumer values. In this model, goods continued to indicate status but they did so more indirectly by signifying consumers' taste for certain values that in turn expressed status. In other words, what had once been a relatively tight link between consumption and status was loosened to accommodate a more expansive

[14] Mark Overton et al., *Production and Consumption in English Households*.
[15] Martha Howell, *Commerce before Capitalism in Europe, 1300–1600* (Cambridge, 2010), ch. 4.
[16] Jean-Yves Grenier, "Une économie de l'identification: Juste prix et ordre des marchandises dans l'Ancien Régime," in Alessandro Stanziani, ed., *La Qualité des produits en France (XVIIIe–XIXe siècles)* (Paris, 2003), 25–53.

role for consumer taste, the possession of which allowed consumers to associate themselves with specific status-enhancing values.

To understand how this worked, we must reconsider the period's material culture. The study of material culture, as practiced by anthropologists, archaeologists, art historians, and historians, examines the relationship between people and things. As historian Ann Smart Martin puts it:

> The study of material culture is about the way people live their lives through, by, around, in spite of, in pursuit of, in denial of, and because of the material world. The venture is premised on the proposition that artifacts are integral to cultural behavior. Humans use them to create, learn, and mediate social interaction and relations. Human-made things are far more than mere tools; they are complex bundles of individual, social, and cultural meanings grafted onto something that can be seen, touched, and owned.[17]

Not all scholars of material culture conduct their work the same way: some emphasize the materiality of artifacts; others their representations in word and image; and still others the practices through which humans interact with them. But all strive to understand how humans engage with the material world to derive, make, and communicate meaning.[18] From this perspective, the meaning of consumption cannot be reduced to the role of signaling social status. Material things also articulate ideas about gender, sexuality, politics, ethnicity, race, and individual identity. They trigger memory, mark stages of the life cycle, evoke sentiment, and bestow significance on rituals and ceremonies. Acknowledging the myriad ways in which people lived their lives through material objects opens up new possibilities of interpretation and allows us to see how the rise of consumption in the long eighteenth century generated a host of new values.

The Meaning of Consumption

Historians have discovered the vestiges of countless ideas, values, and expressions of identity embedded in the material and commercial culture of the long eighteenth century. Although none were revolutionary in and of themselves, collectively they suggest the development of a new consumer sensibility. Indeed, some historians argue that what was truly transformative about the so-called consumer revolution was not so much

---

[17] Ann Smart Martin, "Material Things and Cultural Meanings: Notes on the Study of Early American Material Culture," *William and Mary Quarterly* (WMQ) 52 (1996), 5.

[18] For current approaches to material culture, see Anne Gerritsen and Giorgio Riello, eds., *Writing Material Culture History* (London, 2015); Daniel Miller, *Stuff* (Cambridge, 2010).

the proliferation of goods as the development of a new "culture of consumption."[19] Although "the process of growth in consumption was evolutionary," James Riley contends, "its effect was revolutionary."[20]

Recent research maintains that the eighteenth century experienced a broad cultural shift to modern forms of consumption. Rather than simply classifying new commodities as "populuxe" goods, cheap versions of aristocratic amenities acquired by nonelites interested in emulating their social superiors, it is more productive to consider how contemporaries themselves characterized the ever rising number of goods swirling around them.[21] Producers, traders, and consumers – and a multitude of self-proclaimed professional experts like interior decorators, fashion merchants, retailers, doctors, and writers – used language to articulate the values of a forward-looking material culture that often reflected the ideas of the eighteenth-century Enlightenment.

What follows is an exploration of a number of values that defined the changing consumer culture of the long eighteenth century. To be sure, the following classification of cultural meanings is too tidy. Goods were invested with multiple meanings, many of which cut across the divisions I lay out. Readers are therefore encouraged to disaggregate, recombine, and add to these categories while they reflect on the linkages and tensions among the manifold ideas attributed to eighteenth-century goods.

Novelty and Fashion

The theme of novelty manifested itself in documents ranging from probate inventories to print advertisements to philosophical essays. The use of the terms "new" and "modern" became remarkably common in probate inventories from areas with vibrant consumer cultures, such as Kent, England, and Antwerp, the Netherlands.[22] In newspapers and bills

[19] Natacha Coquery, *Tenir Boutique à Paris au XVIIIe siècle* (Paris, 2011), 24.
[20] James Riley, "A Widening Market in Consumer Goods," in Euan Cameron, ed., *Early Modern Europe: An Oxford History* (Oxford, 1999), 257. Daniel Roche, *The People of Paris*, trans. Marie Evans (Berkeley, CA, 1987), 128, likewise asserts that the qualitative importance of changes in consumer habits "may far exceed their quantitative manifestations."
[21] Cissie Fairchilds, "The Production and Marketing of Populuxe Goods in Eighteenth-Century Paris," in John Brewer and Roy Porter, eds., *Consumption and the World of Goods* (London, 1993), 228–248.
[22] Overton et al., *Production and Consumption in English Households*, 115; Bruno Blondé, "Cities in Decline and the Dawn of a Consumer Society: Antwerp in the 17th–18th Centuries," in Bruno Blondé and Natacha Coquery, eds., *Retailers and Consumer Changes in Early Modern Europe: England, France, Italy and the Low Countries* (Tours, 2005), 37–52.

of trade, shopkeepers increasingly emphasized all kinds of wares as "new and elegant," "in the newest taste," "*à la mode*" ("in the latest fashion"), "new fashioned" (as opposed to "old fashioned"), and "modern."[23] Strikingly, the use of the word "modern," which in this period meant contemporary or belonging to the present aesthetic moment in contrast to a past often depicted as outmoded and crude, was applied to goods large and small. Cabinetmaker Thomas Malton claimed that fellow tradesmen who displayed "a little modern taste" would be more successful. Mary Lamar, who was helping her brother Henry Hill design a townhouse in Philadelphia in accordance with the "present taste" of London, urged him to opt for the "Modern Style, not grand but Elegant and Convenient."[24] The great *philosophe* Denis Diderot did not hesitate to apply the term to the fashionable bagwig, "the most modern" wig of all because it was short and convenient unlike the grotesquely large wigs of the past.[25]

This "mania for the new," as one eighteenth-century German critic called it, was closely related to that of fashion.[26] French dictionaries from the period defined "la mode" as "everything which changes according to time and place" and "the manner that is, or once was, in vogue."[27] To be "à la mode," an expression that quickly passed into other European languages, was to be up-to-date in your appearance and taste. Such definitions spoke to the phenomenon of the fashion cycle, which by all accounts was accelerating in the eighteenth century. Naturally, the speed of any given fashion cycle varied according to the type of goods involved. Clothing, personal accessories, and certain household furnishings like earthenware danced to the tune of fashion more nimbly than heavy and expensive furniture, but even certain models of furniture such as writing tables were now subject to voguish trends. As one carpentry manual declared, "with each change in fashion, each person makes it their duty to conform, even if it means getting rid of pieces of good Furniture for

---

[23] Nancy Cox, *The Complete Tradesman: A Study of Retailing, 1550–1820* (New York, 2000), 220; Joan DeJean, *The Age of Comfort: When Paris Discovered Casual – And the Modern Home Began* (New York, 2009), 147.

[24] Quoted in Clive Edwards, "The Upholsterer and the Retailing of Domestic Furniture, 1600–1800," in Blondé and Coquery., eds., *Retailers and Consumer Changes in Early Modern Europe*, 63; quoted in Amy Henderson, "A Family Affair," in John Styles and Amanda Vickery, eds., *Gender, Taste, and Material Culture in Britain and North America, 1700–1830* (New Haven, CT, 2006), 271.

[25] Denis Diderot and Jean Le Rond d'Alembert, eds., *Encyclopédie, ou Dictionnaire raisonné des sciences, des arts, et des métiers*, seventeen vols. (Paris, 1751–1765), s.v. "perruque."

[26] Quoted in Michael North, *"Material Delight and the Joy of Living": Cultural Consumption in the Age of Enlightenment in Germany*, trans. Pamela Selwyn (New York, 2008), 45.

[27] Antoine Furetière, *Dictionnaire universel* (The Hague, 1690), s.v. "la mode"; *Le Dictionnaire de l'Académie française* (1694), s.v. "la mode."

new, perhaps less good ones, and this for the simple reason that is almost shameful not be as fashionable in one's furnishings as in one's dress."[28]

Some items were redesigned annually for the first time in history. In the 1660s and 1670s, the French silk industry in Lyon established annual or even seasonal fashion cycles. In the eighteenth century, the Parisian shop Le Petit Dunkerque marketed new snuffboxes every year, often commemorating current events such as the death of Louis XV in 1774.[29] To help consumers keep up with the increasing rate of fashion, magazines with relatively wide readerships provided illustrated fashion prints of the latest styles and hairdos. Indeed, for those of means who wished to be fashionable, keeping up with new designs became, in the words of one observer from Montpellier, "truly an occupation" unto itself (see Figure 4.1).[30] According to historian William Sewell, consumers who actively read and talked about fashion performed a special type of labor that enhanced the surplus value of goods in much the same way that discussion of products on the Internet generates consumer demand today.[31]

The greatest thinkers of the age were astonished by the quickening pace of fashion, this "the mania for the new."[32] One of Montesquieu's characters in *Persian Letters* commented hyperbolically that "a woman who leaves Paris to spend six months in the country comes back looking as antiquated as if she had been away for thirty years."[33] But it was Diderot who most sensitively explored the culture of novelty in "Regrets on Parting with My Old Dressing Gown," in which he confessed to becoming a "slave" to fashion. Diderot observed how, after receiving the gift of a brand-new scarlet dressing gown, he felt compelled not only to abandon his old gown, but to replace his old furnishings, one after the other, ultimately redecorating his entire office. Each substitution made the remaining objects appear that much more obsolete and repugnant. In a frantic effort to restore aesthetic coherence, he bought (on credit of course) a whole series of new items: an armchair covered with

---

[28] Quoted in Natacha Coquery, "Language of Success: Marketing and Distributing Semi-luxury Goods in Eighteenth-Century Paris," JDH 17 (2004), 85. Furniture designer André Jacob Roubo said that "it was disgraceful for one's furniture not to be as up-to-date [à la mode] as one's clothing." DeJean, *The Age of Comfort*, 105.

[29] Carolyn Sargentson, *Merchants and Luxury Markets: The Marchands Merciers of Eighteenth-Century Paris* (London, 1996), 121.

[30] Quoted in Shovlin, "The Cultural Politics of Luxury in Eighteenth-Century France," 586.

[31] William Sewell, "The Empire of Fashion and the Rise of Capitalism in Eighteenth-Century France," PP 206 (February 2010), 81–120.

[32] Quoted in North, *"Material Delight and the Joy of Living,"* 46.

[33] Montesquieu, *Persian Letters*, trans. C. J. Betts (London, 1993), letter 99.

Figure 4.1 Pietro Antonio Martini after Jean-Michel Moreau Le Jeune, *La Petite Toilette*.

Courtesy of the Metropolitan Museum of Art. At his "toilette" or dressing table, a gentleman has his hair done as he considers a fashionable jacket presented to him by a tailor. Although eighteenth-century commentators claimed that women were particularly susceptible to the lure of fashion, men eagerly consumed fashion goods as well

Moroccan leather that "usurped" his old straw chair; a fancy inlaid cabinet that supplanted his sagging bookcase; an expensive new desk with drawers for organizing his affairs that replaced his paper-strewn wooden table; and, for good measure, a pendulum clock, a writing desk, and two paintings that added luster to the workspace. "Change means throwing things away, turning things upside down, and building something new," Diderot declared.[34] His shrewd analysis of how the introduction of a single new object of fashion can induce one to indulge in an obsessive cascade of consumption was so insightful that economists today call the phenomenon the "Diderot effect."

Individuation, Selfhood, and Domesticity

In addition to novelty, certain scholars have associated the growth of consumption in this era with the emergence of individuality. Philosopher Gilles Lipovetsky, deviating from a long-standing critical tradition that emphasizes the moral pitfalls of modern consumption, claims that since the Middle Ages, fashion has encouraged consumers to break free of tradition in the pursuit of freedom, democracy, and "secular individualism."[35] Unsurprisingly, early modern historians have found this linear view of history problematic. Many consumer decisions were taken by couples or families, not isolated individuals. Shopping itself was as much a collective social experience as an individual one. For the laboring classes, furthermore, many forms of consumption were involuntary rather than the result of individual choice: domestic servants did not always choose their own clothing; city folk who rented furnished rooms did not select their furniture; soldiers and sailors received uniforms and food rations; recipients of charity took what they could get; and the enslaved in the Americas were given cheap rough clothing. In sum, it is wise to avoid teleological histories of consumer individualism. Any sort of self-fashioning that took place through consumption did so "in dialogue with different groups" and through socially constructed norms.[36]

Nevertheless, certain consumer practices and discourses in the eighteenth century did indeed reflect a valorization of the concept of self. It is possible to identify three related aspects of selfhood in the material culture of the day: individuation; reflexivity; and sentimentalism.

[34] Denis Diderot, *Rameau's Nephew and Other* Works, trans. Jacques Barzun and Ralph Bowen (Indianapolis, 2001), 312.
[35] Gilles Lipovestky, *The Empire of Fashion: Dressing Modern Democracy*, trans. Catherine Porter (Princeton, NJ, 1994), 7.
[36] Ulinka Rublack, *Dressing Up: Cultural Identity in Renaissance Europe* (Oxford, 2010), 10.

Individuation, a process by which individuals differentiate themselves from groups, is perhaps most obvious in changing practices of dining. In the Middles Ages, men and women shared drinking goblets and ate food from common serving dishes. Gradually across Europe in the seventeenth and eighteenth centuries, however, elites and the middling sort began to use separate, individualized drinking glasses, plates, and utensils. In the eminently collective ritual of dining, individual place settings became the order of the day. Abbot Kitowitcz observed this phenomenon among Polish nobles, who had once shared cups without hesitation. But because glasses were now "set separately before each place setting," a sense of "disgust for the mouth of the other" arose and drinking henceforth became individuated.[37] Restaurants in Paris took this one step further by inviting customers "to sit at his or her *own* table, to consult his or her *own* needs and desires, to concentrate on that most fleeting and difficult to universalize sense: taste."[38] Clothing and accessories, too, became more individualistic. Family account books began to list acquisitions of apparel by the names of each family member, and advertisements promoted goods that were customized to individual tastes.[39] Even promenading through the city, a collective activity once reserved for groups of aristocrats, began to undergo a process of individuation. City guides in the second half of the eighteenth century no longer described public promenades in terms of their social function – namely, to see and be seen in high society – but in terms of the diversity of amusements on offer to any reader with the time and inclination to experience the city personally for him or herself.[40]

Many scholars argue that this process of self-differentiation was related to the emergence of a reflexive and sentimental self. Sociologist Anthony Giddens contends that in late modern society, as traditional social forces waned, individuals constructed distinct selves by consciously choosing particular consumer lifestyles, often in consultation with professional experts.[41] Building on Giddens, theorist Celia Lury suggests that consumer culture provides a "particular set of material circumstances in which individuals come to acquire a reflexive relation to identity."[42]

---

[37] Quoted in Meyzie, *L'Alimentation en Europe à l'époque moderne*, 104.

[38] Rebecca L. Spang, *The Invention of the Restaurant: Paris and Modern Gastronomic Culture* (Cambridge, MA, 2000), 75.

[39] Michael Kwass, "Big Hair: A Wig History of Consumption in Eighteenth-Century France," AHR 111 (June 2006), 653–656; Styles, *The Dress of the People*, 242.

[40] Laurent Turcot, *Le promeneur à Paris au xviiie siècle* (Paris, 2007), ch. 5.

[41] Anthony Giddens, *Modernity and Self-identity: Self and Society in the Late Modern Age* (Stanford, CA, 1991).

[42] Ceila Lury, *Consumer Culture* (New Brunswick, NJ, 2011), 29.

Again, early modern historians remain skeptical of such blanket assertions about the rise of the reflexive self, but many suggest that, for certain elites and intellectuals, a new sense of self did develop in the context of rising consumption. If we accept the definition of the modern self as a producer and consumer of stories that "place [one's] self at the center of the system of relations, discursive and otherwise," it is not difficult to find examples of modern, reflexive, consuming selves in the eighteenth century.[43] As this chapter's epigraph recounts, William Hutton, a poorly paid stockinger's apprentice who scraped together enough money through overtime pay and credit to buy "a genteel suit of clothes," found that "the girls eyed me with some attention" but that "I eyed myself as much as any of them."[44] He may well have looked at himself in one of the countless household mirrors that proliferated in the age of Enlightenment. Self-reflection of a more figurative type was evinced by women's interests in letter-writing, which in elite households involved the purchase of writing desks, ink stands, and fine paper. Correspondence allowed women "to retreat to a space of privacy in which to reflect, and from which they could … launch themselves through time and space beyond the limits of their daily lives."[45] Private correspondence allowed women to develop habits of self-reflection as well as a sense of both individual autonomy and wider social connection.

Sentimentalism also seems to have informed ideas and practices of selfhood. Although the Enlightenment has often been cast as an age of reason, it is now clear that sensibility, the notion that individuals could be moved by deep inner feeling, shaped ideas of morality, society, and the arts. The precise connection between sentimentalism (what the French called *sensibilité*, the Germans *Empfindsamkeit*) and consumption became clear in the second half of the eighteenth century when some men and women began to experiment with new styles of casual dress that were meant to express their inner selves. In Germany, young middle-class men wore blue frock coats and yellow waistcoats to signal their identification with the ill-fated, ultrasensitive protagonist of Goethe's *Sorrows of Young Werther*.[46] In France, Jean-Jacques Rousseau dramatically changed his wardrobe, abandoning finery for simple woolen clothing; for the self-proclaimed "citizen of Geneva," dressing down meant rejecting the artifice of Parisian high society and adopting a truer, more

---

[43] Quoted in Dena Goodman, *Becoming a Woman in the Age of Letters* (Ithaca, NY, 2009), 323.
[44] Quoted in Styles, *The Dress of the People*, 1.
[45] Goodman, *Becoming a Woman in the Age of Letters*, 335.
[46] North, *"Material Delight and the Joy of Living,"* 57.

Figure 4.2 Élisabeth Vigée-Lebrun, *La Reine en gaulle*, 1783.
Courtesy of the National Gallery of Art, Washington, DC. This painting of
Marie-Antoinette in a simple muslin gown and straw hat caused a stir when
displayed publicly at the Salon of 1783

authentic mode of living. Even Queen Marie-Antoinette donned simple
white muslin dresses at the Petit Trianon at Versailles, the more private,
informal palace where she claimed that she could be herself. When
Élisabeth Vigée-Lebrun painted the queen in just such an outfit without
court dress, makeup, or diamonds – that is, without any marks of royal
station – it caused a scandal (see Figure 4.2). However, many women
would adopt the informal style and, with it perhaps, the notion that it
enabled them to express their individual selves more fully.[47] The idea of
sensibility also had implications for family life, for it was in the domestic
sphere that parents were to raise virtuous sons and daughters with the
proper balance of sensibility and decorum (see Figure 2.1). Practices like
family reading, whereby parents and children read aloud to one another,
ensured that the strong individual emotions evoked by reading would be

[47] Caroline Weber, *Queen of Fashion* (New York, 2006), 160–163.

held in check by close familial ties.[48] Sentimentalism encouraged domesticity as well as individuality, even if these values remained largely aspirational for many households.[49]

Comfort, Convenience, Pleasure

We sometimes forget that physical comfort – defined as "self-conscious satisfaction with the relationship between one's body and its immediate physical environment"[50] – is historically conditioned. There is no fixed universal sense of comfort across time and space because the concern for comfort is a socially constructed product of history. The period of the late seventeenth and eighteenth centuries was particularly important in this regard, as the discourse of producers, traders, consumers, and commentators shifted from Renaissance values of magnificence (embodied in status-boosting architectural splendor) to Enlightenment-era comfort, a quality hailed by its proponents as a harbinger of a new, modern age. As one eighteenth-century author reflecting on man's progress in the arts remarked, "comfort had replaced magnificence."[51]

Although the French and British both lay claim to the invention of comfort, the history of the word "comfort" reveals the concept's transnational origins. In France, from the 1670s, the semantic range of the word "*commodité*," which originally connoted convenience, expanded to include a sense of physical ease – what we would now call comfort. The English not only anglicized the French term ("commoditie") to refer to the quality of convenience but in the late eighteenth century transformed the French term *confort*, meaning help or solace, into "comfort," indicating physical ease and well-being. The French eventually followed suit in the middle of the nineteenth century, adopting the meaning of the English word comfort for the older French term *confort*. Such vagaries of the terminology reflect the cross-border construction of the concepts of convenience and comfort in the age of the consumer revolution.

From the 1670s, the idea of comfort and convenience emerged in relation to changing forms of architecture, furniture, apparel, and accessories. As wealthier homeowners increasingly compartmentalized interior space – yet another sign of individuation and privacy – they assigned

---

[48] Abigail Williams, *The Social Life of Books: Reading Together in the Eighteenth-Century Home* (New Haven, CT, 2017).

[49] Julie Hardwick, "Fractured Domesticity in the Old Regime: Families and Global Goods in Eighteenth-Century France," AHR 124 (October 2019), 1267–1277.

[50] John Crowley, "The Sensibility of Comfort," AHR 104 (June 1999), 750; John Crowley, *The Invention of Comfort: Sensibilities and Design in Early Modern Britain and Early America* (Baltimore, 2001).

[51] Quoted in DeJean, *The Age of Comfort*, 233.

Figure 4.3 Commode. Victoria and Albert Museum. This neoclassical commode or chest of drawers was made by the Parisian cabinetmaker Pierre Denizot around 1775.

specific functions to different rooms (parlors, bedrooms, kitchens, etc.) and filled spaces with upholstered furniture designed to make bodies comfortable. Both the easy chair and the sofa were invented in Paris but spread rapidly to courts and cities throughout Europe. The heavy cushioning of chairs allowed sitters to sink into furniture as they socialized or read, while the sofa, amply padded on all surfaces, was large enough to accommodate two reclining sitters or to permit a single sitter to stretch out and prop up their legs. The affluent could change the upholstery seasonally to match the latest fashions and, in winter, use closed stoves instead of open fireplaces to ensure a warmer, less smoky, and more cozy home environment.[52]

Furniture expressed convenience as well as comfort. No item of furniture better captures the vogue for convenience than the chest of drawers (Figure 4.3). In fact, the French name for the chest of drawers, the *commode*, literally meant "convenient." Unlike its ancestor the chest, the *commode* allowed its users to store things in and retrieve them from

[52] DeJean, *The Age of Comfort*.

easy-to-use separate compartments. It was the perfect piece of furniture for organizing an ever expanding world of objects. This premium on convenience was also apparent in the proliferation of small functional tables: night tables, writing tables, gaming tables, and dressing tables, all of which reflected the age's concern for domestic life. Home furniture became more specialized, functional, and utilitarian, even at court where utility had not always been uppermost in the minds of kings and aristocrats.

The pursuit of comfort also redefined clothing. While men donned loose-fitting, kimono-style dressing gowns called banyans or *robes de chambre* around the house, women dared to wear more comfortable dress in public. Starting in the 1670s, elite women gradually abandoned formal court dress for a simpler, looser, one-piece gown called a mantua. Comfort was paramount. As a Parisian newspaper observed, "since everyone in France today wants to be comfortable, people hardly get dressed up anymore ... [Court dress] is now used only for ceremonial occasions ... and no longer when one drops in on one's friends or just to go for a walk."[53] The mantua's light fabric was worn over stays that, while restrictive by today's standards, were not as binding as traditional bodices. Produced by women for a broad social spectrum of female consumers, the casual mantua was an immediate hit. Similar attention to lightness and comfort in women's fashion appeared in the loose-fitting sack dress (*robe volante*), in the casual style of "undress" (*déshabillé négligé*), and in the loose muslin gowns of the 1770s, all of which contrasted vividly with the rigid formality of the court. As Joseph Addison declared in the *Spectator* as early as 1711, "the fashionable world is grown free and easy; our manners sit more loose upon us; nothing is modish as an agreeable negligence."[54]

In addition to comfortable furniture and clothing, consumers partook of a host of "convenient" personal gadgets and accessories: fans, canes, snuffboxes, pocket watches, nail clippers, candle snuffers, retractable carriage steps, and so on. Take the umbrella, a convenience of Asian origin that spread to Europe and the Americas. In the seventeenth century, the umbrella was an unwieldy exotic item held by servants (often depicted as dark-skinned) to protect pale aristocratic ladies from the sun. Its associations with exoticism and whiteness never disappeared, but in 1705 a Parisian purse maker invented the first lightweight, collapsible, waterproof umbrella that provided protection from the rain. As an

---

[53] Quoted in DeJean, *The Age of Comfort*, 190.
[54] Quoted in Keith Thomas, *In Pursuit of Civility: Manners and Civilization in Early Modern England* (New Haven, CT, 2018), 326. Crowston, *Fabricating Women*, 36–41.

advertisement for the invention emphasized, the umbrella weighed only six ounces, would fit easily inside one's pocket, and was tastefully trimmed. "Thus each person can, without inconveniencing himself, have one of them on him as a precaution against bad weather."[55] Although the umbrellas were quite costly at first, Parisians could soon acquire cheap knock-offs in clandestine markets. The utilitarian fashion spread to Germany and, of course, Britain, where it would eventually become a symbol of Englishness.

For philosophers and scientists, artisans and interior decorators, such quotidian conveniences like the umbrella were associated with core Enlightenment concepts of utility, happiness, and pleasure. Benjamin Franklin noted that "happiness consists more in small conveniences or pleasures that occur every day, than in great pieces of good fortune that happen but seldom to a man in the course of his life."[56] Indeed, small conveniences and simple pleasures went hand-in-hand. "It is certain that physical needs are the source of the pleasures of the senses," wrote scientist Madame du Châtelet, "and I am persuaded that there are more pleasures in a modest fortune than in total abundance: a box, a porcelain, a new piece of furniture are the true pleasures for me."[57] Châtelet, like her intellectual partner and lover Voltaire, extolled tasteful material pleasures while criticizing gaudy aristocratic display.

Nature, Simplicity, Authenticity

In the second half of the eighteenth century, an aesthetic movement prizing simplicity expressed itself in art and architecture, as the whimsical curves of the rococo gave way to the sober angles of neoclassicism. At the level of everyday consumer culture, a parallel shift took place from purportedly fanciful and artificial goods to those deemed genuine and natural. This trend is visible in everything from food to apparel, but the cosmetic industry provides a particularly clear example. Originating in the courts of Renaissance Italy, the use of cosmetics spread to the French court in the seventeenth century and quickly diffused to elites throughout Europe. Both male and female aristocrats applied white paint to their faces, rouge to their cheeks, and powder and pomade to their hair.

---

[55] Joan DeJean, *The Essence of Style* (New York, 2006), 226 (figure 11.3). See also Fairchilds, "The Production and Marketing of Populuxe Goods in Eighteenth-Century Paris," 235–236.

[56] Quoted in Crowley, "The Sensibility of Comfort," 174.

[57] Quoted in Goodman, *Becoming a Woman in the Age of Letters*, 165. For pleasure, see Thomas M. Kavanagh, *Enlightened Pleasures: Eighteenth-Century France and the New Epicureanism* (New Haven, CT, 2010); Roy Porter, *The Creation of the Modern World: The Untold Story of the British Enlightenment* (New York, 2000).

Whiteness, long associated in Christianity with the purity of the soul, signified moral and social superiority, distancing elites from dark-skinned, purportedly impure peasant laborers in the countryside and enslaved laborers in the colonies.[58] Bright red circles on the cheek were meant to highlight the whiteness around them and draw the attention of admirers. None of this was supposed to look natural. One was supposed to apply rouge to the cheeks "with abandon," remarked Casanova. "One did not want the rouge to appear natural."[59] In the eighteenth century, as the European market for cosmetics expanded to include urban servants, artisans, shopkeepers, and shop clerks, moral critics denounced the artificial quality of makeup, claiming not only that it was immoral to hide one's face but that the use of metallic-based paint was physically harmful. Jean-Jacques Rousseau and other writers who decried the artificiality of cosmetics celebrated the virtues of natural beauty.

We might expect such critiques to dampen sales of cosmetics but in the 1770s and 1780s, cosmetic producers adapted to this critique by marketing "natural," vegetable-based cosmetics that enhanced nature instead of covering it up. My rouge "perfectly imitates natural colors," touted Parisian hairstylist Bellangier.[60] Consumers responded in turn: women went for a more natural look, foregoing white paint or applying it and rouge more subtly, while men gave up on makeup altogether and opted instead for scented soap. The same imperative to appear natural influenced other consumer goods as well. Men abandoned the towering wigs of the past for those that imitated "natural" hair.[61] The Enlightenment idea of nature as a morally sound and ontologically secure foundation of the world could not help but shape consumer culture, especially as it regarded the body. As one writer put it, "Our way of dressing, of styling our hair, & of wearing our shoes is more analogous to the construction of our body than it has ever been."[62] Eighteenth-century fashion sought to anchor itself in the human body, establishing a

---

[58] The perceived quality of the sugar produced by the enslaved in the Americas was also based on its whiteness, which affirmed the social status of its consumer. Maud Villeret, *Le goût de l'or blanc: Le sucre en France au xviiie siècle* (Rennes, 2017), 277.

[59] Quoted in Melissa Lee Hyde, "Beautés rivales: les portraits de Madame Du Barry et de la reine Marie-Antoinette," in Catherine Lanoë et al., eds., *Cultures de cour, cultures du corps, XIVe–XVIIIe siècle* (Paris, 2011), 194.

[60] Quoted in Catherine Lanoë, *La Poudre et Le Fard: Une Histoire des Cosmétiques de la Renaissance aux Lumières* (Seyssel, 2008), 323. See also Morag Martin, *Selling Beauty: Cosmetics, Commerce, and French Society, 1750–1850* (Baltimore, 2009).

[61] Kwass, "Big Hair," 652.

[62] C. S. Walther, *Manuel de la toilette et de la mode*, three vols (Dresde, 1771–1780), vol. 2, pt. VI, ch. 9, 59–60.

paradoxical yet enduring link between modern consumption and the pursuit of natural authenticity.

The move from courtly display to nature, simplicity, and authenticity had important implications for the construction of gender. In 1930, psychologist and psychoanalyst J. C. Flügel argued that nineteenth-century European men renounced extravagant dress in favor of sober costume that symbolized the denial of beauty and pleasure and the embrace of duty, self-control, and work. Women, by contrast, continued to wear colorful and ostentatious clothing, becoming the principal agents of conspicuous consumption. Elaborating on Flügel's theory, some historians of dress have extended its reach backward into the eighteenth century, when, they suggest, sexual differentiation sharpened and a division between a male public sphere and female private sphere widened.[63] There is certainly much truth to this argument. In the late eighteenth century, for example, the dark English *frac* coat swept European male fashion, anticipating the somber suits male elites wear throughout the world today. But we should be careful not to press the idea of an eighteenth-century "masculine renunciation" too far. Although dress continued to denote gender, the aesthetics of masculine and feminine clothing were often shaped by the same underlying cultural trends, including that of simplicity; men did not claim a monopoly on natural authenticity. Historians should therefore think twice before adopting Flügel wholesale. If a renunciation did take place, it seems to have unfolded in two stages. In the eighteenth century, men *and* women sought to move beyond courtly forms of consumption to create a consumer ethic consistent with Enlightenment ideas of simplicity, utility, nature, and self. Only during the second stage, largely in the nineteenth century, would European society witness a full-scale redefinition of masculinity and a hardening of gender boundaries that expressed itself in a material culture split between bourgeois male sobriety and female conspicuousness, though even that formulation may well be exaggerating the case.

Authenticity in fashion, moreover, could express national identity. In the second half of the seventeenth century, as European power shifted from Spain to France, the French court extended its influence across the continent and the French luxury trades dramatically expanded; fashion became largely a French affair. Indeed, as we have seen, the very expression for fashion – "la mode" – was French. Over the course of the

---

[63] Jennifer Jones, *Sexing La Mode: Gender, Fashion, and Commercial Culture in Old Regime France* (Oxford, 2004); David Kuchta, *The Three-Piece Suit and Modern Masculinity* (Berkeley, CA, 2002); Daniel Purdy, *The Tyranny of Elegance: Consumer Cosmopolitanism in the Era of Goethe* (Baltimore, 1998).

eighteenth century, however, the French and other Europeans increasingly took an interest in Britain, this rough island nation across the channel to the north that had produced John Locke and Isaac Newton and, astonishingly, defeated France in the Seven Years' War (1756–1763). In the world of fashion, French reactions to Britain's rise to power took various forms. One response on the part of consumers was to tap into rising nationalist sentiment and express loyalty to the French *patrie*. During the War of American Independence, elite French women commemorated a decisive French naval victory by wearing models of a famous frigate, *Belle Poule*, in their abundant hair. Alternatively, many consumers abandoned themselves to "Anglomania" by imitating English fashions in food, clothing, and gardening that they characterized as natural, unfussy, and authentic. In the 1780s, the followers of the duke d'Orléans, a great admirer of the English constitution, wore unadorned English-style riding coats ("redingotes" in French) to express their political loyalties. Just as the redingote embodied "English" simplicity and virtue, "English" gardens, which replaced rigidly symmetrical "French" gardens across Europe, evoked less formal, more natural landscapes. Perceived differences in national identity became part of European-wide fashion in the eighteenth century, a trend that would become fully politicized in the age of revolution. As an American in Paris observed in 1789, "Every Thing is *à l'Anglois* and a Desire to imitate the English prevails alike in the Cut of a coat and the Form of a Constitution."[64]

Cleanliness, Health, Hygiene

Unlike today, when norms in many parts of the world demand regular bathing, washing was not a high priority in early modern Europe. Water was scarce and perceived to be dangerous. According to medical theory at the time, warm water dilated skin pores, opening a channel through which dangerous diseases could pass.[65] The virtue of cleanliness was reserved first and foremost to the soul which, the church urged, should be kept free from the stain of sin.

Beginning in the sixteenth century, however, civility manuals began to apply religious concepts of purity and cleanliness to the exterior of the human form. They instructed readers to wash their hands, face, and

[64] Quoted in Ashli White, *Revolutionary Things* (New Haven, CT, forthcoming).
[65] Georges Vigarello, *Concepts of Cleanliness: Changing Attitudes in France since the Middle Ages*, trans. Jean Birrell (Cambridge, 1988). However, Vigarello's thesis has recently been challenged by Susan North, *Sweet and Clean?: Bodies and Clothes in Early Modern England* (Oxford, 2020).

clothing, the condition of which reflected the inner state of the soul. Clothing, Erasmus wrote, "is the body's body and gives an idea of the soul's disposition."[66] Gradually, at court and among urban elites, clean clothing came to denote morality and social respectability. In the long eighteenth century, as clothing consumption expanded beyond the court, concern for cleanliness encouraged the accumulation of linen undergarments like white shirts and shifts. Tantamount to a dry bath, the frequent changing of linens removed the impurities of sweat, dirt, and oil from the skin and provided a respectable veneer. When sixteen-year-old John Keys was accused of stealing a shirt in London in 1789, he defended himself by saying that he found the garment on the ground: "I picked it up and took it home; having a dirty shirt on, I put on that [which] I found, being clean, as I was going to my master the next morning."[67] Keys evidently believed that he would cut a finer figure before his master if he was wearing a clean white shirt. Clean clothes certainly improved the prospects of Jane Field, who applied for lodging in Westminster in 1793. Her landlord recalled that "she appeared rather poor but the clothes she had on were very clean; I thought her a working person as she said she was."[68] A poor person who wore clean clothes and had a regular job was entitled to a degree of respect.

The premium on cleanliness also explains why cotton became such an appealing textile. Unlike silk or wool, cotton cloth imported from India and increasingly produced in Europe was eminently washable. Indian dyeing techniques ensured that the textile's vivid colors were colorfast and would hold up after repeated washing, a feature that amazed Europeans (see Figure 4.4). Indeed, enthused one French philosopher, far from losing their brilliance after being washed, the colors "become only more beautiful."[69] Hence, cotton came to be associated with cleanliness, which itself signified respectability. As one Briton asked, "Is there a wench above sixteen who does not find herself more acceptable to others when she looks clean [in cotton] than when she is obliged to wear woolen, which never looks so clean?"[70]

Finally, the norm of cleanliness stimulated consumption of household linens. Much has been made of the cleanliness of the Dutch, whose

---

[66] Quoted in Daniel Roche, *A History of Everyday Things: The Birth of Consumption in France, 1600–1800*, trans. Brian Pearce (Cambridge, 2000), 159.
[67] Quoted in Styles, *The Dress of the People*, 78.
[68] Quoted in Styles, *The Dress of the People*, 78.
[69] Louis de Jaucourt, "toile peinte des Indes," in Diderot and le Rond d'Alembert, eds., *Encyclopédie, ou dictionnaire raisonné des sciences, des arts et des métiers*, vol. 16 (Neufchastel, 1765), 370.
[70] Quoted in Styles, *The Dress of the People*, 114.

Figure 4.4 Giacomo Ceruti (il Pitocchetto), *The Laundress*, 1736.
Copyright Getty Images. The labor that produced cleanliness was intensive and
gendered: women did the work of cleaning laundry. The laundress portrayed
here, a middle-aged woman in ragged clothes, stares directly at the viewer

pristine and orderly domestic interiors, which inspired Vermeer and
other painters, radiated a moral commitment to godliness and national
providence. But we should not put too much stock in national stereo-
types, for the cult of domestic cleanliness extended well beyond the
Netherlands. Better-off households across Western Europe accumulated
unprecedented quantities of household linens (bed sheets, table covers,
cloths, napkins, and so on), which projected virtue and respectability. In
the Americas, Euro-Americans' concern for white linens and undergarments grew all the more intense as they sought to distinguish themselves
from African-Americans and Native Americans. In the Atlantic context,
interest in cleanliness (whiteness) developed in parallel with hardening

racial hierarchies and slavery, the shirt serving as a kind of public skin used to differentiate between the European body and the African or indigenous body.[71]

Cleanliness was entangled with themes of health and hygiene. Today's pervasive commercialization of physical well-being has roots in the eighteenth century, when many health-related goods and services became available through the market. Apothecaries, grocers, physicians, surgeons, and unlicensed charlatans offered a variety of services and remedies for those concerned with their health. The health sector of the economy, though nowhere near the size it is today, was certainly expanding in the eighteenth century. Consumers hired dentists to clean and whiten (rather than simply pull) their teeth, participating in what Colin Jones has called the "smile revolution." A healthy white-tooth smile "came to be viewed as a symbol of an individuals' innermost and most authentic self."[72] In the same vein, other "artisans of the body" such as barber-surgeons, hairdressers, and wigmakers offered services to a widening clientele eager to have their hair cut, shaved, whitened, or curled in the latest style or according to the particular "air" of the individual customer.[73] Then there were the myriad health and beauty products: remedies, elixirs, tonics, powders, soaps, and perfumes as well as toothpicks, ear-cleaners, tongue-scrapers, and handkerchiefs. Racheal Pengelly, the wife of an English merchant, regularly spent money on a variety of remedies her doctor prescribed.[74] Concern for health also explains the success of overseas commodities such as coffee, tea, chocolate, sugar, and tobacco, the ingestion of which was initially perceived to have medicinal benefits. Noncommercial homemade remedies did not disappear, especially in rural areas, but middling men and women in towns across Europe purchased unprecedented quantities of health, beauty, and personal care products.

Exoticism

During the Middle Ages, most Europeans construed difference in terms of time, imagining a past Golden Age or a prelapsarian Eden. Only a tiny

---

[71] The proliferation of linen laid a heavy burden on working-class women, who labored ceaselessly in their own homes and as domestic servants and laundresses to keep this new mass of linen and undergarments clean. The costs and benefits of the consumer revolution were not shared equally. Kathleen Brown, *Foul Bodies: Cleanliness in Early America* (New Haven, CT, 2009).

[72] Colin Jones, *The Smile Revolution in Eighteenth-Century Paris* (Oxford, 2014), 3–4, 62.

[73] Sandra Cavallo, *Artisans of the Body in Early Modern Italy: Identities, Families and Masculinities* (Manchester, 2007).

[74] Weatherill, *Consumer Behaviour and Material Culture in Britain*, 127.

elite of princes, lords, and clergy put a premium on geographical distance, collecting "exotic" goods (silk, spices, ceramics, tapestries, pearls,
jewels, and religious artifacts) from the "orient," a vast, vaguely defined
region that stretched from the Levant to Japan. Over the course of the
early modern period but especially the late seventeenth and eighteenth
centuries, the circulation of "exotic" objects widened beyond wealthy
elites as East Indies companies traded intensively with Asia, Atlantic
commerce boomed, and Europeans fabricated imitations of imported
goods. Imports from distant lands became everyday goods for millions
of Europeans. Historians are now just beginning to understand how such
imports shaped European material culture.

The consumption of exotic goods reflected a new level of imaginative
engagement with the world beyond Europe. For propertied women who
decorated their homes with chinoiserie (porcelain vases, tea sets,
pagodas), such objects were "emissaries of a distant world that expanded
their horizons."[75] Anthropological theory can help us understand what
these foreign goods might have meant to the Europeans who appropriated them. Igor Kopytoff explains, "what is significant about the adoption of alien objects – as of alien ideas – is not the fact that they are
adopted, but the way they are culturally redefined and put to use."[76]
Anthropologists typically apply this methodology to illuminate how indigenous peoples actively shape the meanings of the Western goods that
they encounter. Historians are now taking a similar approach to the flow
of goods in the other direction to study Europe's past adoption of non-
European goods. One conclusion that they have drawn is that European
engagement with remote lands was mediated by innumerable producers,
merchants, experts, state officials, and consumers themselves, who
helped to domesticate or "indigenize" the exotic world.

In the eighteenth century, commercial, cultural, and state brokers
modulated the strangeness and familiarity of exotic goods at almost every
point in the commodity chain. East Indies companies collaborated with
Indian producers to tame the exotic origins of Indian cloth by adding
familiar European themes.[77] Chinese producers decorated porcelain
with scenes of China as Europeans imagined it, while consumers placed
such "Chinese" pieces next to locally made objects for a culturally mixed

---

[75] Goodman, *Becoming a Woman in the Age of Letters*, 178.

[76] Igor Kopytoff, "The Cultural Biography of Things: Commoditization as Process," in
Arjun Appadurai, ed., *Social Life of Things: Commodities in Cultural Perspective*
(Cambridge, 1986), 67.

[77] Beverly Lemire, "Domesticating the Exotic: Floral Culture and the East India Calico
Trade with England, *c.* 1600–1800," *Textile* 1 (2003), 64–85.

home environment. Europeans who sipped tea "adapted the Chinese conviction that drinking tea led to bodily health, psychic contentment, and a more poetic, productive, and sober self," just as Europeans who snorted or smoked tobacco borrowed certain Native American associations with the leaf, such as healing and sociability, while rejecting Amerindian cosmologies on which those associations had for centuries been based.[78]

As Europeans domesticated the exotic, they radically simplified the complexity of the overseas world. From 1670 to 1730, geographic books published in the Netherlands collapsed a diversity of distant lands into an "agreeably exotic world for a universally European consumer."[79] Marked in print by shorthand icons like palm trees and parasols, the tropical world beyond Europe was portrayed as eminently consumable. Even as plantation slavery deepened in the Americas over the course of the eighteenth century, representations of an agreeably exotic world persisted. British tobacco advertisements showed hybrid African-Native Americans freely trading in the leaf, effacing the role of slave labor in the production process.[80] Similarly, wood and cotton harvested in Caribbean slave societies were finished with exotic Asian themes just as cafés that sold coffee and sugar from the Caribbean advertised the hot drink as Turkish or Arabian (see Figure 4.5). Motifs of "eastern" luxury, civility, comfort, and sensuality predominated, even when the majority of overseas goods now came from the Americas. The brutally exploitative system of plantation slavery, which was responsible for so much of the efflorescence of consumption, remained partly hidden behind anodyne images of an exotic "Orient" as East and West Indies were amalgamated into a strange and distant landscape.[81] We might add that, for consumers, the environmental degradation wrought by colonial monoculture remained equally obscure.

The meanings attributed to specific ingested imports (coffee, tea, chocolate, sugar, and tobacco) are particularly revealing. When first imported into Europe in tiny quantities, these psychoactive products were largely understood to be medicinal. In sixteenth-century Spain,

[78] Marcy Norton, *Sacred Gifts, Profane Pleasures: A History of Tobacco and Chocolate in the Atlantic World* (Ithaca, NY, 2008); Erika Rappaport, *The Thirst for Empire: How Tea Shaped the Modern World* (Princeton, NJ, 2017).
[79] Benjamin Schmidt, *Inventing Exoticism: Geography, Globalism, and Europe's Early Modern World* (Philadelphia, 2015), 15.
[80] Catherine Molineux, "Pleasures of the Smoke: 'Black Virginians' in Georgian London's Tobacco Shops," WMQ 64 (April 2007), 327–376.
[81] Madeleine Dobie, *Trading Places: Colonization and Slavery in Eighteenth-Century French Culture* (Ithaca, NY, 2010); Emma Spary, *Eating the Enlightenment: Food and the Sciences in Paris, 1670–1760* (Chicago, 2012).

Figure 4.5 Woodcut of a coffeehouse from *A Broadside against Coffee*, London, 1672.

Folger Shakespeare Library. Turkish associations with coffee are underscored in this early woodcut, which condemns the foreign drink as immoral. Such attacks would dissipate in the eighteenth century as coffee drinking became part of many Europeans' daily life

for example, medical experts legitimized the consumption of American chocolate and tobacco by incorporating the substances into humoral theory, a basis of medical science since Ancient Greece. The European courtiers who first sampled tobacco as snuff took it to cure a host of ailments from stomachaches to asthma. As these ingested goods circulated ever more widely in the late seventeenth and eighteenth centuries, their medical applications gave way to what we would today call recreational use. They became associated with prevailing Enlightenment notions of domesticity, pleasure, and polite sociability. In fact, coffee and tea became so well domesticated in France and Britain that the drinks eventually became nationalized; coffee was ultimately seen as "French" and tea "British." Within the space of a century, these two hot drinks went from being rarefied exotic medicines to everyday national comforts.

Finally, exoticism was linked to quality and authenticity. Even as the purchase of exotic goods became routine, retailers and consumers continued to use place names (*Chinese* porcelain and tea, *Virginian* tobacco, and *Turkish* coffee) to underscore their genuine quality.[82] In an age when imported goods were often copied or adulterated, exotic place names distinguished the authentic from the ersatz, both of which were available to urban consumers. Modest artisans could browse shops that sold European imitations of Chinese porcelain, which still evoked an exotic Asia, while wealthier shoppers could opt for the Chinese original over the European copy. The same could be said for high-quality coffee from Mocha and ordinary coffee from the Caribbean; elites could opt for the genuine article, while the middling and labor classes drank affordable lower-quality versions. Even cheaper versions of exotic Asian goods produced in the Americas or Europe were often hailed by retailers as "true" imitations.[83]

Piety

Lest we think that the emerging consumer culture completely detached itself from traditional moorings, it is important to acknowledge the role of piety in consumption. As Frank Trentmann observed of the twentieth

---

[82] It should be noted that exoticism ran in both directions, with Chinese elites collecting exotic European goods. See Ming Wilson, "Chinese Fantasies of Europe" in Anna Jackson and Amin Jaffer, eds., *Encounters: The Meeting of Asia and Europe 1500–1800* (London, 2004), 338–347.

[83] Natacha Coquery, "Selling India and China in Eighteenth-Century Paris," in Maxine Berg, Felicia Gottmann, Hanna Hodacs, and Chris Nierstrasz, eds., *Goods from the East, 1600–1800: Trading Eurasia* (Houndmills, 2015), ch. 15.

century, economic development is "not only a challenge for religion but also an opportunity."[84] In Catholic Europe, where the Counter-Reformation Church encouraged the use of material aids to enhance private religious devotion in the home, commercially produced religious objects, images, and texts enjoyed wide circulation. Households acquired increasing numbers of sacred objects, notably crucifixes that symbolized the mystery of redemption, a theme underscored by the post-Tridentine Church. Pious images depicting Christ, the Virgin, and the saints also adorned middling households, as did sundry books of devotion. With rosary beads in hand and eternal redemption in mind, women became particularly avid consumers of religious goods as piety became increasingly feminized in this period, yet another indication of women's active role in the creation of new modes of consumption.[85]

The story of Protestant Europe is more complicated. In *The Protestant Ethic and the Spirit of Capitalism*, German sociologist Max Weber argued that modern capitalism was rooted in the Protestant religion, particularly Calvinism, which encouraged hard work and frugality.[86] Calvinist values of thrift and self-denial, so the argument goes, acted as a powerful brake on consumption, as the simple dress of Quakers and Methodists demonstrates, enabling the accumulation of profits, saving, and investment. Weber argued that this new propensity to save would give rise to modern capitalism in northern Europe and North America.

Weber's thesis has been hotly contested. While we owe Weber a debt of gratitude for his profound insight that capitalism has cultural as well as economic origins, his particular argument that Protestants eschewed consumption in favor of saving has proven less convincing. Simon Schama has shown that despite Calvinist jeremiads against luxury, Dutch culture in the Golden Age "was not the austere pleasure-denying

[84] Frank Trentmann, *Empire of Things: How We Became a World of Consumers, from the Fifteenth Century to the Twenty-First* (New York, 2016), 621.
[85] Charly Coleman, *The Spirit of French Capitalism: Economic Theology in the French Enlightenment* (Stanford, 2021), ch. 5; Cissie Fairchilds, "Marketing the Counter-Reformation," in Christine Adams, Jack R. Censer, and Lisa Jane Graham, eds., *Visions and Revisions of Eighteenth-Century France* (University Park, PA, 1997), 31–59; Arlette Farge, *Fragile Lives: Violence, Power, and Solidarity in Eighteenth-Century Paris*, trans. Carol Shelton (Cambridge, MA, 1993), 210; David Garrioch, "Varieties of Religious Behavior in Eighteenth-Century Paris: The Material Culture of Leaders of Confraternities," in Mita Choudhury and Daniel J. Watkins, eds., *Belief and Politics in Enlightenment France* (Oxford, 2019), 181–196; Annik Pardailhé-Galabrun, *The Birth of Intimacy: Privacy and Domestic Life in Early Modern Paris*, trans. Jocelyn Phelps (Philadelphia, 1991), ch. 7. Fairchilds and Garrioch note differences in the material subcultures of traditional "baroque" Catholics, Jansenists, and "enlightened" Catholics.
[86] Max Weber, *The Protestant Ethic and the Spirit of Capitalism*, trans. Stephen Kalberg (New York, 2011).

culture of historical cliché. In fact it seems likely that the market for decorative and applied arts was more highly developed in Holland than anywhere else in mid-seventeenth-century Europe."[87] To be sure, the Dutch rejected the kind of conspicuous consumption on display at European royal courts, but they did not refrain from indulging in what Jan de Vries calls the "new luxury" of domestic comfort and refinement.[88] Nor did Protestantism in England dampen the enthusiasm for luxury goods there, even during the English Civil War.[89] Protestants could consume as avidly as Catholics, though their patterns of consumption might be different. Protestants owned more Bibles and Catholics more crucifixes, just as Jews in Europe acquired apparel and accessories particular to their religion, but the overall rise of consumption appears to have transcended confessional divisions.

Modernity and Social Order

Historians believe that eighteenth-century consumer culture constituted an important step on the road to modernity. For McKendrick and his peers, it represented the dawn of a consumer society driven by social and economic forces that would ultimately lead to mass consumption in the twentieth century.[90] For Daniel Roche, it was part of a larger cultural transformation in which the values of a rigid and stationary Christian economy gave way to the egalitarianism and individualism of modern commodity culture.[91] For Jennifer Jones, it reflected a shift to modern essentialist notions of gender difference.[92]

I would suggest that eighteenth-century consumer culture was related to modernity in two fundamental ways. First, as more and more consumer goods circulated among Europeans, such goods took on meanings – comfort, selfhood, fashionability, cleanliness, domesticity, nature, authenticity, and exoticism – that have come to define consumer cultures across much of the world today.[93] Many of these consumer values are with us still in one form or another, though their specific meanings have evolved during the intervening centuries.

---

[87] Simon Schama, *Embarrassment of Riches: An Interpretation of Dutch Culture in the Golden Age* (New York, 1987), 298, 304.

[88] Jan de Vries, *The Industrious Revolution: Consumer Behavior and the Household Economy, 1650 to the Present* (Cambridge, 2008), 44–45.

[89] Linda Levy Peck, *Consuming Splendor: Society and Culture in Seventeenth-Century England* (Cambridge, 2005), ch. 6.

[90] McKendrick, Brewer, and Plumb, *The Birth of a Consumer Society.*

[91] Roche, *A History of Everyday Things.*   [92] Jones, *Sexing La Mode.*

[93] Lury, *Consumer Culture*; Trentmann, *Empire of Things.*

Second, eighteenth-century consumer culture can be called modern insofar as it contributed to the construction of a new form of historical consciousness that valorized present over past. Dan Edelstein has recently argued that the Enlightenment was defined by a self-reflexive historical narrative that declared the present age enlightened. In other words, "the Enlightenment seems to have been the period when people thought they were living in an age of Enlightenment," a notion, he claims, that emerged in the late seventeenth century during a literary quarrel between the Ancients and the Moderns.[94] I would add that such a feeling of presentness, of living in a new age, enjoyed broader material-cultural resonance over the course of the eighteenth century as daily life echoed ideas of human progress found in many Enlightenment texts. Fashion producers, merchants, retailers, and consumers – as well as fashion commentators who bridged the commercial and literary worlds – seized on the notion that they were living through a turning point in history, a moment in which society was liberating itself from an archaic past and embracing a new forward-looking cultural aesthetic. Indeed, contemporaries did not hesitate to use the word "modern" in this sense to describe current trends in the arts, product design, and new kinds of architecture and furniture, all of which were placed in stark contrast to the purportedly crude, artificial, and restrictive material culture of the medieval and courtly past. If part of being modern is *feeling* modern and committing oneself to present over past, then there was undoubtedly something very modern in the consumer culture of the eighteenth century.[95]

Of course, Enlightenment ideas of progress did not go unchallenged. Moralists like Rousseau railed against the notion that society was steadily improving, arguing instead that it was becoming ever more corrupt. But this counter-narrative, which is as essential to modernity as the narrative of progress itself, was absorbed by the very consumer culture that Rousseau and others attacked. In the second half of the eighteenth century, values of naturalness, simplicity, and authenticity comingled with those of comfort and utility to lend consumer goods an air of moral legitimacy. Consumer culture was supple enough to incorporate the critiques of luxury that aimed to destroy it, a process that remains alive and well in our own day.

---

[94] Dan Edelstein, *The Enlightenment: A Genealogy* (Chicago, 2010), 73. See also François Hartog, *Regimes of Historicity*, trans. Saskia Brown (New York, 2017), which puts forward a different chronology of Europe's sense of time.

[95] This understanding of modern progress was articulated – and contested – by the many writers who engaged in the luxury debate, which is examined in Chapter 6.

Socially, the ramifications of eighteenth-century consumer culture were complex. More than mere props in a game of emulation, goods carried a variety of meanings that infused the material life of millions of Europeans and others. At the same time, however, it would be naïve to assume that goods ceased to mark the social status of those who acquired, used, and displayed them. Although cultural brokers who promoted new consumer values sometimes flirted with the fiction that personal consumption was no longer about class – was there not something modern in this as well? – their rhetoric should not be taken at face value.[96] The growth of consumption may not have leveled social order but it did transform it. Indeed, a new social hierarchy based on both aesthetic knowledge (or "taste") and the financial capacity to consume goods that embodied such knowledge was overtaking an older hierarchy of raw sociolegal rank and its display. I hesitate to call this new order "bourgeois" because nobles and laborers participated in it as well as middling folk, but it was nevertheless based largely on urban wealth and consumer competency, and, as such, constituted a challenge to an aristocratic society founded on the ideal of birth and lineage. Those who had the economic and cultural resources to participate in the new consumer culture – to appear clean, to express individuality, to look natural, to live comfortably, and to perform domesticity – did not hesitate to claim the social status that identification with such values conferred.

Nor did certain "cultural omnivores" in the eighteenth century fail to claim the status that came with appropriating both high and low forms of culture. A cultural omnivore is someone who has the wealth, time, education, and cultural competency to consume in multiple social registers and does so to gain prestige as well as amusement.[97] Marie Antoinette was not the only aristocrat who might wear elaborate court costume one day only to dress down the next. As sociologists emphasize, cultural omnivores possess the knowledge and means to graze across cultural forms, incorporating high and low, formal and informal, and, to some extent, masculine and feminine (Marie Antoinette wore male hunting outfits and refused to ride side-saddle). Although cultural omnivores may seem egalitarian in spirit, their self-reflective versatility demonstrates a kind of competence that became a marker of distinction for

---

[96] The *Magasin des modes nouvelles* declared in 1788 that "new fashions are for all classes ... Every women may forget her social status, the conditions of her birth, and even the extent of her wealth, [and] go to a ball in the most expensive, the smartest dress, without fear of serious rebuke." Quoted in Jennifer Jones, "The Taste for Fashion and Frivolity" (PhD thesis, Princeton University, 1991), 221–222.

[97] Tony Bennett, Mike Savage, Elizabeth Silva, et al., *Culture, Class, Distinction* (New York, 2009).

certain eighteenth-century elites, as it has become for a much larger proportion of the population today, including for corporate executives clad in jeans, t-shirts, and hoodies.

Sociologist Pierre Bourdieu famously wrote that "taste classifies, and it classifies the classifier." In other words, taste is not a matter of innocent cultural preference but a reflection of class and education that marks one's place in the social order.[98] Bourdieu's model of social distinction does not, however, fully account for competing economies of worth. In the eighteenth century, one emerging order of taste that contemporaries called "modern" seems to have been overtaking – or at least competing with – another order centered around the court, even if courtiers often adopted new modes of consumption.[99] This emerging cultural order appears highly egalitarian in light of its rejection of courtly consumption and the relatively wide social range of consumers who participated in it. Indeed, historian William Sewell argues that consumer capitalism fostered abstract social relations conducive to the ideas of civic equality that shaped the French Revolution.[100] Sewell's thesis is compelling: commercial society was undoubtedly eroding an older society of orders based on status and face-to-face relationships. But we should not exaggerate the emancipatory or egalitarian effects of this transformation, for rising consumption did not necessarily entail boundless social mobility, abstract social anonymity, or radical change. Members of the middling and laboring classes who managed to participate in new forms of consumption did not suddenly leap-frog into categorically higher status groups, as moralists feared they were doing (in a corpus of eighteenth-century literature on which the social emulation thesis would later be built). Many men and women bought into the world of goods simply to shore up horizontal claims of respectability, honor, and civility within their social milieux. Hutton, the stockinger's apprentice, described his "genteel suit of clothes" as "fully adequate to the sphere in which I moved."[101] He had no delusions of grandeur; he merely wanted to appear respectable within his own social circle, a goal shared by consumers at all social levels, even the humblest. The concern for civility, honor, and respectability that operated across the eighteenth-century

[98] Pierre Bourdieu, *Distinction: A Social Critique of the Judgement of Taste*, trans. Richard Nice (Cambridge, MA, 1984), 6. For a critique, see Bennett, Savage, Silva, et al. *Culture, Class, Distinction*.

[99] Antoine Lilti, *The World of the Salons*, trans. Lydia G. Cochrane (Oxford, 2006), 123, 236, makes a similar argument about the coexistence of rival criteria of social classification in the eighteenth century.

[100] William Sewell, *Capitalism and the Emergence of Civic Equality in Eighteenth-Century France* (Chicago, 2021).

[101] Quoted in Styles, *The Dress of the People*, 1.

social order was not necessarily driven by cross-class emulation or an abstract desire for social equality.[102]

Finally, it is worth remembering that while elites, middling folk, and many ordinary people assembled physical manifestations of respectability, legions of Europeans could not afford to express such status-enhancing consumer values as novelty, cleanliness, and fashion.[103] The price was far too high for countless underemployed laborers in urban and especially rural areas, to say nothing of enslaved peoples in the Americas who faced unrelenting exploitation. Those who did not have the financial and cultural resources to become "'proficient' in the art of living" due to lack of work, a fixed domicile, education, and freedom were stigmatized by their social superiors as poor, ignorant, vicious, uncivilized, and dangerous, characterizations that rendered their lives all the more precarious.[104] Historians should therefore be careful when assessing eighteenth-century consumer culture: what looks like emergent egalitarianism may be better understood as inequality transformed.

---

[102] Thomas, *In Pursuit of Civility*, ch. 2.; Woodruff Smith, *Consumption and the Making of Respectability* (New York, 2002); Styles, *Dress of the People*; de Vries, *The Industrious Revolution*; Fernand Ramos, "Révolution industrielle, identité, et effet trickle-down dans une économie sous-développée," in *Consommateurs & consommation XVIIe–XXIe siècle: Regards franco-espagnols* (Perpignan, 2015), 47–78. Adam Smith noted that necessities included "whatever the custom of the country renders it indecent for creditable people, even of the lowest order, to be without." Hence in Europe "a creditable day-labourer would be ashamed to appear in publick without a linen shirt, the want of which would be supposed to denote that disgraceful degree of poverty, which, it is presumed, no body can fall into without extreme bad conduct." Smith, *Wealth of Nations*, II, 870.

[103] Julie Hardwick, "Fractured Domesticity in the Old Regime," stresses that many households were excluded from partaking of the value of domesticity.

[104] DeJean, *The Age of Comfort*, 229.

5   Consuming Enlightenment

> Everyone in Paris is reading ... Everyone, but women in particular, is
> carrying a book around in their pocket. People read while riding in
> carriages or taking walks; they read at the theatre during the interval,
> in cafés, even when bathing. Women, children, journeymen and
> apprentices read in shops. On Sundays people read while seated at the
> front of their houses; lackeys read on their back seats; coachmen up on
> their boxes, and soldiers keeping guard.[1]

The Enlightenment was an intellectual and cultural movement that swept
Europe between 1680 and 1800. For generations, liberal scholars hailed
the Enlightenment as the birthplace of the modern world, an era in which
great thinkers like Voltaire vanquished superstition, disseminated natural
philosophy (science), and freed the individual from the oppressive intellectual constraints of the past. Although many historians today tend to be
suspicious of such grandiose interpretations of the period, they still cling to
the idea of the eighteenth century as the threshold to modernity. Rather
than defining modernity in terms of a particular philosophical or literary
canon, however, scholars now emphasize how new social and cultural
practices flourished in the hothouse environment of rising consumption.[2]
Many argue that the expansion of print and the development of new forms
of sociability in the eighteenth century softened traditionally rigid social
hierarchies, generated a public sphere of critically minded citizens, and
produced modern understandings of self and society. This chapter
explores connections between consumption and Enlightenment by examining, first, the dramatic expansion of print and, second, the rich material
environments in which new sites of sociability thrived.

---

[1] Quoted in Reinhard Wittmann, "Was There a Reading Revolution at the End of the
Eighteenth Century?" in Guglielmo Cavallo and Roger Chartier, eds., *A History of
Reading in the West*, trans. Lydia Cochrane (Cambridge, 1999), 285.
[2] John Brewer, *Pleasures of the Imagination: English Culture in the Eighteenth Century* (New
York, 1997); Roy Porter, *The Creation of the Modern World: The Untold Story of the British
Enlightenment* (New York, 2000); Daniel Roche, *France in the Enlightenment*, trans. Arthur
Goldhammer (Cambridge, MA, 1998).

Books: A Special Sort of Consumer Good?

As for many other goods, the production and consumption of books climbed to new heights in the eighteenth century. Composed of printed words and images, books were capable of carrying enormously rich, complex, and powerful meanings, which is why historians have long sought to apprehend the cultural impact of the rise of print in the age of the Enlightenment. Older liberal accounts stressed how the proliferation of books broadened access to knowledge, diffused forward-looking ideas, and set Europe on a progressive path toward modernity. Scholars stressed that during the Enlightenment's early decades, certain European thinkers used the printed word to challenge traditional Christianity and advance more rational models of understanding the world. Pierre Bayle's skepticism, John Toland's Deism, John Locke's call for limited religious toleration, and Voltaire's anticlericalism all questioned fundamental religious beliefs and institutions, leading to a "crisis" of the European mind.[3] The high Enlightenment of the late eighteenth century may have fielded fewer intellectual mavericks, but its literature was nonetheless important and heavily reformist in tone. Authors called on readers to use their reason to better the condition of man in this world, not the afterlife, through all manner of political, social, and moral reform. Reformers demanded broad religious toleration, support for scientific projects, the remodeling of the criminal justice system, the implementation of new economic policies, and the gradual abolition of the slave trade. The goal was to improve humanity by changing "men's common way of thinking," as Diderot put it, and modernizing a jumble of obsolete institutions.[4] Although authors rarely called for revolutionary change, their ardent reformism had far-reaching implications for what was still in many ways a traditional society.[5]

Departing from older interpretations that focused on "enlightened" ideas found in a retrospectively constructed canon of books, historians have more recently argued that the enhanced circulation of the printed word contributed to two fundamental cultural transformations in the eighteenth century: (1) a "reading revolution" that changed the

---

[3] Paul Hazard, *The Crisis of the European Mind, 1680–1715*, trans. J. Lewis May (New York, 2013).

[4] Denis Diderot, *Rameau's Nephew and Other Works*, trans. Jacques Barzun and Ralph Bowen (Indianapolis, 2001), 296.

[5] Peter Gay, *The Enlightenment: An Interpretation*, two vols. (New York, 1969). Recent work on Enlightenment reformism includes John Robertson, *The Case for the Enlightenment: Scotland and Naples 1680–1760* (Cambridge, 2005); and Michael Kwass, *Contraband: Louis Mandrin and the Making of a Global Underground* (Cambridge, MA, 2014), ch. 11.

relationship between reader and book and (2) the formation of a "public sphere" that was independent of the state.

Both theories are predicated on the indisputable fact that the volume and variety of literature expanded dramatically during the Enlightenment. Although a truly mass reading public would not take shape until steam-powered printing overtook the hand-press in the nineteenth century, there is little doubt that more books were published, purchased, and read in the eighteenth century than ever before. Britain led the way as the number of titles published annually jumped from 1,916 in 1703 to 6,801 in 1793, thanks largely to successive growth spurts after 1763.[6] In Germany, a printing industry that had been devastated by the Thirty Years' War came roaring back to produce 175,000 titles over the course of the eighteenth century, two-thirds of which were published after 1760.[7] In France, where censorship was strong, the number of titles nonetheless climbed from 500 a year in 1700 to 1,000 in 1771, not including a heavy flow of illicit books smuggled in from Holland and Switzerland, including inexpensive editions of Diderot's *Encyclopédie*.[8] French book production would skyrocket after revolutionaries dismantled the regime of state censorship in 1789–1790. In Eastern and Southern Europe, the book trade was less buoyant, but even these regions experienced modest growth. In Russia, titles rose from a meager 17 a year in the 1720s to well over 300 a year in the 1780s and 1790s. Colonial America was also slower to expand than Western Europe, but in British America, imports from the metropole, in addition to a thriving newspaper trade in Boston and Philadelphia, made print available in towns.

One factor behind the development of the book trade was rising literacy among a growing population. Thanks to urbanization and efforts on the part of Protestant and Catholic churches to educate their flocks, literacy widened considerably in eighteenth-century Europe. The incidence of male literacy was higher than female literacy, but rates went up for both sexes. In England, where around 30 percent of adult men were literate in the 1640s, 60 percent of them – and 45 percent of adult

[6] Michael Suarez, "Towards a Bibliometric Analysis of the Surviving Record, 1701–1800," in Michael Suarez and Michael Turner, eds. *The Cambridge History of the Book in Britain* (Cambridge, 2009), 43–44. See also, James Raven, "The Book as a Commodity," in Suarez and Turner, eds., *The Cambridge History of the Book in Britain*, 83–117.
[7] T. C. W. Blanning, *The Culture of Power and the Power of Culture: Old Regime Europe 1660–1789* (Oxford, 2002), 142.
[8] Blanning, *The Culture of Power and the Power of Culture*, 141. Robert Darnton, *The Business of Enlightenment: A Publishing History of the Encyclopédie 1775–1800* (Cambridge, MA, 1979). Simon Burrows, *The French Book Trade in Enlightenment Europe II: Enlightenment Bestsellers* (London, 2018), ch. 9, states that 50 percent of books circulating in France on the eve of the Revolution were technically illegal.

women – could read by 1800.[9] In France, the adult male and female literacy rates likewise rose from 29 percent and 14 percent, respectively, in the late seventeenth century to 48 percent and 27 percent by the late 1780s.[10] Rates for adults in Germany gradually rose too, from 10 percent in the mid-eighteenth century to 25 percent in 1800.[11] These averages mask huge differences between urban and rural Europe: literacy was nearly universal for men in cities like London, Paris, and Amsterdam, while it remained stubbornly low in rural Eastern Europe. A similar urban–rural divide existed in the Americas.

With the rise in literacy and the expansion of the book trade, more and more people in the middling and laboring classes came to own books. In France, the size of merchants' libraries caught up to those of traditional elites, as traders amassed books on their profession, science, technology, and geography. About half of the 3,000 Parisian households studied by Annik Pardailhé-Galabrun possessed books in the second half of the eighteenth century.[12] Master craftsmen, shopkeepers, and servants were more likely to own texts than lower-order journeymen, day laborers, and other casual workers, but the gap was closing.[13] In Germany, more and more townspeople owned increasing numbers of books; even Swabian peasants enlarged their libraries to fourteen books on average by the 1780s.[14] In Britain, only the wealthiest had been able to afford books on a regular basis before the late seventeenth century, but the market expanded to include the middling classes as the book became increasingly commodified over the course of the following century.[15]

Book ownership is only part of the story. Although their high price put many books beyond reach of all but the wealthiest, people did not necessarily have to own a book in order to read it. They could borrow a volume from relatives, friends, and neighbors, or they could make use of two new vital institutions: reading societies and lending libraries. Reading societies were self-managed, noncommercial organizations that made books and periodicals available to dues-paying members.

---

[9] Suarez, "Towards a Bibliometric Analysis of the Surviving Record," 44.

[10] Roger Chartier, *The Cultural Origins of the French Revolution*, trans. Lydia Cochrane (Durham, NC, 1991), 69.

[11] Rietje van Vliet, "Print and Public in Europe 1600–1800," in Simon Eliot and Jonathan Rose, eds., *A Companion to the History of the Book* (Oxford, 2007), 251.

[12] Annik Pardailhé-Galabrun, *The Birth of Intimacy: Privacy and Domestic Life in Early Modern Paris*, trans. Jocelyn Phelps (Philadelphia, 1991), 175.

[13] Daniel Roche, *The People of Paris: An Essay in Popular Culture in the 18th Century*, trans. Marie Evans (Berkeley, CA, 1987), ch. 7.

[14] James van Horn Melton, *The Rise of the Public in Enlightenment Europe* (Cambridge, 2001), 83.

[15] Raven, "The Book as a Commodity."

Figure 5.1 Isaac Cruikshank, *The Lending Library*, 1800–1811.
Yale Center for British Art. Women borrowing books from a lending library.
The shelves display several popular genres: novels, sermons, romances, tales,
voyages and travels, and plays

Membership was not cheap, but for middling men and women who could afford it, reading societies provided access to large print collections and promoted a sociable environment for reading. Lending (or circulating) libraries, on the other hand, were commercial enterprises run by booksellers who provided materials to a broad public (see Figure 5.1). Most towns by the 1790s had at least one lending library that allowed subscribers to borrow books for a fixed period of time. Subscription rates were relatively affordable, giving professionals, merchants, and skilled artisans access to an array of popular genres, from novels to chivalric romances to crime literature.[16]

---

[16] Wittmann, "Was There a Reading Revolution at the End of the Eighteenth Century?," 306–312.

Not only were more books available to a broader section of the population than ever before, but the *kinds* of books people were reading were changing. Religious books remained a staple of literary consumption – the age of Enlightenment was not nearly as secular as some scholars have claimed – but proportionally, as a share of the total number of books produced, religious works declined as other types of printed literature came to the fore. Texts on law, politics, and history; medicine and science; agriculture and trade; and philosophy, ethics, and education were all on the upswing. Meanwhile, at a lower yet intersecting social level, all manner of ephemeral popular literature, such as inexpensive chapbooks, almanacs, woodcuts, pamphlets, and song sheets, flourished. Perhaps the quintessential literary genre of the eighteenth century was the novel, a relatively new form of fictional narrative written in prose. Best selling novels such as Samuel Richardson's *Pamela* (1740), Jean-Jacques Rousseau's *La Nouvelle Héloïse* (1761), and Johann Wolfgang von Goethe's *The Sorrows of Young Werther* (1774) had a profound emotional impact on their readers. Such novels drew readers into imagined yet seemingly real worlds inhabited by characters wrestling with love, social class, and virtue. Indeed, the novel's intense focus on the individual experience of social and familial relationships in a contemporary setting intrigued women as well as men, and inspired many women to become novelists themselves. Françoise de Graffigny's enormously successful *Letters from a Peruvian Woman* (1747) explored themes of virtue, corruption, and friendship that Rousseau would later appropriate without attribution in his own work.

As successful as novels were, the fastest growing sector of eighteenth-century publishing was the periodical.[17] Often funded by subscribers, monthly or weekly serial publications, featuring articles on literature, science, agriculture, commerce, art, or music, spread ideas and tastes far and wide. Some, like the *Journal des sçavans* and the *Philosophical Transactions*, could be quite scholarly, while others had a lighter, more entertaining touch. In this latter category, journals reflecting on society and manners figured prominently, the most famous of which was *The Spectator*, which, edited by Joseph Addison and Richard Steele, dwelled on the moral peculiarities of modern life in the big city of London. Composed of essays intended to stimulate polite conversation over tea or coffee, the ad-filled *Spectator* deliberately cultivated a female as well as male readership. "There are none to whom this paper will be more useful than to the female world," the journal's tenth edition proclaimed.[18]

---

[17] Andrew Pettegree, *The Invention of News: How the World Came to Know About Itself* (New Haven, CT, 2014), ch. 13.
[18] Quoted in ibid., 280.

The same could be said of fashion journals like the *Cabinet des Modes* and *Journal des Luxus und der Moden* that illustrated the latest trends in clothing and accessories.

What are we to make of all this new printed work? Departing from older accounts, proponents of the reading revolution thesis focus less on the content of books than on how they were read. Many historians now doubt that books have straightforward, direct effects on readers, as if the act of reading is already inscribed in the text. According to this more skeptical approach to book history, gaps existed between the meaning writers assigned to a given text and the interpretation of that text by readers. Rather than passively absorbing texts, readers actively and creatively appropriated particular meanings for themselves. Calling into question the simple transmission of ideas from author to reader, then, historians have become more interested in *how* people read than in *what* they read.[19]

In this vein, it has been suggested that Europe has experienced three reading revolutions. We are currently in the midst of the third revolution as more and more readers across the world use electronic screens and access digital texts through social media and the Internet. It appears that the relationship between reader and text is undergoing fundamental change, with dramatic repercussions for politics and society. However, this is not the first time in history that modes of reading have changed. The first reading revolution began in the Middle Ages, when silent (as opposed to oralized) reading became common among monastic scribes, university professors, and eventually the aristocracy and men of letters. The second revolution occurred in the eighteenth century. While the introduction of the printing press and moveable type in the fifteenth century enabled the written word to circulate far beyond the parameters of medieval scribal culture, shaping the diffusion of religious ideas in the age of the Reformation and Counter-Reformation, it was not until the late eighteenth century, when the volume of print rose to unprecedented levels, that a second reading revolution unfolded.[20]

Historian Rolf Engelsing, a founding father of the reading revolution thesis, argues that in certain parts of Germany in the second half of the eighteenth century, reading shifted from being "intensive" to "extensive." Intensive reading had revolved around a small canon of texts, such

[19] Guglielmo Cavallo and Roger Chartier, "Introduction," in Cavallo and Chartier, eds., *A History of Reading in the West*, 1–36.
[20] Rolf Engelsing, *Der Burger als Leser: Lesergeschichte in Deutschland, 1500–1800* (Stuttgart, 1974); Wittmann, "Was There a Reading Revolution at the End of the Eighteenth Century?"

as religious works like the Bible, which were repeatedly read and recited. Readers invested these texts with a sacred quality and accorded them substantial normative authority. By contrast, extensive reading involved more freely perusing a wider body of literature, much of it new and ephemeral, for the purposes of entertaining oneself; the sacred quality of the text dissolved. Proponents of the reading revolution thesis contend that extensive reading steadily replaced intensive reading in the eighteenth century as readers encountered a larger and more diverse corpus of books, which now included smaller portable formats for readers on the go (much like today's diminutive screens). In the French case, contends Roger Chartier, extensive reading forged a new relationship not only between readers and texts but between readers and the larger world around them (see Figure 5.2). Extensive reading was "disrespectful of authorities, in turn seduced and disillusioned by novelty, and, above all, little inclined to belief and adherence." Engendered by the ubiquity, accessibility, and variety of printed texts, this new mode of reading

Figure 5.2 Jean François de Troy, *Reading from Molière*, 1728.
Copyright Bridgeman Art Library. Painter Jean François de Troy's depiction of contemporary mores portrayed reading as integral to sociability, leisure, and comfort

encouraged critical perspectives on the world and ultimately prepared the way for revolutionary change.[21]

Yet, the concept of a reading revolution is controversial. To be sure, the increasing volume and variety of printed material in the Enlightenment stimulated extensive reading; readers browsed, moved between genres, and skimmed excerpts. But intensive reading did not disappear. On the contrary, it blossomed with the spread of the novel, a genre of literature that inspired intensely emotional modes of reading. Set in the present or recent past, novels offered fictional narratives about characters whose life experiences seemed authentic and compelling. Readers immersed themselves in these narratives to gain access to the inner emotional lives of protagonists with whom they often sympathized. Some scholars suggest that the experience of reading novels was so intense that it encouraged readers to cultivate their own interior feelings and to sympathize with others outside the world of the book, others to whom they now attributed deep emotional lives as well. Epistolary novels in particular, Lynn Hunt argues, trained readers to tap into the suffering of others, enabling them to imagine new political conceptions such as human rights.[22] Whatever the political repercussions, novels appear to have fostered the same culture of selfhood, intimacy, and feeling that the architecture and furniture of private domestic space engendered in many households. Small wonder that painters and writers often represented women reading novels and writing letters in intimate interiors (bedrooms, closets, boudoirs), comfortable private spaces where they were free to explore their emotional selves. Critics of the sentimental novel warned that such solitary reading would lead women astray because female readers who over-identified with characters were vulnerable to the same vicious temptations to which fictional protagonists succumbed.

Thus, modes of reading in the eighteenth century did not shift in a linear fashion from intensive to extensive so much as expand to include multiple types of reading that existed side by side: oral and silent; solitary and communal; intensive and extensive. Reading in the home (and as we shall see in cafés) was as much conducted aloud in small groups of family and friends as it was alone in boudoirs and bedrooms.[23] Readers

---

[21] Chartier, *The Cultural Origins of the French Revolution*, 91. Hugh Armory and David Hall, eds., *A History of the Book in America*, vol. 1, *The Colonial Book in the Atlantic World* (Cambridge, 2000), 5, 399–404, are reluctant to apply the reading revolution thesis to American colonies, although the success of circulating libraries of Philadelphia suggests a major change in modes of reading.

[22] Lynn Hunt, *Inventing Human Rights* (New York, 2007).

[23] Abigail Williams, *The Social Life of Books: Reading Together in the Eighteenth-Century Home* (New Haven, CT, 2017).

employed various techniques of reading to navigate the fragmenting media landscape of the period, as the following letter from Luise Meyer, who worked in Holstein as a lady's companion to the Countess of Stolberg, attests:

Breakfast at ten o'clock. Then Stolberg reads out a chapter from the Bible, and a song from Klopstock's *Lieder*. Everyone retires to his or her bedroom. Then I dip into the *Spectator* or *Physiognomy*, and a few books the Countess has given me. She comes downstairs while Lotte translates, and I spend an hour reading her Lavater's *Pontius Pilate*. While she has her Latin lesson, I copy for her or read to myself until dinner is served. After dinner and coffee, Fritz reads from the *Lebensläufen*, then Lotte comes downstairs and I read Milton with her for an hour. Then we go back upstairs and I read to the Count and Countess from *Plutarch* until teatime at around nine o'clock. After tea Stolberg reads a chapter from the Bible and one of Klopstock's *Lieder*, then it's "goodnight."[24]

The enthusiasm for, and variety of, reading exhibited in the Stolberg household worried moral critics like clergyman Johann Rudolph Gottlieb Beyer, whose anxious words anticipate criticisms of screen-obsessed readers and viewers today:

Readers of books who rise and retire to bed with a book in their hand, sit down at table with one, have one lying close by when working, carry one around with them when walking, and who, once they have begun reading, are unable to stop until they have finished. But they have scarcely finished the last page of a book before they begin looking around greedily for somewhere to acquire another one; and when they are at their toilet or at their desk or some other place, if they happen to come across something that fits with their own subject or seems to them to be readable, they take it away and devour it with a kind of ravenous hunger. No lover of tobacco or coffee, no wine drinker or lover of games, can be as addicted to their pipe, bottle, games or coffee-table as those many hungry readers are to their reading habit.[25]

In addition to the reading revolution, a second highly influential theory concerning the cultural impact of print in the age of Enlightenment was articulated by German philosopher Jürgen Habermas.[26] Habermas' conception of the public sphere derives from Immanuel Kant's celebrated 1784 essay "What is Enlightenment?," which made an important distinction between the public and private use of reason. For Kant, the public use of reason, by which he meant the use of reason by learned men (literally "men" in Kant's gendered analysis) before a reading public,

---

[24] Quoted in Wittmann, "Was There a Reading Revolution at the End of the Eighteenth Century?," 298.
[25] Quoted in ibid., 285.
[26] Jürgen Habermas, *The Structural Transformation of the Public Sphere*, trans. Thomas Burger (Cambridge, MA, 1989).

would gradually free man from his "self-incurred tutelage." Following Kant, Habermas argued that a "bourgeois public sphere" flourished in the late seventeenth and eighteenth centuries, first in England and then elsewhere, as private individuals assembled to form a public that, through reasoned debate, generated "public opinion," a term that began to circulate widely in the eighteenth century. According to Habermas, the production and consumption of books, pamphlets, and especially newspapers contributed to the formation of a robust and critical public that, once politicized, was capable of opposing state authority. Although Habermas claimed that the public sphere ultimately degenerated in the nineteenth and twentieth centuries as it succumbed to mass culture, he believed that its eighteenth-century incarnation had enabled the reading public to openly discuss pressing issues of the day, which produced rational public opinion, and to recognize itself as a legitimate authority independent of state power.

Habermas had a profound impact on Enlightenment studies, especially after his 1962 book, *The Structural Transformation of the Public Sphere,* was translated from German into French in 1978 and English in 1986. The work inspired important research on the development of the idea of public opinion in political discourse and on the emergence of voluntary associations that mediated the relationship between state and society. Nevertheless, Habermas has been challenged by two trenchant critiques. First, historians have doubted the specifically "bourgeois" character of a public sphere that included nobles, clergy, office holders, and professionals – not exactly the classic Marxian bourgeoisie to which Habermas referred. Further, members of the laboring classes also engaged with print and discussed pressing public issues. Although they may not have subscribed to the *Encyclopédie* or attended salons, many craftspeople, farmers, and domestic servants read inexpensive printed texts (such as almanacs, chapbooks, and devotional works), regularly exchanged ideas in streets, marketplaces, and taverns, and expressed important political ideas of their own. Like Kant before him, however, Habermas overlooked this plebeian public sphere and neglected to explore how it intersected with or countered other publics. It is now clear that multiple overlapping publics coexisted in the age of the Enlightenment.

Nor was the eighteenth-century public sphere inherently oppositional to the state, as Habermas claimed. Examples abound. Monarchs and state officials, now forced to compete in a public sphere crowded with interlocutors, increasingly turned to print to build popular support for their programs. French minister of finance Jacques Necker sought to inspire financial confidence in the state when, in 1781, he broke with precedent and published the royal budget, which became an instant best seller. Necker deployed the printed word to build support for the monarchy. Consider, too, an example close to Habermas' heart: the newspaper press, to which, according to the German sociologist, members of the public immediately laid claim "for use against the public authority itself."[27] It is true that from the 1760s, European newspaper editors grew more daring and began to cover contentious domestic politics. In England, where party politics were stormy and censorship relatively lax, the outspoken radical journalist John Wilkes used his pro-Whig newspaper, *The North Briton*, to attack government ministers and King George III. American and French revolutionaries would likewise turn to the newspaper to cultivate enthusiasm for their political movements. Often read aloud to reach the semiliterate and illiterate, newspapers could mobilize extraordinarily large sections of the citizenry. However, for the most part, newspapers steered clear of controversy and instead covered the glories of military battle, the twists and turns of ministerial rivalries and international diplomacy, and the latest deeds of celebrity aristocrats, scarcely the sort of political material to whip up opposition to the state. On the whole, the press tended to be quite supportive of king and country, especially in times of war when news sold well and large segments of the population rallied to imperial, proto-nationalist causes. As state officials and critics both understood, print could cut both ways, serving the regime or undermining it, depending on the circumstances.[28]

Although Habermas may have not have gotten everything right, his main insight about the importance of publicity in the Enlightenment has been borne out. A dialectical relationship between privacy and publicity developed in this period wherein private life was simultaneously deepened in domestic environments and increasingly publicized in novels, biographies, crime literature, and exposés of scandalous behavior. Historian Antoine Lilti suggests that one of the most important consequences of publicity was not so much the formation of rational public opinion à la Habermas but the advent of a society of celebrity in which editors, writers, and journalists increasingly publicized the private lives of others for commercial or political purposes.[29] A surprising legacy of Enlightenment publicity, the cult of celebrity continues to inform the contemporary world.

Historians have long treated the book as a special kind of consumer good. In the older liberal historiography of the Enlightenment, it was assumed that

---

[27] Jürgen Habermas, "The Public Sphere: An Encyclopedia Article," *New German Critique* 3 (1974), 52–53.

[28] Tabatha Leigh Ewing, *Rumor, Diplomacy and War in Enlightenment Paris* (Oxford, 2014), 163–180; Pettegree, *The Invention of News*.

[29] Antoine Lilti, *The Invention of Celebrity*, trans. Lynn Jeffress (Cambridge, 2017).

exposure to books challenging Christianity, advocating for natural religion and religious toleration, and offering useful knowledge for the improvement of humanity suddenly changed the belief systems of their readers. While historians today are doubtful that books impressed ideas on their readers in such a direct manner, there is no denying that writers during the Enlightenment exploited the printed word to demand deep reforms in society, culture, and politics. Print gave voice to eighteenth-century reformism. Further, historians have problematized the relationship between reading and belief to suggest that how people read was just as important as what they read. The growing consumption of books, periodicals, and other printed matter in eighteenth-century towns encouraged multiple forms of reading, including extensive reading that connected readers to a wide world of ideas and knowledge. Meanwhile, the intensive reading of novels provided readers access to what they understood to be the interior emotional lives of human beings, both fictional and real, creating ties of sentimental sympathy. In sum, the proliferation of the book contributed to important developments in both public and private life during the Enlightenment.

Sociability

As the growth in the consumption of print attests, Europeans in the long eighteenth century engaged in increasingly commercialized forms of leisure. Beyond the world of work, new kinds of social interaction – what scholars call "sociability" – shaped the cultural life of the Enlightenment. For Habermas, sociability was every bit as important as the press for the development of the public sphere. Mediating between the family and the State, he argued, a host of associations (academies, salons, assemblies, cafés, clubs, Masonic lodges) spurred intellectual exchange and the development of rational public opinion. Following Habermas, historians stress how sites of sociability burgeoned over the course of the eighteenth century to facilitate broader social interaction; spark literary, philosophical, and political debate; and cultivate liberal and democratic ideas and practices. However, some scholars challenge Habermas' idealistic model of Enlightenment sociability, countering that new sites of social interaction could be highly exclusive in terms of class and gender (let alone race) and did not always produce the kind of polite rational debate Habermas prized. Moreover, like popular literature, popular sociability in the street, tavern, and marketplace produced its own version of public opinion, which did not necessarily align with that of elites.[30] Finally,

[30] James Brophy, *Popular Culture and the Public Sphere in the Rhineland 1800–1850* (Cambridge, 2007); Arlette Farge, *Subversive Words: Public Opinion in Eighteenth-Century France*, trans. Rosemary Morris (Cambridge, 1994).

scholars are examining the particular material environments that afforded new forms of sociability, a previously overlooked subject that is crucial to any analysis of the relationship between the Enlightenment and the consumer revolution.

We will approach the question of sociability by focusing on three particular sites: salons, cafés, and public promenades. Of the three, salons were by far the most exclusive and least commercialized. They were also one of the most important institutions of the Enlightenment. Often hosted by women but frequented by mostly male writers, artists, and elites, they stimulated literary and philosophical conversation, encouraged the dissemination of print, and helped aspiring writers find well-heeled patrons. The origins of the salon lay in the royal courts of the sixteenth and seventeenth centuries, where nobles, high bourgeois, and writers came together to discuss literature and socialize. In the eighteenth century, salons gained a measure of independence from courts and established themselves in capital cities throughout Europe (Paris, London, Milan, Rome, Madrid, Vienna, and Berlin). Women of wealth and high social position were instrumental in their creation. In England, Elizabeth Montagu established the Bluestockings, a circle of female writers and critics who met regularly to discuss literature. In Vienna, Charlotte Greiner and then Fanny von Arnstein, a Jewish woman, brought together aristocrats, reformist officials, professors, and writers in a relaxed atmosphere. Jewish women also hosted salons in Berlin, providing for the unprecedented if temporary social mixing of German nobles and Jews. In Paris, women such as Marie Thérèse Rodet Geoffrin, Julie de Lespinasse, and Suzanne Necker became salonnières, hosting weekly salons to advance the intellectual exchange at the heart of the Enlightenment project.

The material culture of salons reflected the part that they played in the Enlightenment. As Dena Goodman explains, the Parisian town houses where salonnières invited men of letters to dine were "characterized spatially by a new articulation of public and private, in the manner of the Republic of Letters."[31] Salons were private insofar as they took place in a domestic space, the salonnière's home, rather than in a state building or on a commercial street, but they were public insofar as guests from outside the household met in sitting rooms to constitute fora for the exchange of ideas or, as Kant would put it, the public use of reason. The classic mid-century salons were decorated in the rococo style, which featured comfortable furniture, paintings by contemporary artists, elaborate coffee and tea services, and mirrored walls. They were also

---

[31] Dena Goodman, *The Republic of Letters: A Cultural History of the French Enlightenment* (Ithaca, NY, 1994), 84.

structured around meals. Geoffrin, who invented the Enlightenment salon, organized her weekly meetings (Monday for artists, Wednesday for men of letters) around leisurely afternoon dinners, though, according to Goodman, "discourse, not dining, was their defining function."[32] Goodman argues that the material culture of the salon reflected the pivotal role of the salonnière, who not only organized the gatherings and planned the meals, but also set the agenda for the discussion and guided the conversation to ensure polite, reciprocal, and productive exchanges among men of different social rank – a difficult task given the combative style of debate instilled by educational institutions of the day. In this way, the salonnière was able to secure her own education in an age of limited formal learning for women while promoting the broader philosophical project of the Enlightenment. In Goodman's feminist interpretation, salons were at the center of the Enlightenment, and women were at the center of salons.

Antoine Lilti also pays close attention to the material world of the salons, the life of which, he writes, "was actually a lot less ethereal than one imagines."[33] Rejecting Goodman's image of the female-centered philosophical salon, Lilti insists that salon-goers were as interested in socializing, play, and entertainment as they were in discussing ideas. They dined, gambled, listened to concerts, put on plays, and sang songs. For Lilti, the salons were part of a world of civility and refinement that belonged as much to Versailles as it did to any purportedly egalitarian public sphere. Privileging Elias over Habermas, Lilti displaces salons from the center of the Enlightenment (implicitly diminishing women's role in the movement) to foreground the salons' courtly social life and consumption.

Lilti's discussion of dining is illustrative. Salon gatherings were built around fine meals – afternoon dinners and late night suppers – during which hostesses lavished guests with expertly prepared plates of fish, fowl, vegetables, and salads. Geoffrin oscillated between pampering guests with luxurious cuisine and offering simple fare such as spinach omelets that did not distract from deep intellectual exchange. But Lilti dismisses what he considers a false dichotomy between gastronomic refinement and intellectual integrity. Salons where the philosophes had the most influence did not shy from the pleasures of the table. The arts of speaking and of eating were "integrated in the life of high society and in

---

[32] Ibid., 91.
[33] Antoine Lilti, *Le monde des salons: sociabilité et mondanité à Paris au XVIIIe siècle* (Paris, 2005), 225.

forms of civility."[34] Lilti concedes that salon civility was less rigid than that delineated in books on court etiquette but, he contends, salons were hardly instantiations of an egalitarian and autonomous public sphere. Ultimately, they were extensions of the hierarchical royal court where the concern for "worldly distinction" dominated.

The scholarly dispute between Lilti and Goodman, besides guaranteeing further debate on the role of women in the Enlightenment, raises important questions about the cultural significance of rising consumption in the eighteenth century. Did consumption facilitate the spread of courtly civility into a broader urban social milieu, as Lilti would have it, or did it stimulate the development of an alternative, middling, and oppositional (or at least autonomous) cultural sphere, as Goodman claims? I would suggest that the growth of consumption reflected a tense fusion of the two. Undoubtedly, the aristocratic French court radiated outward into city life in a society that remained steeply hierarchical, but, at the same time, affluent people who lacked ancient noble lineage yet had nonetheless mastered the arts of polite society could now claim a public voice and degree of cultural authority that undermined the traditional order. The tension between these two aspects of eighteenth-century life defined much of the Enlightenment.

More commercial and less exclusive than salons, cafés were quintessential institutions of the public sphere because they encouraged the circulation of news and political and literary critique. Modeled on cafés in the Ottoman Empire, Europe's first cafés appeared in the seventeenth century in such cities as Venice, London, Amsterdam, Marseille, Paris, Hamburg, and Vienna. Not that coffee was an instant sensation. In England, coffeehouses were initially frequented by small groups of virtuosi, gentleman scholars driven by what they called "curiosity," a fascination for the rare, novel, and (often Orientalist) exotic. Only after the virtuosi touted the intellectual virtues of this strange and bitter drink – and after apothecaries, physicians, and other commentators promoted its medicinal benefits – did the European café take root.[35] At first, in the late seventeenth and early eighteenth centuries, coffeehouse owners drew customers by playing on associations between coffee and an exotic East, giving their establishments Turkish names ("The Turk's Head"), dressing waiters in Turkish attire, and offering Turkish baths on the side to create an enticingly luxurious and subversive atmosphere in the heart

[34] Ibid., 233.
[35] Brian Cowan, *The Social Life of Coffee: The Emergence of the British Coffeehouse* (New Haven, CT, 2005); Emma Spary, *Eating the Enlightenment: Food and the Sciences in Paris, 1670–1760* (Chicago, 2014).

of the European city. By the middle of the eighteenth century, coffee's exotic associations with the Orient faded as bean cultivation swung from the Middle East to the Caribbean, where production expanded, and townspeople got used to the idea of seeing coffeehouses in their neighborhoods. In fact, cafés became so common in French towns by the end of the century that coffee was considered by some a French national beverage, in much the same way that Chinese tea was indigenized as "British." Like tea (and sugar and tobacco), coffee morphed from an exotic curiosity into an everyday commodity.

What truly sustained the coffeehouse over the long eighteenth century was not its exoticism but its ability to offer a drink that did not intoxicate. Before the café, public drinking establishments in Europe furnished customers with ales, beers, wines, and other alcoholic beverages. What set the coffeehouse apart was that in addition to alcohol, it offered a drink that, far from intoxicating those who ingested it, left them perfectly sober – even sharper of mind, it seemed. French botanist Antoine Laurent de Jussieu thought of coffee as a psychoactive medicine. Unlike wine, he observed, the bean "seems to cheer [the mind], make it more fit for work, recreate and dissipate its cares."[36] This medicinal understanding of coffee enabled the coffeehouse to become a space of public sobriety where respectable middling and elite men could gather to discuss news, talk politics, and conduct business in a "civilized" manner.[37] In London, there were specialized coffeehouses in which political partisans could talk strategy, stock market financiers could strike deals, merchants could conduct business, and writers could reflect on the world of letters. Zimmerman's Coffee House in Leipzig was known for staging evening concerts.[38] In Paris, upscale cafés replaced taverns as the preferred meeting places for scientists, academicians, men of letters, and musicians, even if, at the plebeian level, the difference between neighborhood coffeehouses and traditional wineshops might not have been so sharp.[39] Many cafés drew regular customers who simply wanted to socialize, play board games, read the latest newspapers and newsletters

[36] Quoted in Spary, *Eating the Enlightenment*, 80.
[37] Steve Pincus, "'Coffee Politicians Does Create': Coffeehouses and Restoration Political Culture," JMH 67 (December 1995), 833.
[38] Michael North, *"Material Delight and the Joy of Living": Cultural Consumption in the Age of Enlightenment in Germany*, trans. Pamela Selwyn (New York, 2008), 156.
[39] David Garrioch, *Neighborhood and Community in Paris, 1740–1790* (Cambridge, 1986), 180–191; Thierry Rigogne, "Readers and Reading in Cafés, 1660–1800," FHS 41 (2018), 473–494; Spary, *Eating the Enlightenment*, ch. 3. Craig Koslovsky, "Parisian Cafés in European Perspective," *French History* (FH) 31 (2017), 39–62, suggests that, initially at least, cafés in Paris were more aristocratic than they were in England, the Netherlands, and Germany.

(often provided for free), and strike up conversations about matters of common interest from the latest war raging in the colonies to domestic politics.

Much of the reading in cafés was done aloud in small groups, "thus giving rise to multiple publics, which taken together – and along with publics forming at the same time in other settings – came to be seen as a unitary 'public' or 'public opinion.'"[40] Such publics could form spontaneously in cafés because customers in effect rented a physical infrastructure – complete with candles, mirrors, stoves, chairs, and tables – that was conducive to reading and conversation.[41] Such infrastructure was, moreover, available day or night thanks to strides in urban street illumination and policing, which made it safer for "respectable" people to go out after sunset and patronize cafés, salons, theaters, shops, restaurants, or, as we shall see, public gardens, as part of a cultural process by which "consumers of leisure colonized the night."[42] No wonder the café caught Habermas' eye.

Yet, we need not accept Habermas' argument about sociability wholesale. First, the German philosopher's discussion of Enlightenment sociability puts the accent on inclusion, suggesting that the status-oriented rules about who should be allowed to interact with whom and how, which governed the world outside the café (and the Masonic lodge), were temporarily suspended inside them. However, coffeehouses were inclusive and exclusive at the same time. To be sure, there were no legal barriers to entering a café, so elites did mingle with middling professionals (clerks, shopkeepers, and master artisans) as they sipped hot beverages, but there were nevertheless acute gender and social divides. In England, coffeehouses were predominantly male. Women might run or peddle pamphlets in cafés, but the spaces were masculine by design; coffee-drinking men engaged in commercial, political, learned, and social discussion to the exclusion of women. Laboring women who

---

[40] Rigogne, "Readers and Reading in Cafés," 488.
[41] Ibid., 485. Rigogne's notion of infrastructure is consistent with my discussion in Chapter 1 about clusters of consumption. It also applies to clubs like the Salon des Échecs, where, for five louis a year, "one finds several well-heated rooms, all the journals, writing materials equal to those at home, and refreshments such as tea, lemonade, or syrup drinks." Quoted in Antoine Lilti, *The World of the Salons*, trans. Lydia G. Cochrane (Oxford, 2006), 223.
[42] Craig Koslovsky, *Evening's Empire: A History of the Night in Early Modern Europe* (Cambridge, 2011), 184. Paris was the first city to inaugurate street lighting, but as the technology improved, other European and colonial cities (Amsterdam, London, Leipzig, Berlin, Cologne, Boston, New York, Philadelphia, and Cap-Français) followed suit. See Darrin M. McMahon, "Illuminating the Enlightenment: Public Lighting Practices in the *Siècle des Lumières*," PP 240 (August 2018), 119–159.

worked in or passed through cafés risked physical abuse and accusations of sexual promiscuity, while fashionable ladies did their best to avoid such places by taking their coffee at the window of their carriages or serving the beverage at home.[43] In France, by contrast, women appear to have patronized cafés, though usually in the company of male family members.[44]

Before the nineteenth century, cafés were also socially exclusive, especially the fancier ones decorated with wooden paneling, marble counters, and mirrors. It is true that at literary cafés verbal skill could take priority over social rank as middling men of talent and ambition (such as French philosopher Denis Diderot) impressed elites and found patrons, but most laboring men continued to frequent taverns as their social superiors abandoned local drinking haunts for more respectable cafés. Even as social mixing among the middle and upper orders occurred in cafés, the café/tavern divide reflected a widening sociocultural chasm between the propertied elite and the laboring classes.[45]

Finally, coffeehouses were not always bastions of polite respectability and rational debate. Frank conversations among men of different social standing could easily lead to personal insult and violence. The chevalier de Mailly observed how heated conversation in one Parisian café suddenly turned into a brawl: "The Glasses & Cups were smashed, the tables and Coffee-pots overturned, the Chandeliers & Mirrors broken, & for a quarter of an hour there was nothing but disorder, & blows struck on one side or another."[46] So much for calm rational debate. In fact, the notion many historians have of polite coffeehouse conversation ultimately comes from the idealized versions of the café that commentators such as Joseph Addison and Richard Steele imposed on what they must have known was a much messier reality. Through their magazines, which offered aspiring middle-class readers guidance for navigating the world of polite sociability, Addison and Steele painted a model portrait of coffeehouse customers as "men who have business or good sense in their faces, and come to the coffeehouse either to transact affairs or enjoy conversation," serious men whose "entertainments are derived rather from Reason than Imagination."[47] But this triumphal image of the sober, rational coffeehouse, which Habermas later developed into a full-blown theory of the

[43] Phil Withington, "Where Was the Coffee in Early Modern England?" JMH 92 (March 2020), 40–75.
[44] Koslovsky, "Parisian Cafés in European Perspective"; Rigogne, "Readers and Reading in Cafés."
[45] Peter Burke, *Popular Culture in Early Modern Europe* (New York, 1978).
[46] Quoted in Spary, *Eating the Enlightenment*, 119.
[47] Quoted in Cowan, *The Social Life of Coffee*, 245.

public sphere, did not always match the reality of the eighteenth-century café. As one historian of the institution concludes, the voice of the coffee-house "sounded much more like the confused chatter of the tower of Babel than it did the product of a sober, rational, ideal speech situation."[48]

The last key site of sociability we will consider is the public promenade. The physical space of cities changed dramatically as leisure became increasingly commercialized over the course of the long eighteenth century. For much of the early modern period, the affluent did not take leisurely strolls through city streets the way that they do today. Most streets were narrow, crooked, unpaved, and had no sidewalks; they served as sewers for neighborhood waste and turned to mud when it rained. Aristocrats who wanted to take a leisurely walk or carriage ride escaped to the majestic gardens and alleys of royal palaces. However, in the late seventeenth and eighteenth centuries, new sorts of public space opened up in and around affluent neighborhoods. In addition to the emergence of the fashionable shopping districts discussed in Chapter 3, public promenades and pleasure gardens started to appear as zones of sociable amusement and consumption that catered to a relatively broad public.

In London, Vauxhall pleasure gardens, on the south bank of the Thames river, consisted of several acres of trees and plants that offered alleys and paths for shady walks, popular entertainments, and food and drink (see Figure 5.3). In 1728, entrepreneur Jonathan Tyers acquired the gardens and turned it into a successful enterprise by adding a touch of musical respectability. He remodeled the gardens, installed an organ in the orchestra, and, in 1738, added a life-size statue of George Frederic Handel. He also began to charge a modest entrance free of a shilling to supplement the income from food and beverage concessions. Illuminated at night, the walkways and bandstand at Vauxhall drew large and diverse crowds; 12,000 people turned out in 1749 for a rehearsal of Handel's "Music for the Royal Fireworks." But its socially diverse clientele put some people off. Anna Larpent, a prosperous and cultured Londoner, found Vauxhall "a most disagreeable place" after her first visit in 1780.[49] She preferred Ranelagh, one of a number of pleasure gardens to spring up in the wake of Vauxhall's success. Ranelagh had a higher entrance fee and was therefore more exclusive, but those who could afford the price of admission could stroll through the leafy grounds, partake of various refreshments, and hear a full orchestra play in a rotunda. Mozart performed there in 1764.

---

[48] Cowan, *The Social Life of Coffee*, 254.
[49] Quoted in Brewer, *Pleasures of the Imagination*, 65.

Figure 5.3 John S. Muller, *Vauxhall Gardens Shewing the Grand Walk* ..., after 1751.
Yale Center for British Art. Orchestra music accompanies men, women, and children promenading along the main walkway of Vauxhall gardens

Commercialized leisure space opened up in Paris, too.[50] The Jardin des Tuileries, once the private garden of the Tuileries palace, is a typical example of the way inclusion and exclusion functioned in eighteenth-century public space. The once strict etiquette of the royal garden was relaxed to welcome all polite and well-dressed people – bourgeois as well as noble – who wished to walk along its tree-lined paths or sit on its shady benches to take in the latest fashions. But such mixing among the propertied was based on a formal act of exclusion: Swiss guards remained at the gate to block entry to servants and laboring people. The shift from strictly regulated and ritualized courtly leisure to a more open form of polite urban sociability involved the formal exclusion of the lower orders.

However, not all public leisure space in Paris proved to be so restrictive. In the late eighteenth century, the Tuileries lost ground to the more inclusive and commercialized area known as the Boulevards in the northern part of the city. With no entrance fee (or Swiss guards), the

[50] Laurent Turcot, *Le promeneur à Paris au xviiie siècle* (Paris, 2007).

Boulevards provided ample space for strolls and coach rides amid a string of cafés offering everything from lemonade to ice cream and a plethora of popular entertainments, including theaters, street singing, circuses, magic shows, and science exhibitions. The main attractions were the inexpensive little theaters, which featured pantomimes, acrobats, tight-rope walkers, dancing, and farcical plays. Although such acts were aimed at the lowborn, every social type could be found in the audience, from bejeweled duchesses to unskilled artisans. The social diversity of revelers on the Boulevards far exceeded that of the exclusive salons and the more professional cafés. It was the same with the Palais-Royal, the legal enclave belonging to the house of Orléans, where high and low mixed and consumers could buy anything from banned books to sex.

Extraordinarily large and diverse urban crowds formed to witness the most public scientific experiments of the age: balloon ascents. Throngs in Paris, London, Frankfurt, Hamburg, and provincial cities gathered to watch the great ballooning events of the 1780s. Blurring the boundaries between elite and plebeian publics, wealthier ticket holders crossed paths with ordinary spectators to witness the latest demonstrations of Enlightenment science in which hot air and hydrogen balloons ascended from city parks to unimaginable heights before sailing beyond the city and descending on some unsuspecting village of peasants in the hinter-land. "Never before was a philosophical experiment so magnificently attended," observed Benjamin Franklin of the Paris balloon ascent of December 1, 1783.[51] Ten thousand spectators with tickets filled the Tuileries, but many more (200,000 according to Mercier) packed city streets, stood at windows, lined the Seine, and sat on rooftops to catch a glimpse of the balloon "whirling aloft like a planet, … the most astounding achievement the science of physics has yet given the world," remarked the usually sardonic Mercier.[52] Thrilled spectators could pur-chase any number of commemorative fans, pocket watches, and plates to keep the memory of the spectacle alive.

The stunning diversity of the Boulevards and other public spaces has provoked much scholarly reflection. Robert Isherwood, stressing social integration and the cultural convergence of high and low theater, questions Peter Burke's claim that a gulf opened up between elite and popular culture in the early modern period.[53] For Isherwood, the Boulevards mitigated

[51] Quoted in Mi Gyung Kim, *The Imagined Empire: Balloon Enlightenments in Revolutionary Europe* (Pittsburgh, 2016), 94.

[52] Quoted in ibid., 95.

[53] Robert Isherwood, *Farce and Fantasy: Popular Entertainment in Eighteenth-Century Paris* (Oxford, 1986).

distinctions between "high" and "low" forms of expression, fostering a counterculture that defied the traditional order. William Sewell likewise emphasizes the diversity of the Boulevards but argues instead that such social mixing, combined with the anonymity that came with urban commercial society, reflected the development of capitalistic commodification. The spread of the commodity form in places such as public gardens, he hypothesizes, gave rise to abstract forms of social relations that ultimately made the civic equality of the French Revolution conceivable.[54] Sewell's work is inspired by Marx's theory of the commodity, but Colin Jones makes a similar argument based on Habermas that the commercial press posited "an open and relatively egalitarian social organization," which ran counter to older social logics of birth, privilege, and corporate status.[55]

We will have ample opportunity to discuss the relationship between revolution and consumption in Chapter 7. Suffice it to say here that the elite did in fact widen in the eighteenth century to include well-off bourgeois and professionals. But this broader elite, based on wealth, education, and consumer competency as well as birth, nonetheless remained exclusive, pulling away from the laboring classes, as Burke suggests, even if the broader elite occasionally encountered the plebeian public in various "contact zones."[56] Certainly, aristocrats and shop clerks crossed paths on the Boulevards and in pleasure gardens, but they could all tell who was who. Contact and integration are two very different things. Alarmist comments by eighteenth-century writers about the illegibility of rank in open public spaces were prescriptive exaggerations, literary tropes in a debate on luxury, not clinical social descriptions.

At the same time, however, many urban elites did in fact dabble in popular consumer culture, a phenomenon that invites further reflection. Rather than seeing in such mixing the existence of an egalitarian public sphere that encompassed rich and poor alike, it might be instructive to refer back to the concept of the cultural omnivore.[57] We have already noted how Marie-Antoinette donned simple white cotton dresses, playing at sartorial simplicity. The same sort of behavior occurred at the Boulevards, where aristocrats avidly partook of popular

---

[54] William Sewell, "Connecting Capitalism to the French Revolution: The Parisian Promenade and the Origins of Civic Equality in Eighteenth-Century France," *Critical Historical Studies* 1 (Spring 2014), 5–46; William Sewell, *Capitalism and the Emergence of Civic Equality in Eighteenth-Century France* (Chicago, 2021).

[55] Colin Jones, "The Great Chain of Buying: Medical Advertisement, the Bourgeois Public Sphere, and the Origins of the French Revolution," AHR 101 (February 1996), 14; Colin Jones, "Bourgeois Revolution Revivified: 1789 and Social Change," in Colin Lucas, ed., *Rewriting the French Revolution* (Oxford, 1991).

[56] Kim, *The Imagined Empire*.

[57] Tony Bennett et al., *Culture, Class, Distinction* (New York, 2009).

entertainments. Even the king and queen of France themselves attempted to recreate the raucous atmosphere of the Boulevards at the palace of Versailles. We should be careful, however, not to take such cultural phenomena as evidence of a new egalitarian public sphere, for cultural omnivores who participated in popular consumption had no intention of diminishing their social status. If anything, their cultural promiscuousness may have enhanced their status in the eyes of peers as it became fashionable to display one's cross-cultural competencies. The majority of townspeople in the eighteenth century did not have the money or education to consume across a wide range of cultural levels. Whereas high society could and often did access the culture of the laboring classes, the laboring classes could not access the culture of high society, even in an age of expanding consumption. That distinction is worth remembering because it underscores the limits of egalitarianism in the eighteenth-century public sphere.

The growth of consumption in the eighteenth century helped produce a raft of new cultural practices associated with the Enlightenment. The proliferation of books and their increasing variety encouraged a multiplicity of modes of reading that, revolutionary or not, changed the relationship between readers and texts, private and public life, and self and society. While novels invited intensive reading and the belief in an inner world of emotions, books, newspapers, and ephemeral literature stimulated extensive reading and the formation of a vibrant public sphere. Although the public was not as bourgeois, rational, and oppositional as Habermas imagined, the elevated circulation of printed work did broaden discussion of pressing issues of reform and pose a serious challenge to rulers, many of whom now felt obliged to enter the public fray to compete for the attention of readers.

Consumption shaped Enlightenment sociability as well. The material environments in which townspeople interacted afforded the creation of multiple sites of social and intellectual exchange. Men and women ate meals at salons, drank coffee at cafés, and sported new fashions in public gardens, all of which gave rise to robust conversational publics. Such polite sociability softened social hierarchies insofar as it created a relatively broad sociocultural elite among the nobility and the professional classes, but it also created new forms of exclusion on the basis of wealth, property, and taste. Plebeian sociability continued apace, sometimes intersecting with that of elites but often unfolding in separate marginalized arenas of the tavern, street, and marketplace. Gender, too, remained a vector of exclusion, though wealthier women devised creative ways to organize salons and attend other public gatherings. With the growth of print and the emergence of new forms of sociability, sovereigns, writers, and philosophers increasingly referred to "the public" as a source of authority, but the question of who exactly constituted the public was scarcely a settled matter. Kant believed that the public would peacefully and gradually expand, and that rulers would learn to listen to what it had to say, but the German philosopher's definition of the public excluded women, uneducated men, and people of color. Whose voices were supposed to carry weight in the rapidly developing public sphere? Numerous political battles since the eighteenth century have been fought over precisely this question.

6   The Luxury Debate

As the proliferation of things sustained the Enlightenment, Enlightenment thinkers reflected on the proliferation of things. Observing the rise of European consumption with varying degrees of enthusiasm and alarm, philosophers, political economists, novelists, and others felt compelled to write about it. While they rarely used the word "consumption," they spoke incessantly of "luxury," a multivalent term that became the principal idiom through which writers reflected on the moral, social, and political implications of consumption in the eighteenth century. Indeed, the controversy over luxury was a proxy for the first modern debate on consumption, the intellectual twin of the consumer revolution and the commercial capitalism that fueled it.

As Figure 6.1 shows, printed discussions of luxury spiked in eighteenth-century Europe, a curious cultural phenomenon that raises a series of questions. What was at stake in this flurry of polemical literature? How did writers fathom the expanding world of goods in which they found themselves and characterize its effects on the human condition? How did they discuss the perils and promises of a rapidly developing consumer culture?

Although many scholars have examined the eighteenth-century luxury debate, their treatment of it remains fragmentary.[1] Studies tend to examine either the pro-luxury or anti-luxury side, focus on a particular country, analyze a limited set of thinkers, or consider either fiction or nonfiction.[2] The seminal work of J. G. A. Pocock on classical

---

[1] The few general overviews include: Maxine Berg and Elizabeth Eger, eds., *Luxury in the Eighteenth Century: Debates, Desires and Delectable Goods* (New York, 2002); Christopher Berry, *The Idea of Luxury: A Conceptual and Historical Investigation* (Cambridge, 1994); Istvan Hont, "The Early Enlightenment Debate on Commerce and Luxury," in Mark Goldie and Robert Wokler, eds., *The Cambridge History of Eighteenth-Century Political Thought* (Cambridge, 2006), 379–418; John Sekora, *Luxury: The Concept in Western Thought, Eden to Smollett* (Baltimore, 1977).

[2] For Spain, see Belén Moreno Claverías, "L'inégalité comme norme: Modèles de consommation dans l'Espagne préindustrielle," in *Consommateurs & consommation XVIIe–XXIe siècle: Regards franco-espagnols* (Perpignan, 2015), 36–38. For France,

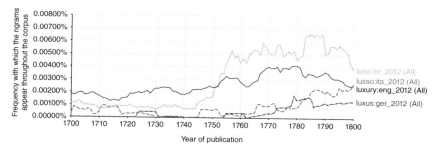

Figure 6.1 Google Ngram of the Words "luxe," "luxury," "lusso," and "luxus" in French, English, Italian, and German publications, respectively.

republicanism provided a framework for further research on critiques of luxury in early modern thought.[3] More recently, scholars have brought questions of gender into the discussion, an important and fruitful intervention because so much of the luxury debate hinged on gendered rhetoric.[4] And a resurgence in the study of political economy and empire

Charly Coleman, *The Spirit of French Capitalism: Economic Theology in the Age of Enlightenment* (Stanford, CA, 2021), ch. 6; Michael Kwass, "Ordering the World of Goods: Consumer Revolution and the Classification of Objects in Eighteenth-Century France," *Representations* 82 (Spring 2003), 87–116; Michael Kwass, "'Le superflu, chose très nécessaire': Physiocracy and Its Discontents in the Eighteenth-Century Luxury Debate," in Steven L. Kaplan and Sophus Reinert, eds., *The Economic Turn: Recasting Political Economy in Enlightenment Europe* (London, 2019), 117–138; Sarah Maza, "Luxury, Morality, and Social Change: Why There Was No Middle-Class Consciousness in Prerevolutionary France," JMH 69 (June 1997), 199–229; André Morize, *L'Apologie du luxe au XVIIIe siècle et "Le Mondain" de Voltaire* (Geneva, 1970); Philippe Perrot, *Le luxe: une richesse entre faste et confort, XVIIIe–XIX siècle* (Paris, 1995); Audrey Provost, *Le luxe, les Lumières et la Révolution* (Seyssel, 2014); Ellen Ross, "Mandeville, Melon, and Voltaire: The Origins of the Luxury Controversy in France," *Studies on Voltaire and the Eighteenth Century* (SVEC) 155 (1976), 1897–1912; John Shovlin, *The Political Economy of Virtue: Luxury, Patriotism, and the Origins of the French Revolution* (Ithaca, NY, 2006). Studies of particular thinkers include: Renato Galliani, *Rousseau, le luxe et l'idéologie nobiliaire* (Oxford, 1989); Felicia Gottman, "Du Châtelet, Voltaire, and the Transformation of Mandeville's *Fable*," *History of European Ideas* 38 (2012), 218–232; E. G. Hundert, *The Enlightenment's Fable: Bernard Mandeville and the Discovery of Society* (Cambridge, 1994); Michael Kwass, "Consumption and the World of Ideas: Consumer Revolution and the Moral Economy of the Marquis de Mirabeau," *Eighteenth-Century Studies* 37 (Winter 2004), 187–214; Anthony Strugnell, "Diderot on Luxury, Commerce and the Merchant," SVEC 217 (1983), 83–93.

3 J. G. A. Pocock, *The Machiavellian Moment: Florentine Political Thought and the Atlantic Republican Tradition* (Princeton, NJ, 1975); J. G. A. Pocock, *Virtue, Commerce, and History* (Cambridge, 1985). Shovlin, *The Political Economy of Virtue*, for example, extends Pocock's work to eighteenth-century France.

4 Berg and Eger, *Luxury in the Eighteenth Century*, part IV; Clare Haru Crowston, *Credit, Fashion, Sex: Economies of Regard in Old Regime France* (Durham, NC, 2013); Jennifer

has shed additional light on the role that the idea of luxury played in eighteenth-century economic reasoning.[5] This chapter weaves together these threads to formulate a brief but balanced overview of the luxury debate.

As John Sekora emphasized, luxury had been the object of intense criticism since antiquity.[6] For ancient Greek philosophers, luxury was a symptom of imbalance and disorder in the city caused by excessive human appetites that no longer respected need-based desires. From the very beginning, this critique was gendered: men who overindulged in luxury became effeminate and unfit to wage war, the ultimate test of masculinity. Greek critiques of luxury were further developed by Roman philosophers, who would have enormous influence on early modern thought. Cicero claimed that men who were unable to control their appetites were brutes addicted to material and sensual pleasures. Instead of leading frugal, austere, and sober lives, they succumbed to "luxury, softness, and effeminacy" and, in so doing, endangered the welfare of the collective polity.[7] This understanding of luxury pervaded histories of Rome, which suggested that once the Roman people had been exposed to foreign luxury, namely the luxury of "Asia" and the Greeks, they became weak, corrupt, feminine, and vulnerable to foreign enemies. The excessive pursuit of pleasure extinguished civic virtue, the quality by which men acted on behalf of the public good, precipitating the decline and fall of Rome.

In the Middle Ages, Christian thinkers added further layers of criticism. No longer a mere vice, luxury became a religious sin, the antithesis of an ascetic ideal embodied in monasticism. Luxury, moreover, was not just any sin: Saint Augustine tied luxury to the sin of lechery, which he defined as the pursuit of sexual pleasure uncoupled from the duty of procreation. Throughout the early modern period, both Catholic and Protestant theologians made it abundantly clear that Christians had to choose between fleeting pleasure in this world and eternal salvation in the next. They beseeched their flocks to avoid the evils of luxury even as, in the case of Enlightenment France, clerics began

Jones, *Sexing La Mode: Gender, Fashion, and Commercial Culture in Old Regime France* (Oxford, 2004); Maza, "Luxury, Morality, and Social Change."
[5] For example, Anthony Brewer, "Luxury and Economic Development: David Hume and Adam Smith," *Scottish Journal of Political Economy* 45 (1998), 78–98; Gottman, "Du Châtelet, Voltaire, and the Transformation of Mandeville's *Fable*"; Kwass, "'Le superflu, chose très necessaire'"; Anoush Fraser Terjanian, *Commerce and Its Discontents in Eighteenth-Century French Political Thought* (Cambridge, 2016).
[6] Sekora, *Luxury.*   [7] Quoted in Berry, *The Idea of Luxury*, 66.

to rethink the relationship between terrestrial consumption and the celestial riches that awaited.[8]

While ancient and medieval critiques persisted across the early modern period, a growing scholarly consensus contends that the discussion of luxury shifted decisively at the turn of the eighteenth century. At that time, two writers – François de Fénelon and Bernard Mandeville – laid the foundations for a vigorous Enlightenment debate on luxury and its effects on state and society.[9] In *The Adventures of Telemachus, Son of Ulysees* (1699), an adaptation of Homer's *Odyssey* that would become an eighteenth-century bestseller, French Archbishop Fénelon drew heavily on classical and Christian ideas to argue that luxury destroys kingdoms. Taking aim at Jean-Baptiste Colbert, the minister of Louis XIV who had actively supported the luxury trades, Fénelon claimed that the consumption of expensive fashionable goods corrodes virtue, wreaks havoc with the social order, and saps the power of nations. As preceptor Mentor warns Telemachus, luxury "corrupts manners" by encouraging a vicious culture of material display that renders men "slaves" to false desires as it spreads through the social hierarchy. "All live above their rank and income, some from vanity and ostentation, and to display their wealth; others from false shame, and to hide their poverty ... Even those who are poor will affect to appear wealthy, and spend as if they were so: they will borrow, they will cheat, they will have recourse to a thousand indirect methods" to obtain the trappings of the elite.[10]

Excessive consumption not only raised moral issues for individuals but had a profoundly disorienting social effect: as commoners usurped higher rank through false appearances, they increasingly rendered the social hierarchy illegible. How could one know who was who in a society where the rampant circulation of signs of status obscured the underlying social order? Moral decay and social illegibility would inevitably yield chaos, Fénelon strenuously asserted. But the archbishop had a solution. As exemplified by his fictional kingdom of Salentum, polities could reform themselves by banishing luxury, nurturing agriculture, and instilling in their populace the virtues of frugality, industriousness, and public spirit. Only then could the state avoid social disorder and moral decline, and endure.

---

[8] Coleman, *The Spirit of French Capitalism*.
[9] Hont, "The Early Enlightenment Debate on Commerce and Luxury"; Hundert, *The Enlightenment's Fable*; Shovlin, *The Political Economy of Virtue*.
[10] François de Fénelon, *Telemachus, Son of Ulysses*, ed. and trans. Patrick Riley (Cambridge, 1994), 296–297.

Although Fénelon was enormously influential throughout the eighteenth century, encouraging countless jeremiads against the social disorder of "luxury" – precisely the kind of jeremiads that McKendrick would use as evidence of a consumer revolution – the archbishop's ideas were directly and powerfully challenged by Bernard Mandeville, a Dutch physician living in England who brushed aside screeds against material excess and advanced a bold apology for luxury. Taken together, Mandeville's witty poem, *The Grumbling Hive: Or, Knaves Turn'd Honest* (1705), and his extensive prose commentary, *The Fable of the Bees: or Private Vices, Publick Benefits* (1714, 1723), built on the arguments of earlier English economic writers Nicolas Barbon and Dudley North to make an astonishing intellectual intervention (see Figure 6.2). The story of *The Grumbling Hive* begins with a morally flawed yet thriving society of bees, a hive "full of Vice, Yet the whole Mass a Paradise." The political and economic success of the hive was driven by vice, especially the desire for luxury, which "Employ'd a Million of the Poor." One day, however, bees troubled by the hive's moral shortcomings prayed for a new era of "Honesty," an appeal that "Jove" happily granted. The god expunged all vice from the hive, and the bees immediately began to behave virtuously. The public effects of such virtue, however, were catastrophic. The economy plummeted as elites curbed spending on luxury goods; artisanal employment dried up; fashion cycles disappeared; lawyers failed to find clients; and military spending was slashed. As a result, merchants and artisans went bankrupt and large numbers of bees emigrated, leaving the depleted hive vulnerable to invasion. Enemies soon conquered the hive and massacred all those who remained. The moral of the story could not have been more clear: if one wanted to enjoy the benefits of a prosperous and strong polity, one would have to live with "fraud, luxury, and pride."[11] You could not have it both ways.

In *The Fable of the Bees*, Mandeville expounded upon his bitterly satirical poem. One important theme on which he elaborated was the role of female consumer desire in an expanding economy – what historians call the "petticoat thesis." According to the physician, women's "fickleness" and "luxury" was a source of enormous economic strength, responsible for as much as a quarter of the entire economy. What made women so economically powerful was their ever expanding understanding of material need. Middling women who "have half a score of suits of clothes, two or three of them not the worse for wearing, will think it a

---

[11] Bernard Mandeville, *The Fable of the Bees: or Private Vices, Publick Benefits*, vol. 1, F. B. Kaye, ed. (Indianapolis, 1988), 24, 25, 27, 36.

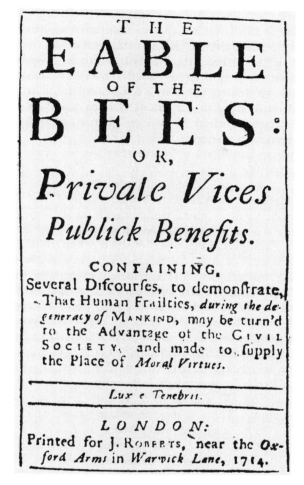

THE
FABLE
OF THE
BEES:
OR,
Private Vices
Publick Benefits.

CONTAINING,

Several Difcourfes, to demonftrate,
That Human Frailties, *during the degeneracy of* MANKIND, may be turn'd
to the Advantage of the CIVIL
SOCIETY, and made to fupply
the Place of *Moral Virtues.*

Lux e Tenebris.

LONDON:

Printed for J. ROBERTS, near the Oxford *Arms* in *Warwick Lane*, 1714.

Figure 6.2 Cover of Bernard Mandeville, *The Fable of the Bees*,
1714 or 1724.
Copyright Getty Images

sufficient plea for new ones, if they can say that they have never a gown or
petticoat, but what they have been often seen in, and are known by." The
ardent feminine desire to be seen in new clothes, combined with the "vile
stratagems" women employed to bend husbands to their will, were
responsible for "an opulent, powerful, and ... flourishing kingdom."[12]

[12] Ibid., vol. 2, 226–228.

Again, the message was unequivocal: wealth and power were sustained by vice, particularly the feminine vice of consumer desire. Although steeped in Augustinian notions of human sin, Mandeville relished the moral irony that vice mimicked virtue by contributing to the public good. If subjects of mighty and prosperous kingdoms wished to continue to thrive, they would simply have to live with this painful moral irony. Thus, the book turned on its head the venerable classical and Christian idea that vice or sin necessarily destroys polities, provoking howls of moral outrage from scandalized readers.

The luxury debate continued to evolve after the inaugural works of Fénelon and Mandeville. From the 1720s to the 1750s, a series of major thinkers – the third earl of Shaftesbury, Jean-François Melon, Montesquieu, Madame du Châtelet, Voltaire, and David Hume – softened Mandeville's caustic moral irony to craft an apology for luxury that associated high levels of consumption with cultural progress. Luxury was portrayed as a benign manifestation of the flowering of the arts and sciences, the refinement of taste, the enhancement of sociable exchange among men and women, and the expansion of human happiness. Shaftesbury asserted that humans were naturally social; their appetite for food, pleasure, wealth, and material goods derived from natural sentiments and did not necessarily lead to greed and luxury. The right sort of education in sociability could prevent men and women from overindulgence and moral decay. In *Persian Letters* (1721), Montesquieu, through the voice of Usbek, reiterated Mandeville's arguments about the public benefits of luxury consumption and explicitly rejected the notion that such consumption effeminates men. Luxury generates "universal industry and ingenuity. Where is the effeminate nation which you talk about so much?"[13] In his magnum opus *Spirit of the Laws*, Montesquieu stressed that "the effect of commerce is wealth; the consequence of wealth is luxury; that of luxury is the perfection of the arts."[14] For his part, Melon emphasized that society progressed as the basic needs of ordinary consumers expanded to include "secondary necessities," goods that were once perceived as luxuries but were now considered everyday conveniences.[15] Luxury was concerned with the basic comforts of life, not the ostentatious overindulgence to which its critics constantly

---

[13] Montesquieu, *Persian Letters*, trans. C. J. Betts (London, 1993), letter 106.
[14] Montesquieu, *De l'esprit des lois* (Paris, 1979), book 21, ch. 6. In this same work, Montesquieu argued that commerce polishes and softens manners. See Albert O. Hirschman, *The Passions and the Interests: Political Arguments for Capitalism before Its Triumph* (Princeton, NJ, 1977), 56–63.
[15] Jean François Melon, *Essai politique sur le commerce* (1736), 113, 121. Before Melon, Fénelon, *Telemachus*, 297, had observed how superfluities turned into necessities over

referred. By associating luxury with morally temperate concepts such as comfort and convenience, apologists like Melon attempted to legitimize luxury and incorporate it into a broader narrative of Enlightenment cultural progress.

As the case of Melon suggests, pro-luxury writers went to great lengths to demonstrate the relativity of luxury. Mandeville had played brazenly with the categories of necessity and luxury, offering a strict biological definition (luxury was all that was not immediately necessary for man to survive) before entertaining an expansive cultural one (almost everything was a necessity according to certain women). "In one Sense every Thing may be call'd [luxury], and in another there is no such thing at all."[16] For Mandeville, the irony generated by juxtaposing two conflicting definitions was meant to challenge the semantic coherence of the word luxury itself and neutralize one of moralists' favorite linguistic weapons. How could one criticize luxury when the term itself had no stable meaning?

After Mandeville, apologists tended to restrict the category of necessity to the bare minimum in order to highlight the capaciousness of the category of luxury. Luxury not only contained morally dubious ostentation, Georges Marie Butel-Dumont pointed out, but also "the useful, the convenient, the agreeable, an infinity of everyday things." There was nothing excessive about it. It encompassed a large set of banal comforts and conveniences well beyond moral reproach. Butel-Dumont went so far as to classify a common comestible for many Parisians, white bread, as a luxury. We only think of it as a necessity, he explained, because with the passage of time people falsely reclassify what were once novel luxuries as necessities. History proved, however, that the apparent necessities of the current age (such as white bread) were in fact luxuries whose very banality bore witness to the progress of society. A survey of the world beyond Europe demonstrated the same thing. The bow and arrow of the "savage," Butel-Dumont observed, was an "instrument of convenience," a type of luxury not unlike an eighteenth-century carriage; both inventions spared men the trouble of running. Such cross-cultural comparisons between Europeans and Africans, Native Americans, and Pacific Islanders made luxury seem utterly natural and harmless, certainly not the scourge of a decaying, overly refined nation.[17]

The most vivid celebrations of luxury were penned by Voltaire, whose poems *Le Mondain* ("The Man of the World," 1736) and the *La Défense*

time, but the archbishop came to the opposite conclusion: that the expanding category of necessity was a sign of corruption.
[16] Mandeville, *The Fable of the Bees or Private Vices*, vol. 1, 107–108, 123.
[17] Georges Marie Butel-Dumont, *Théorie du luxe*, vol. 1 (n.p., 1771), 50, 111.

du Mondain ou l'apologie du luxe ("The Defense of the Man of the World or the Apology of Luxury," 1737) unabashedly extolled modern comforts. Borrowing heavily from scientist and mathematician Émilie du Châtelet, who extrapolated on Mandeville's *The Fable of the Bees* in 1735 as she translated it, Voltaire dismissed the idea that early man and citizens of ancient civilizations were more virtuous than present-day Parisians.[18] Ancients had lived an ascetic life out of poverty, not virtue: "Do not therefore with simplicity call virtue that which was poverty." Eager as always to attack traditional Judeo-Christianity, Voltaire went so far as to depict Adam and Eve in the Garden of Eden as brutes with filthy overgrown fingernails, unkempt hair, and tanned skin. The first man and woman ate nothing but water, millet, and acorns, had shamefully base sex, and slept on the ground. "There is your state of pure nature," Voltaire mocked. Contrast such "wretched" conditions with life in eighteenth-century Paris, where men and women of taste lived in beautiful buildings, adorned them with fine paintings and tapestries, promenaded in pleasant gardens, and traveled by gilded coaches ("rolling houses") to delightful operas and gourmet dinners. France in the eighteenth century was the very height of civilization, he insisted, thanks to three historical forces: overseas trade, which brought wine from the Canary Islands, coffee from Arabia, porcelain from China, and silver from Potosi; the industriousness of ambitious workers, fueled by their social aspirations; and the firm guidance of Colbert, who "knew that luxury enriches our State". Forget Eden, forget ancient Rome: "the terrestrial paradise is where I am."[19]

Drawing on Voltaire's notion of material and cultural progress, the great Scottish philosopher David Hume synthesized a formidable defense of luxury in 1752. In an essay first entitled "Of Luxury" but later changed, tellingly, to "Of Refinement in the Arts," Hume abandoned the poetry of Mandeville and Voltaire to lay out the arguments in favor of luxurious consumption in lucid prose. He flatly asserted "that the ages of refinement are both the happiest and most virtuous." Differentiating himself from Mandeville, Hume did not dwell on the moral irony that vice was ultimately advantageous to society. Rather, like Voltaire, his argument rested on the notion that the development of luxury was of a piece with intellectual, cultural, political, and commercial progress:

---

[18] Gottman, "Du Châtelet, Voltaire, and the Transformation of Mandeville's *Fable*."

[19] Voltaire, *Le Mondain* (1736) (https://artflsrv03.uchicago.edu/philologic4/toutvoltaire/navigate/262/1/2/ [accessed July 20, 2021]) and *Défense du Mondain* (1737) (https://artflsrv03.uchicago.edu/philologic4/toutvoltaire/navigate/262/1/3/?byte=9669&byte=9678&byte=9681 [accessed July 20, 2021]).

"the same age, which produces great philosophers and politicians, renowned generals and poets, usually abounds with skillful weavers, and ship-carpenters."[20] And, like Montesquieu, Hume clarified the gender implications of his argument. The classical and Christian critique of luxury as a cause of effeminacy and corruption was not a concern. In advanced societies, "both sexes meet in an easy and sociable manner; and the tempers of men, as well as their behavior, refine apace." In "the more luxurious ages," such cross-gender sociability fostered "humanity" as well as industry and knowledge. Implicit in Hume's analysis was a new model of masculinity according to which men of the middling classes could be cosmopolitan and sociable without fear of becoming feminized and unproductive.[21]

Going further, Hume emphasized that military and political power expanded with the growth of production and consumption: armies grew in size; laws improved; and mind and body strengthened. The example of ancient Rome touted by "severe moralists" was badly misunderstood. Rome did not fall due to its adoption of "Asiatic luxury" but rather from "an ill modelled government, and the unlimited extent of conquests." "Progress in the arts," by which he meant agriculture and industry as well as the liberal arts and sciences, "is rather favourable to liberty" and the health of the polity because it supports "the middling rank of men, who are the best and firmest basis of public liberty."[22] Hume's defense of luxury associated it with happiness, sociability, industry, refinement, martial strength, and the political virtues of the middling classes.

Not everyone accepted such arguments. Indeed, following Fénelon, a growing number of philosophers, moralists, political economists, agronomists, journalists, clerics, and novelists warned readers about luxury's deleterious effects on individuals, society, and the state. Ironically, with the expansion of print in the age of Enlightenment, anti-luxury tracts reached the public in unprecedented numbers. Although the majority of critiques simply rehashed ancient and early modern themes, many emphasized with new urgency the social disorientation caused by emulative consumption. The perception that the quickening circulation of consumer goods was subverting traditional

---

[20] Such ideas of cultural advancement would feed stadial theories of human progress elaborated by Adam Smith and Jacques Turgot, who claimed that humanity progressed through successive stages of social development.

[21] David Hume, "Of Refinement in the Arts," in Henry Clark, ed., *Commerce, Culture, and Liberty: Readings on Capitalism before Adam Smith* (Indianapolis, 2003), 360–361.

[22] Ibid., 365–367. Voltaire, too, validated the urban middle classes, though in cultural, not political, terms. See Hont, "The Early Enlightenment Debate on Commerce and Luxury," 415.

social hierarchies induced a flood of exaggerated warnings like this one
from Henry Fielding:

while the Nobleman will emulate the Grandeur of a Prince and the Gentleman
will aspire to the proper state of a Nobleman, the Tradesman steps from behind
his Counter into the vacant place of the Gentleman. Nor doth the confusion end
there: It reaches the very Dregs of the People, who aspire still to a degree beyond
that which belongs to them.[23]

Most social critiques of luxury conceded that it was customary and
proper for men and women of high birth to express their status through
the display of luxury. The problem began when common people emulated their superiors and consumed beyond what their status allowed, a
misappropriation of signs that was tantamount to the usurpation of status
itself. As I've stated, it was the ubiquity of this sort of complaint in the
literature of the period that inspired McKendrick to formulate the emulation thesis in the first place.

Some anti-luxury essayists went beyond long-standing arguments by
expanding the intellectual dimensions of the debate or deploying new
literary forms. Chief among those who deepened the terms of debate was
Jean-Jacques Rousseau, who in the mid-century broke with fellow
Enlightenment philosophers to advance a blistering attack on luxury
and the supposed cultural progress with which it was associated.[24]
Rousseau's initial assault on luxury was prompted by the Dijon
Academy's essay contest question "Has the Restoration of the Sciences
and Arts Contributed to the Purification of Morals?" Rousseau's
Discourse on the Sciences and the Arts (1751), the essay that made him
famous, replied with a resounding "no!" Characterizing himself as a
simple "Citizen of Geneva," a tiny republican city-state across the border
from the grand kingdom of France, Rousseau argued that the development of the arts and sciences – and the rise of luxury that necessarily
accompanied it – did not improve human morality. On the contrary, the
development of knowledge, high culture, and a commercial economy
corrupted morals and weakened the state. Rousseau was well aware that
Mandeville and other writers of note had valorized luxury. He granted
that "luxury is a certain sign of riches; that, if you like, it even serves to
increase them." But who could deny that "good morals are essential if
empires are to endure, and that luxury is diametrically opposed to good
morals? ... The ancient politicians forever spoke of morals and virtue;

---

[23] Quoted in E. G. Hundert, "Mandeville, Rousseau and the Political Economy of
Fantasy," in Berg and Eger, eds., *Luxury in the Eighteenth Century*, 32.
[24] Galliani, *Rousseau*.

ours speak only of commerce and of money... According to them, a man is worth to the State only what he consumes in it," a logic Rousseau energetically sought to refute. Harking back to ancient republican themes, he argued that military strength depended not on riches but on the masculine patriotism of its citizens. Hence luxurious Sybaris "was subdued by a handful of peasants" whereas austere Sparta "caused Asia to tremble." In his own day, "as the conveniences of life increase, the arts improve, and luxury spreads," learned men sacrifice their taste to women, "the Tyrants of their freedom," and, as a result, "the military virtues vanish." For Rousseau, the growth of luxury produced a fatal reversal of the gender order and, by extension, undermined the capacity of men to act in the public interest. Rebutting Melon's argument about the natural progression of "secondary necessities," he bluntly asserted that "Everything beyond the physically necessary is a source of evil."[25]

Rousseau refined his ideas on luxury in his *Discourse on the Origin and the Foundations of Inequality among Men* (1755), a more sophisticated work of social theory. In it, Rousseau speculated on man's transition from the state of nature, a precivil existence that Thomas Hobbes had described as a war of all against all, to a political state with a developed society and government. Unlike Hobbes, Rousseau depicted a relatively benign state of nature. "Savage" man had limited needs, which he could satisfy rather easily, leaving his calm, self-regarding soul intact. However, this peaceful and free state of nature broke down once agriculture and metallurgy were introduced and, with them, the evils of the division of labor, dependency, and social stratification – in a word, inequality. Luxury, or at least the emergence of consumer desires beyond what was physically necessary to survive, was integral to this transition from nature to society. As humans began to build huts for lodging, develop sentimental ties with family members, and establish elementary forms of property, they used their leisure time "to acquire several sorts of conveniences unknown to their fathers; and this was the first yoke which, without thinking of it, they imposed on themselves, and the first source of evils they prepared for their Descendants." (Karl Marx, a close reader of Rousseau, would later write that "the production of new needs is the first historical act.")[26] The desire for such conveniences, Rousseau continued, "degenerated" into true needs, the pursuit of which both created and reflected a tightly bound, conflict-ridden society that was sharply divided between rich and poor. Gone was the strictly need-based,

---

[25] Jean-Jacques Rousseau, *The Discourses and Other Early Political Writings*, ed. and trans. Victor Gourevitch (Cambridge, 2016), 18–20, 84.
[26] Karl Marx, *The German Ideology*, ed. C. J. Arthur (London, 1974), 49.

self-regarding, serene man of the state of nature. He was replaced by "sociable man," a creature with constantly expanding desires and ambitions whose sense of self (*"amour propre"*) derived exclusively from the judgment of others. When the rich tricked the poor into entering political society, they locked into place not only vast differences in wealth and property but also a malignant culture of luxury, "the worst of all evils in any State, large or small." For, while the state "grows rich on the one hand," it "gets weak and depopulated on the other," eventually becoming "the prey of the poor Nations that succumb to the fatal temptation to invade them, and grow rich and weak in their turn, until they are themselves invaded and destroyed by others." The cycle of luxury, corruption, and military defeat would perpetually continue.[27]

While Rousseau rigorously laid out his critique of luxury in his political discourses, it was through his bestselling novel *La Nouvelle Héloïse* that his ideas on the subject reached a broad and enthusiastic audience. Indeed, as a literary form, the novel constituted an extraordinarily effective tool for diffusing critiques of luxury throughout the eighteenth century. Consider one of the most famous anti-luxury novels of the period: *The Expedition of Humphry Clinker* (1771) by Tobias Smollett.[28] Smollett was revolted by the social changes of his day: the spectacular growth of London, the rise of middle-class spa towns like Bath, the intensification of commerce, and the venality of parliamentary politics – all of which, he believed, undermined an orderly, unified, and simpler world in which social identity was fixed and hierarchy respected. Commerce and consumption were blessings when kept within proper channels, "but a glut of wealth brings along with it a glut of evils: it brings false taste, false appetite, false wants, profusion, venality, contempt of order, engendering a spirit of licentiousness, insolence, and faction, that keeps community in continual ferment, and in time destroys all the distinctions of civil society; so that universal anarchy and uproar must ensue." For Smollett, a "general tide of luxury" had "overspread the nation, and swept away all, even the dregs of the people."[29]

[27] Rousseau, *The Discourses and Other Early Political Writings*, 164–165, 201–202. Similarly, Gabriel de Mably's *Observations sur le gouvernement et les lois des États-Unis* (1784) identified three stages in commercial development, the last of which inevitably engenders luxury, avarice, and the corruption of the nation.

[28] Sekora, *Luxury*, analyzes Tobias Smollett, *The Expedition of Humphry Clinker* (Athens, GA, 2014), at length. For the place of novels in the German luxury debate, see Matt Erlin, *Necessary Luxuries: Books, Literature, and the Culture of Consumption in Germany, 1770–1815* (Ithaca, NY, 2014).

[29] Smollett, *The Expedition of Humphry Clinker*, 36, 269.

The Expedition of Humphry Clinker follows Matthew Bramble and his family as they leave their estate in southwest England and travel through the towns of England and Scotland. At each point in their peregrination, members of the family are exposed to the ills of tasteless luxury from which they must extricate themselves if they are to continue their journey and make it home with their moral selves intact. The patriarch Bramble is particularly disgusted by the foul smells he encounters among middle-class crowds in Bath, where social-climbing nabobs from India, planters from America, war contractors, and financiers put tasteless luxury on display for all to see. His contempt for newly rich American "negro-drivers" does not extend to the institution of slavery itself, as it did for the Abbé Raynal, Denis Diderot, and other philosophers who viewed plantation slavery as a cruel system of production that did nothing but flood Europe with luxuries.[30] However, Bramble does appear to share the widely held opinion that white creoles in American slave societies were physically weak and morally decadent. He does not hide his disdain for the crude ways in which colonial parvenus flaunted their wealth:

Every upstart of fortune, harnessed in the trappings of the mode, presents himself at Bath, as in the very focus of observation – Clerks and factors from the East Indies, loaded with the spoil of plundered provinces; planters, negro-drivers, and hucksters, from our American plantations, enriched they know not how; agents, commissaries, and contractors, who have fattened, in two successive wars, on the blood of the nation; usurers, brokers, and jobbers of every kind; men of low birth, and no breeding, have found themselves suddenly translated into a state of affluence, unknown to former ages; and no wonder that their brains should be intoxicated with pride, vanity, and presumption. Knowing no other criterion of greatness, but the ostentation of wealth, they discharge their affluence without taste or conduct, through every channel of the most absurd extravagance.[31]

Every character in the book confronts the spread of luxury in his or her own way. Bramble's nephew Jery comes around to his uncle's way of thinking, objecting to a nouveau riche who "blazes out in all the tinsel of the times" at the expense of former friends now "too plain and homespun to appear amidst his present brilliant connexions." Bramble's niece Liddy, one of the novel's few young female characters, is drawn to the splendor of luxury and requires vigilant familial protection. In London, her naïve fascination with superficial appearances leads her to misread

---

[30] According to Guillaume-Thomas-François Raynal, *Histoire philosophique et politique des établissements et du commerce des Européens dans les deux Indes*, vol. 1 (Geneva, 1781), book 6: 135, the principal "object" of the Atlantic slave trade was "luxury." See Terjanian, *Commerce and Its Discontents in Eighteenth-Century French Political Thought*, and Sankar Muthu, *Enlightenment against Empire* (Princeton, NJ, 2003).
[31] Smollet, *The Expedition of Humphry Clinker*, 36.

the social order, mistaking notorious prostitutes for ladies of fashion. Jery and Bramble know that they need to marry her to a sensible man quickly if she is to avoid the degeneracy of the age, for women in the novel are portrayed as rampant consumers whose "tyranny" over their husbands drives them to bankruptcy. In a scene describing the taking of tea, one of many foreign goods targeted in misogynistic anti-luxury tracts of the period, two "amazons" distinguish themselves in the pandemonium ("jostling, scrambling, pulling, snatching, struggling, scolding, and screaming") that breaks out when dessert is served.[32] In striking contrast, there is "honest" Humphry Clinker, "the very picture of simplicity," a virtuous common man who works in the stables at an inn. Jery writes, "Humphry may be compared to an English pudding, composed of good wholesome flour and suet, and Dutton [Jery's valet] to a syllabub or iced froth, which, though agreeable to the taste, has nothing solid or substantial."[33]

Thus far, I have presented the luxury debate as if it were an exchange between two well-defined opposing camps. On one side, traditional critics bemoaned how luxury scrambled the social order, effeminized men, corrupted morals, and destroyed states. On the other side, modern apologists argued that luxury boosted the economy, reflected cultural progress, enhanced sociability between the sexes, and strengthened states. However, historians today suggest that discussions of luxury and rising consumption were not always so clear cut. In the second half of the eighteenth century, many thinkers nuanced previously stark arguments or attempted to resolve the debate once and for all.[34]

Few thinkers immersed themselves in the complexities of luxury like Denis Diderot. In *Supplément au Voyage de Bougainville*, the French philosopher contrasted the ceaseless expansion of "superfluous wants" and "false needs" that drove European consumption with the stable and healthy development of Tahitian society, whose customs closely aligned with the laws of nature. The restless consumer desire of Europeans only spurred them to work harder at the cost of their leisure and freedom (an argument that anticipated the industrious revolution thesis). Yet, far from dismissing luxury consumption as an unmitigated evil, Diderot freely explored its seductions in "Regrets on Parting with My Old

---

[32] Erika Rappaport, *A Thirst for Empire: How Tea Shaped the Modern World* (Princeton, NJ, 2017), 51–55, suggests that anti-luxury critiques often targeted colonial goods such as tea, which some writers characterized as an agent of "gender inversion, social upheaval, and racial degeneration."

[33] Smollett, *The Expedition of Humphry Clinker*, 50–51, 65, 143, 202, 281–282.

[34] Terjanian, *Commerce and Its Discontents in Eighteenth-Century French Political Thought*, ch. 1.

Dressing Gown," which, as we have seen, recounts how his receipt of a new scarlet dressing gown set off a frenzy of buying. Rousseau would have interpreted such overindulgence as a grave moral lapse, but Diderot insisted that the material upgrades – armchairs, cabinets, desks, clocks, and paintings – did not corrupt him: "My heart hasn't grown any harder; my head hasn't swelled; and my nose isn't any higher in the air than it used to be."[35] Indulging in luxury might be frivolous, but it did not necessarily lead to moral decay.

While Diderot wallowed in luxury's contradictions, others attempted to offer resolutions to the debate. One strategy employed by Hume and others was to distinguish between good and bad luxury – that is, between reasonable forms of consumption that fostered human happiness and excessive forms of ostentation that brought down individuals, families, and even whole societies. Conceding the existence of bad luxury allowed thinkers to bolster the case for good luxury. In a similar move, Jean-François de Saint-Lambert used the pages of the *Encyclopédie* to urge readers to break through the debate's impasse by shedding "equally the prejudices of Sparta and those of Sybaris."[36] Tacking between rhetorical extremes to chart a sensible middle course, he argued that luxury is perfectly benign if the desire for it is subordinated to the spirit of community, if its presence suits a country's particular economic and social circumstances, and if governments handled it intelligently.

Writers in the emerging field of political economy also sought to resolve the luxury debate.[37] Most eighteenth-century political-economic writers did not accept Mandeville's dictum that private vice led to public benefits; they were not persuaded that a prosperous economy depended wholly on vice-driven consumption. Nor, however, did they agree with critics of luxury that commercial prosperity inevitably destroyed states, for certain forms of commerce and consumption seemed to contribute to the development of thriving and powerful global empires. How then, they wondered, did states generate solid, lasting wealth? How could societies enjoy the benefits of prosperity without undergoing moral degeneration?

---

[35] Denis Diderot, *Rameau's Nephew and Other Works*, trans. Jacques Barzun and Ralph Bowen (Indianapolis, 2001), 313–314.

[36] Jean-François de Saint-Lambert, "luxe" in Denis Diderot and Jean Le Rond d'Alembert, eds., *Encyclopédie ou Dictionnaire raisonné des sciences, des arts et des métiers*, vol. 19 (Paris, 1765), 771. Coleman, *The Spirit of French Capitalism*, 241, suggests that some French clerics also formulated a position of compromise by which they rejected unqualified asceticism and instead "offered new variations on the Catholic ethic of tranquil enjoyment."

[37] I use the term political economy in the broadest sense of the term as it was used in the period, which included questions of wealth, statecraft, morality, and social order. See Reinert and Kaplan, eds., *The Economic Turn*.

Political economists offered a variety of answers to these questions. Some were closely aligned with the pro-luxury camp, while others shared the concerns of luxury's critics. Regardless of orientation, many economic thinkers in the second half of the century sought to solve the problem of luxury by introducing the idea of productive consumption. Two of the most important political-economic systems invented in the age of Enlightenment – one envisioned by the physiocrats, the other by Adam Smith – rested on the notion that certain kinds of consumption helped to reproduce national wealth and other kinds did not. The trick was to figure out which types of consumption were beneficial to nations and should therefore be encouraged and which types were harmful to nations and should therefore be discouraged.

Founded by François Quesnay, the physiocratic movement took root in France in the second half of the eighteenth century and spread to many European countries and colonies. The physiocrats believed that natural laws governed the economy and that such laws, which they described in mathematical diagrams, dictated the nearly complete withdrawal of the government from the economy. Although the physiocrats are best known for their controversial demand to liberalize the French grain trade by allowing the market to set the price of grain and determine its circulation, they also had much to say about luxury, the debate over which they engaged either directly (as in the case of Mirabeau and Baudeau) or indirectly (as in the case of Quesnay).[38]

According to the physiocrats, the natural economic order prescribed specific rules for spending money. These rules were especially important for landowners since, in the physiocratic model of the economy, all wealth derived from the land. The laws of nature prescribed that landowners, whose expenditure drove the economy, should avoid buying too many finished luxury goods (*faste de décoration*) because such spending channeled resources to artisans and merchants, members of the "sterile" classes whose work did not make significant contributions to the national economy. Alternatively, landowners were meant to spend freely on agricultural products (*faste de consommation*), which directed money to agriculture, the only sector of the economy that reproduced national wealth over the long term. Thus, for the physiocrats, the particular ratios by which landowning consumers spent on the "productive" and "sterile" classes directly affected the annual reproduction of wealth.

The physiocratic concept of productive expenditure, expenditure that favored agriculture over industry, offered a resolution to the luxury

---

[38] For a parallel analysis of physiocratic approaches to luxury, see Coleman, *The Spirit of French Capitalism*, 230–235.

debate because it promised both long-term prosperity *and* good morals. Wholesome rural life would flourish as the corrupt overgrown city of Paris declined, no longer diverting resources from their proper destination as ordained by nature. In this respect, physiocracy did not so much supersede as reformulate the anti-luxury language expressed by classical and Christian critics. Landowning provincial nobles who adhered strictly to the laws of natural expenditure were not only serving their own economic interests but the common good as well, and they would be richly rewarded for their efforts. If landowners embraced austerity and eschewed *faste de décoration*, they would once again find themselves at the heart of a thriving monarchy based on solid agrarian foundations. As liberal thinkers who decried state intervention in the economy, the physiocrats never entertained the idea that the state should regulate the expenditure of landowners in order to make the economy grow. Instead, they exhorted readers in heavily moralizing terms to follow the dictates of the laws of nature and avoid spending on nonagricultural luxuries or else the kingdom of France would be lost. Fénelon would have applauded the physiocrats' didacticism in the service of an agricultural monarchy but would have likely been puzzled by their cryptic terminology.

Adam Smith, who was quite familiar with the work of the physiocrats, was equally concerned with the concept of productive consumption but espoused a very different vision of it. In the *Wealth of Nations* (1776), he famously wrote that "Consumption is the sole end and purpose of all production; and the interest of the producer ought to be attended, only so far as it may be necessary for promoting that of the consumer."[39] The problem was that "the mercantile system," which heavily regulated trade through navigation laws, state-charted trading companies, tariffs, and taxes, favored the interests of producers and merchants over consumers. Smith deplored the ways in which producers and merchants exploited the fiscal and regulatory apparatus of the state, but, unlike the physiocrats, he warmly welcomed traders into the ranks of the productive classes, positioning himself much closer to luxury apologists like Hume (and the circle of economists around Vincent de Gournay) than the physiocrats.

However, Smith fervently shared physiocratic preoccupations with maximizing the reproduction of wealth. Like his French counterparts, he believed that certain sectors of the economy were simply better at reproducing wealth than others. Although he did not divide society into productive agricultural and unproductive industrial classes, he did make

---

[39] Adam Smith, *An Inquiry into the Nature and Causes of the Wealth of Nations*, ed. R. H. Campbell and A. S. Skinner (Indianapolis, 1981), II: 660.

a distinction between productive labor, which by definition produced durable goods, and unproductive labor, which did not. According to Smith, unproductive laborers – whether "important" professionals such as military officers, churchmen, lawyers, physicians, and men of letters or "frivolous" workers such as actors, musicians, and dancers – did not add to the national stock of material goods.[40] If the stock of material goods is what truly signified a nation's wealth, then the prosperity of that nation depended on consumers (and investors) to channel resources to productive rather than unproductive economic activity. The idea that national growth hinged on moving resources toward productive sectors of the economy was a signature feature of both physiocratic and Smithian economic systems and would become a chief tenet of classical economics in the nineteenth century.

Smith's understanding of productivity shaped his analysis of saving and spending. Saving money was of utmost importance. Unlike most economic thinkers before him, Smith did not worry about hoarding and could therefore place a theory of saving at the center of his economic thought. Saving, he contended, enabled greater capital accumulation, which led to greater investment in the productive sector of the economy. Hence, turning Mandeville on his head, Smith could assert that "every prodigal appears to be a publick enemy, and every frugal man a publick benefactor."[41] While Smith put a premium on saving, he also acknowledged that consumers would spend some of their money and that such spending decisively shaped the economy. The extent to which consumers contributed to an enduring and prosperous economy, however, depended entirely on how they spent their income. They could consume productively or unproductively. Spending productively meant buying "durable commodities" like furniture and avoiding unproductive nondurables such as domestic service, equipage, and entertainment. Even durable goods that were frivolous (jewels, baubles, fine clothes) were preferable to ephemeral commodities that vanished the moment that they were consumed. Fashionable articles of clothing, for example, lived relatively long lives as the wealthy passed them on secondhand to ordinary people. One could not say the same about a lavish meal or an opera.

Like the physiocrats, Smith wished that wealth would be funneled into dynamic sectors of the economy so that it could better reproduce itself. But, unlike the physiocrats, he had enormous confidence in consumers to spend in a productive fashion. There was no need to teach them about the laws of nature, as the physiocrats attempted to do, because most

[40] Ibid., I: 331.   [41] Ibid., I: 340.

consumers were intrinsically inclined to avoid unproductive forms of luxury. Although landowning magnates might continue to spend unproductively on ephemeral luxuries, a fading legacy of the Middle Ages, the middle classes had fortunately developed healthier financial habits. First, the commercial classes naturally saved money out of the desire to better their condition, "a desire which, though generally calm and dispassionate, comes with us from the womb, and never leaves us till we go into the grave." Because the most obvious way to better their condition was to augment their fortune, and the most likely way to augment their fortune was to save, "the principle of frugality seems not only to predominate, but to predominate very greatly."[42] Frugality allowed for saving, which increased investment, stimulated the division of labor, and maximized the reproduction of wealth. Second, the middle classes were more inclined to spend on durable goods than nondurable ones. They did not waste their resources, as medieval lords had done, on retainers, servants, and hospitality. They were disposed to purchase material goods that lasted, contributing in an enduring way to national wealth. Thanks to middle-class propensities toward saving and productive consumption, Smith did not consider luxury a serious threat in a developed commercial society. Unlike the physiocrats, he felt no need to persuade readers of the moral hazards of luxury; the problem of luxury was resolving itself.

Finally, efforts to resolve the debate on luxury appeared not only in works of philosophy and political economy but, at a deeper level, in everyday commercial practices. Historians have recently observed that producers and retailers incorporated critiques of luxury into the goods that they made and traded, all the better to sell them.[43] In this respect, artisans and shopkeepers offered their own solution to the problem of luxury by characterizing fashionable goods as natural, healthy, and convenient. Whereas seventeenth-century wigmakers, for example, produced ostentatious wigs for royal courtiers interested in display, their

---

[42] Ibid., I: 341–343. For an insightful analysis of the motivations, sentiments, and judgments of economic actors in Smith's work, see Emma Rothschild, *Economic Sentiments: Adam Smith, Condorcet, and the Enlightenment* (Cambridge, MA, 2001). For Smith as a moral thinker, see Donald Winch, "Adam Smith: Scottish Moral Philosopher as Political Economist," HJ 35 (1992), 91–113.

[43] Jennifer Jones, "Repackaging Rousseau: Femininity and Fashion in Old Regime France," FHS 18 (Fall 1994), 939–961; Michael Kwass, "Big Hair: A Wig History of Consumption in Eighteenth-Century France," AHR 111 (June 2006), 631–659; Catharine Lanoë, *La Poudre et le fard: Une histoire des cosmétiques de la Renaissance aux Lumières* (Seysell, 2008); Morag Martin, *Selling Beauty: Cosmetics, Commerce, and French Society, 1750–1830* (Baltimore, 2009); Woodruff Smith, *Consumption and the Making of Respectability* (New York, 2002); Rebecca Spang, *The Invention of the Restaurant: Paris and Modern Gastronomic Culture* (Cambridge, MA, 2001).

eighteenth-century successors advertised their wares as authentic and comfortable, the perfect amenities for the modern man on the go. The "natural" appearance of new wigs distinguished them from the grossly artificial styles of the past and rendered them suitable for an epoch that prized authenticity. Similarly, as the cosmetics market widened beyond aristocrats to include the urban middling classes, retailers turned against the idea of courtly artifice to offer a more natural product. They abandoned lead-based paints, which doctors and scientists declared were harmful, and offered instead new vegetable-based rouges that supposedly nourished the skin, enhanced natural beauty, and let one's individual personality shine through. Late in the century, restaurant owners began to provide simple, healthy meals, claiming that nothing alleviated the ills of fast-paced urban life like a bowl of warm bouillon. To this list of simple, natural, and authentic goods, we could add a host of English-style clothing fashions that swept Europe in the late eighteenth century. Indeed, Anglomania itself could be interpreted in terms of the luxury debate, for English goods symbolized a kind of elegant simplicity that defied old-fashioned continental luxury. As new English goods hit the market, fashion journals like the German *Journal des Luxus und der Moden* promoted the latest taste for understated garments with simple clean lines.[44]

The apparent absorption of the luxury critique did not lead to a decline in consumption. On the contrary, as we saw in Chapter 3, retailers trucked in a variety of eighteenth-century ideas – sensibility, domesticity, individuality, nature, health, cleanliness, authenticity, utility, and comfort – to peddle their goods. As producers and shopkeepers shifted from courtly to Enlightenment principles of consumption, they sustained the growth of retail markets by imbuing goods with a degree of moral authority. Nimbly adapting to the changing cultural climate enabled the fashion industry to flourish in the eighteenth century and beyond.

The eighteenth-century luxury debates initiated a conversation about consumption that would leave an enduring mark on the modern world. The use of the term luxury would decline in the nineteenth century, but controversy over the effects of commerce and consumption hardly abated in the age of industrialization.[45] Marx changed the terms of the debate by emphasizing production over consumption and dismissing consumer

---

[44] Michael North, *"Material Delight and the Joy of Living": Cultural Consumption in the Age of Enlightenment in Germany*, trans. Pamela Selwyn (New York, 2008); Daniel Purdy, *The Tyranny of Elegance: Consumer Cosmopolitanism in the Era of Goethe* (Baltimore, 1998), ch. 3.

[45] Mathew Hilton, "Legacy of Luxury: Moralities of Consumption since the 18th Century," *Journal of Consumer Culture* 4 (2004), 106.

goods as fetishes that masked the social relations of the production that created them. Such a critique fed a broader intellectual movement spanning left and right that, well into the twentieth century, denigrated capitalist mass consumption as alienating and aesthetically empty. The surge in Western consumption that followed World War II had its advocates of course, but many intellectuals continued to harbor doubts, holding to a venerable intellectual tradition that, as we have seen, goes back to the classical world. This was the tradition that Daniel Roche contested in the 1980s and 1990s when, drawing on the work of McKendrick, Brewer, and Plumb, he asserted that commodities in the age of the Enlightenment fostered liberation, not alienation. Today, however, as scholars pay more attention to empire, Atlantic slavery, inequality, and the environment, arguments about the emancipatory effects of consumption are difficult to sustain. Indeed, with health and climate crises looming over the entire planet, individuals, families, cities, nations, and the international community are facing difficult decisions about the global rise of consumption. Debates over the ethics of consumption are still very much alive.[46]

---

[46] Ibid.; Cheryl Kroen, "A Political History of the Consumer," HJ 47 (2004), 709–736; Frank Trentmann, *Empire of Things* (New York, 2016).

7   The Politics of Consumption in the Age of Revolution

The least things are important in revolutions.[1]

Neil McKendrick's original argument about the consumer revolution was profoundly apolitical. Approaching the consumer revolution in much the same way that scholars had analyzed the Industrial Revolution, he and his fellow contributors to *The Birth of a Consumer Society* were more interested in the economic, social, and cultural history of consumption than its political history.[2] Even when the study of consumption migrated to France, where the history of the French Revolution loomed large, it did not venture deeply into politics. Daniel Roche emphasized the cultural dynamism of eighteenth-century urban life but rarely raised political questions or delved into the era of the French Revolution.[3] Similarly, Jan de Vries' discussion of the industrious revolution has little to say about the political implications of the growth of consumption.[4]

However, the consumer revolution did not unfold in a political vacuum. Europe and the Americas experienced intense political strife in the eighteenth century that culminated in the American Revolution (1775–1783), French Revolution (1789–1799), Haitian Revolution (1791–1804), and Latin American revolutions (1810–1824). Did the consumer revolution (lowercase "r") have anything to do with these larger Revolutions (uppercase "R")? It is a difficult question to answer because we tend to think of consumption as an economic, social, and cultural phenomenon and the Atlantic revolutions as, above all, political

[1] French national guardsman quoted in Richard Wrigley, *The Politics of Appearances: Representations of Dress in Revolutionary France* (Oxford, 2002), 103.
[2] Neil McKendrick, John Brewer, and J. H. Plumb, *The Birth of a Consumer Society: The Commercialization of Eighteenth-Century England* (Bloomington, IN, 1982). The one important exception was John Brewer's chapter on "Commercialization and Politics."
[3] Daniel Roche, *A History of Everyday Things: The Birth of Consumption in France, 1600–1800*, trans. Brian Pearce (Cambridge, 2000).
[4] Jan de Vries, *The Industrious Revolution: Consumer Behavior and the Household Economy, 1650 to the Present* (Cambridge, 2008).

180

events. And yet, a number of historians have set out to explore possible connections between consumption and the birth of revolutionary politics.

Some historians of France suggest that the growth of commercial society and consumption did in fact prepare the way for the French Revolution. Rather than tracing the origins of the French Revolution to deepening economic misery among the laboring classes or to the rise of a distinct bourgeois class, as Marxian historians once did, they argue that the rise of commerce and consumption gradually eroded the traditional social hierarchy, softened rigid boundaries between nobility and bour-geoisie, and encouraged the development of a more fluid, forward-looking society founded on wealth, education, and social utility. Further, it has been claimed that the growth of consumption contributed to the formation of an active public sphere that challenged royal absolut-ism and promoted a more open and egalitarian society. Daniel Roche, Colin Jones, Rebecca Spang, Leora Auslander, and William Sewell all assert in one way or another that commercial capitalism gradually under-mined the old regime social order and created the cultural conditions for the French Revolution.[5] In fact, Sewell explicitly uses the term "com-mercial capitalism" (rather than, say, "commercial society") to empha-size that he is building on a Marxian framework in which the development of eighteenth-century capitalism is a dominant historical force but one whose *cultural* effects had more to do with the coming of revolution than class conflict. The interstitial growth of commercial capitalism, he argues, engendered abstract social relations that made the prospect of building a new society based on civic equality thinkable, even desirable. On the American side, T. H. Breen credits consumption in British North America with generating revolutionary

---

[5] Roche, *A History of Everyday Things*; Colin Jones and Rebecca Spang, "*Sans-culottes, sans café, sans tabac*: Shifting Realms of Necessity and Luxury in Eighteenth-Century France," in Maxine Berg and Helen Clifford, eds., *Consumers and Luxury: Consumer Culture in Europe 1650–1850* (Manchester, 1999), 37–62; Colin Jones, "The Great Chain of Buying: Medical Advertisement, the Bourgeois Public Sphere, and the Origins of the French Revolution," AHR 101 (February 1996), 13–40; Colin Jones, "Bourgeois Revolution Revivified: 1789 and Social Change," in Colin Lucas, ed., *Rewriting the French Revolution* (Oxford, 1991), 69–118; Leora Auslander, *Cultural Revolutions: Everyday Life and Politics in Britain, North America, and France* (Berkeley, CA, 2009). I have advanced similar arguments in "Big Hair: A Wig History of Consumption in Eighteenth-Century France," AHR 111 (June 2006), 631–659; and "Ordering the World of Goods: Consumer Revolution and the Classification of Objects in Eighteenth-Century France," *Representations* 82 (Spring 2003), 87–116. The most fully elaborated version of this thesis can be found in William Sewell, *Capitalism and the Emergence of Civic Equality in Eighteenth-Century France* (Chicago, 2021).

solidarity among colonists, who ultimately came to apply the notion of consumer "choice" to the world of politics.[6]

These hypotheses point suggestively to links between consumption and revolution. In the French case, commercial expansion did indeed test the kingdom's traditional social and political order by generating ideas and practices that defied hierarchies of birth, status, and privilege on which the sociopolitical order was founded. But questions remain. Why did such a challenge result in revolution rather than reform? After all, Britain confronted even more dramatic commercial transformation in the eighteenth century without experiencing a metropolitan revolution. Rising consumption in France was just one of several social, political, and cultural conditions that made revolution possible. Further, as we have seen, the consumer culture of this period often ran counter to older aristocratic notions of display, but it did not necessarily foster egalitarianism or abstract social relations. It generated new hierarchies – new inequalities of wealth, property, labor, and taste – that were themselves subject to dispute during and long after the Revolution. Finally, addressing the question of revolutionary origins only carries us so far. Any satisfying model of the role of consumption in the French Revolution must account for the dynamics of the Revolution itself and the ways in which new forms of political activism were invented over the course of the revolutionary decade; the ferment and ambition of the Revolution opened new possibilities for the politics of consumption. As for the thirteen North American British colonies, there is reason to doubt the contention that consumption of imported goods enabled white settlers to transcend entrenched economic, geographic, and cultural divides to create a shared national identity. The additional claim that colonists made a leap from consumer choice to political choice is based on the overly simplistic liberal assumption that economic development and political liberty advance in lockstep, which is not always the case.[7]

This chapter does not claim to resolve all of these historical problems, but it does build on recent work to provide a framework for understanding how goods became implicated in revolutionary (and nonrevolutionary) movements. I argue that during the Age of Revolution, activists politicized consumer goods in three fundamental ways: (1) by protesting political economies of empire; (2) by creating revolutionary republican

---

[6] T. H. Breen, *The Marketplace of Revolution: How Consumer Politics Shaped American Independence* (Oxford, 2004), xvii.

[7] For a critique of Breen, see Sophia Rosenfeld, "Of Revolutions and the Problem of Choice," in David A. Bell and Yair Mintzker, eds., *Rethinking the Age of Revolutions: France and the Birth of the Modern World* (New York, 2018), 236–272.

cultures; and (3) by participating in abolitionist movements. Social scientists studying today's consumer movements, such as boycotts, buycotts, and other conscious efforts to link personal acts of consumption to large-scale structural change, call this type of activism "political consumerism."[8] Any number of recent boycotts could be used to illustrate this phenomenon, from the boycott of Facebook, charged with spreading racism, hate, and misinformation on its platform, to that of the Disney movie "Mulan," the filming of which in Xinjiang in northwest China raised questions about human rights abuses against Uighurs and other Muslim minorities in the territory.[9] Such political consumerism is not an invention of our own era, but appears to have deep historical roots in the age of democratic revolution.

The Political Economy of Empire: States, Markets, and Consumer Activism

Although government consumer agencies and formal consumer associations did not exist in Europe before the late nineteenth century, consumers nevertheless actively engaged in politics.[10] The classic example of early modern consumer politics is the food riot, which became increasingly common in western Europe in the eighteenth century. During periods of real or perceived dearth, rural villagers concerned about "monopolistic" trading practices and the high price of grain joined together in groups not only to stop shipments of wheat from leaving their locality but also to force grain merchants to bring their product to marketplaces where commercial exchanges would be transparent. Meanwhile, townspeople worried about the price of bread formed large crowds to demand that bakers sell it at a "fair price." Such crowds were often led by women, who were responsible for provisioning their households and thus sensitive to the vicissitudes of food prices. Women's naturalized role as family provisioners also meant that they were more likely to escape serious punishment if arrested. Thus, even if ordinary women and men did not refer to themselves as "consumers," they clearly acted collectively to pursue common interests regarding basic consumer needs.

---

[8] Magnus Boström, Michele Micheletti, and Peter Oosterveer, eds., *The Oxford Handbook of Political Consumerism* (Oxford, 2019).
[9] For a partial list of current boycotts, see www.ethicalconsumer.org/ethicalcampaigns/ boycotts, accessed July 12, 2021.
[10] For the discovery of "the consumer" between 1870 and 1900, see Frank Trentmann, *Empire of Things: How We Became a World of Consumers, from the Fifteenth Century to the Twenty-First* (New York, 2016), 146–160.

In 1971, historian E. P. Thompson published a landmark study of the English crowd in which he argued that the expression "food riot" was misleading.[11] The word riot implied that commoners reacted instinctively and spasmodically to hunger by amassing into violent mobs. Thompson insisted instead that crowds of protesters showed considerable restraint and operated according to a particular social and cultural logic: what he called the "moral economy." The moral economy, according to the British historian, was based on old paternalistic laws promulgated in Tudor-Stuart England that had instructed local officials to assure the working poor a minimal subsistence during food shortages and famine. When eighteenth-century crowds reacted to high prices or other threats to food security by demanding that food be sold at a fair price, they were drawing on the memory of these older legal codes to reject a new liberal political economy, espoused by Adam Smith and others, that put property rights and free trade above socioeconomic rights.

Thompson's notion of moral economy has been enormously influential across the social sciences. It has also been heavily criticized. Contesting Thompson's emphasis on old paternalist regulations, John Bohstedt argues that a more general "law of necessity" stood at the core of rioters' claims. Such a law dictated that "when survival hangs in the balance, human subsistence must take precedence over property rights."[12] During subsistence crises, English communities expressed a fundamental right to survive as they negotiated with local authorities over the terms of provisioning, seized grain shipments in transit, and demanded "fair" grain prices. Similarly, in the French case, Steven Kaplan has demonstrated that when grain prices spiked, crowds gathered to remind local officials of their obligation to oversee and regulate the provisioning of the marketplace. Although it was not, according to early modern norms, the government's responsibility to feed the people directly, officials were expected to regulate the market in order "to make sure that [grain] reached the public in 'due time,' in good condition and at a price accessible to the bulk of the population."[13] Hence, French crowds facing real or perceived shortages demanded that officials honor a tacit social contract between an obedient "consumer-people" and a

---

[11] E. P. Thompson, "The Moral Economy of the English Crowd in the Eighteenth Century," PP 50 (February 1971), 76–136.

[12] John Bohstedt, *The Politics of Provisions: Food Riots, Moral Economy, and Market Transition in England, c. 1550–1850* (New York, 2016), 9.

[13] Steven L. Kaplan, *The Stakes of Regulation* (London, 2015), 50–51. See also Jean Nicolas, *La Rébellion française: Mouvements populaires et conscience sociale, 1661–1789* (Paris, 2002), chs. 7–8; and Domonique Margairaz and Philippe Minard, "Marché des subsistances et économie morale: ce que 'taxer' veut dire," AHRF 352 (2008), 53–99.

paternalistic king, who was considered the "baker" of last resort. If royal officials failed to uphold their side of the bargain, rioters would step in and target alleged speculators to secure (sometimes violently) the food supply. Such collective action, both Kaplan and Bohstedt agree, did not signify a rejection of capitalism, as Thompson argued, but rather a desire to tame capitalism, to correct it, so that it met the subsistence needs of local consumers.

The political implications of the food riot expanded dramatically in the Age of Revolution, when activists linked their protests to the nascent concept of popular sovereignty. Subsistence revolts in France, which were exceeded only by antiseigneurial uprisings as the most common form of collective action after 1789, changed the very course of the French Revolution, and more than once.[14] On October 5, 1789, amid bread shortages, rumors that aristocrats at the palace of Versailles had trampled the revolutionary tricolor cockade, and news of the king's wavering support for a new constitutional order, thousands of Parisian women marched to Versailles to demand that bread be made available at fair prices (see Figure 7.1). What began as a seemingly traditional food riot, however, soon turned into a political event of enormous consequence. Under pressure from the large crowd, Louis XVI agreed not only to supply Paris with additional grain but also to approve the Declaration of the Rights of Man, thereby throwing his support behind the drafting of the Constitution. When the women further demanded that "the baker, the baker's wife, and the baker's boy" (the king, queen, and their son) return with them to Paris to live among the people, the king acceded, decamping from Versailles and settling in the metropolis with the National Assembly in tow. Now based in Paris, the crown would be susceptible to the influence of a large and politically active urban populace. In this way, the women's march decisively "expanded the political power of Paris and the 'people' vis-à-vis both king and Assembly" and "shored up the incipient notion of popular sovereignty."[15]

Collective action over the supply and price of food would continue to influence the course of the Revolution as it radicalized between 1792, when the monarchy was replaced by a Republic, and the Terror of 1793–1794. In a period of foreign and civil war, counterrevolution, and high inflation, the provisioning of basic necessities remained a central

---

[14] John Markoff, *The Abolition of Feudalism: Peasants, Lords, and Legislators in the French Revolution* (University Park, PA, 1996).
[15] Suzanne Desan, "Gender, Radicalization, and the October Days: Occupying the National Assembly," FHS 43 (2020), 360.

Figure 7.1 "A Versailles, 5 Octobre."
Courtesy of Musée Carnavalet, Histoire de Paris. Armed with pikes and pulling a canon, Parisian women march to Versailles to demand that the king provision the city's markets

concern for citizens and legislators alike.[16] Members of the influential Jacobin club in Paris increasingly laid stress on socioeconomic rights – health, education, good wages, progressive taxation, and, notably, entitlement to food – eager to build a fairer society in which there would

[16] Albert Mathiez, *La vie chère et le mouvement social sous la Terreur* (Paris, 1973).

"no longer be rich men who are excessively rich, nor poor men who are excessively poor."[17] As the value of paper money plummeted and prices soared, Jacobins struck an alliance with sans-culottes (principally shopkeepers, artisans, and workers) who organized popular protest from the streets. Sans-culotte militants, acting on their belief that hard work and other patriotic contributions to the nation entitled them to a modest but salutary standard of living beyond mere subsistence, demanded that authorities intervene to control the price of bread, flour, sugar, and other essential goods. On September 29, 1793, confronted with sizeable Parisian crowds, the National Convention committed itself to building the material foundations of revolutionary equality by imposing the General Maximum, a law that punished speculators and set price caps across the nation on a variety of foodstuffs – not just grain and flour but also meat, salted fish, butter, oil, salt, sugar, honey, vinegar, brandy, cider, beer, and tobacco. Designed to protect consumers from the ravages of inflation and hoarding, this extensive new policy "cemented Parisian subsistence politics as the cornerstone of national economic policy."[18] A legislative turning point, the Maximum promised to guarantee citizens access to a range of food, drink, and other necessities like leather and candles, dramatically expanding the egalitarian vision of the Revolution.

Historians interpret the General Maximum and the protests leading up to it differently. Florence Gauthier, operating within the moral economy framework, emphasizes that the Maximum drew on notions of a "right to existence" that had long challenged liberal economic ideas about unlimited commercial liberty. She points out that Enlightenment philosophers like Montesquieu, who was no radical, had insisted that the state owes every citizen "guaranteed subsistence, food, suitable clothing, and a way of life which is not contrary to health."[19] For Gauthier, this equitable right to existence was precisely what was at stake during the protests of 1793–1794. Jean-Pierre Gross places the Maximum in a broader context

---

[17] Jeanbon Saint-André as quoted in Jean-Pierre Gross, *Fair Shares for All: Jacobin Egalitarianism in Practice* (Cambridge, 1997), 136. See also Charles Walton, "Why the Neglect? Social Rights and the French Revolutionary Historiography," FH 33 (December 2019), 503–519.

[18] Katie Jarvis, *Politics in the Marketplace: Work, Gender, and Citizenship in Revolutionary France* (Oxford, 2019), 147.

[19] Quoted in Florence Gauthier, *Triomphe et Mort: De la Révolution des Droits de l'Homme et du Citoyen* (Paris, 2014), 63. For an alternative approach that shows how activists added a new political discourse of counterrevolutionary conspiracy to the long-standing rhetoric of the famine plot, see William Sewell, "The Sans-Culottes Rhetoric of Subsistence," in Keith Baker, ed., *The French Revolution and the Creation of Modern Political Culture, vol. 4, The Terror* (Oxford, 1994), 249–270.

than moral economy. He contends that the Maximum's price controls were part of a coordinated egalitarian food policy that, at its most ambitious, aspired to nothing less than, in the words of Deputy Pierre Paganel, "the equal distribution between all Frenchmen of all the resources of the Republic."[20] The Maximum went hand in hand with the remarkable egalitarian social thrust of the moment. Still more critical of the moral economy paradigm, Dominique Margairaz and Philippe Minard assert categorically that Thompson's argument does not apply to the Maximum. Strictly speaking, the notion of moral economy pertains only to specific communal protests that sought to guarantee the fair exchange of necessities in local markets. Margairaz and Minard claim that the General Maximum operated according to a different logic, by which the state sought to regulate a national market to assure a certain quality of life above subsistence. For a brief moment, economic policy shifted toward the modern idea that states have an obligation to sustain the general living standards of their populations.[21] Whatever the larger historiographical debate on the Maximum, it is clear that consumer activism was essential to the radical egalitarian phase of the French Revolution. Moreover, it is evident that such activism was moving beyond its traditional concern with the supply and price of bread to ensure access to a broader range of consumer goods, including colonial commodities like sugar.

It is striking that the target of consumer activism was widening beyond bread in other parts of the Atlantic world as well. Over the course of the eighteenth century, a host of goods, notably new colonial products from overseas, became politicized as objects of both political-economic reflection and collective action. Consider the Boston Tea Party in which North American colonists dumped Chinese tea into Boston harbor, escalating a crisis that would culminate in the American Revolution. Why did tea of all things become invested with such political meaning in this period? Why was the gamut of consumer activism broadening beyond the classic bread riot?

According to Colin Jones and Rebecca Spang, the answer lies in the expansion of the category of "necessity."[22] As we saw in the previous chapter, the set of goods that consumers considered necessities as opposed to luxuries was expanding in the eighteenth century. By the 1790s, for instance, Parisians of all classes had come to count on drinking sugar-laden coffee for breakfast. When the supply of sugar dwindled in

---

[20] Quoted in Gross, *Fair Shares for All*, 79.
[21] Margairaz and Minard, "Marché des subsistances et économie morale."
[22] Jones and Spang, "*Sans-culottes, sans café, sans tabac*"; Rebecca Spang, "What Is Rum? The Politics of Consumption in the French Revolution," in Martin Daunton and Mathew Hilton, eds., *The Politics of Consumption: Material Culture and Citizenship in Europe and America* (Oxford, 2001), 33–49.

1792 following a massive slave rebellion in Saint-Domingue, Parisian crowds (often led by women) attacked retailers for allegedly hoarding the crystal and gouging consumers with high prices. As national guardsman Charles Alexandre recalled in his memoir, sugar had by that time become "an essential foodstuff." Parisians, he explained, feared that merchants would "deprive them of a product on which a part of their subsistence consumption depended, because it was their custom every morning to drink a large quantity of coffee, which kept them going until they returned from work around four or five in the afternoon."[23]

But the expansion of the category of "necessity" does not explain everything. The politicization of consumption was also rooted in the intensification of European imperial rivalries in the seventeenth and eighteenth centuries. As European powers came to prize and compete for commercially valuable overseas territories, their engagement with the global economy deepened, implicating an expanding world of goods in a long, costly, and bellicose struggle for imperial hegemony. Two overlapping frameworks of political economy defined this fierce competition. One framework was "mercantilism," which held that states should aggressively promote national wealth by supporting domestic industry and encouraging favorable balances of trade in which the value of exports would exceed that of imports.[24] Coined in the late nineteenth century and applied retrospectively to early modern states, mercantilism encompassed a loose set of policies that entailed economic protectionism, the creation of state-sponsored overseas trading companies, colonial expansion, and the use of navigation laws to bind new colonial markets to the metropole. The establishment of subordinate colonies came to be seen as crucial to economic growth.[25] Not only did mother countries set out to exploit colonies by extracting raw materials and harvesting agricultural

---

[23] "Women's Participation in Riots over the Price of Sugar, February 1792," in *Liberty, Equality, Fraternity* (http://chnm.gmu.edu/revolution/d/478), accessed February 1, 2019. For French Revolutionary sugar riots, see Rachel Waxman, "Goods Worthy of a Free People: Sugar, Commerce, and Consumer Rights in the French Revolution" (PhD dissertation, Johns Hopkins University, 2021).

[24] The term mercantilism is controversial. See Philip Stern and Carl Wennerlind, eds., *Mercantilism Reimagined: Political Economy in Early Modern Britain and Its Empire* (Oxford, 2014); and Steve Pincus, "Rethinking Mercantilism: Political Economy, the British Empire, and the Atlantic World in the Seventeenth and Eighteenth Centuries," WMQ 69 (January 2012), 3–34. Bullionism, often associated with mercantilism, was indeed waning by the eighteenth century, but the idea that countries should export high value-added products and import low value-added products continued to hold sway in many circles. See Lars Magnusson, *The Political Economy of Mercantilism* (London, 2015).

[25] Paul Cheney, *Revolutionary Commerce: Globalization and the French Monarchy* (Cambridge, MA, 2010); Steve Pincus, "Addison's Empire: Whig Conceptions of Empire in the Early 18th Century," *Parliamentary History* 31 (February 2012), 99–117.

produce, increasingly through the brutal exploitation of enslaved peoples of African descent in the Americas. They also demanded that their colonies (especially settler colonies in the Americas) buy finished goods made in the metropole. Based on elaborate law codes and regulations, such intra-imperial commerce was designed to reap the benefits of colonial production and consumption to the exclusion of rival empires, by military force if necessary.[26]

The other framework for understanding the politicization of consumption was fiscalism, the desire to raise state revenues for funding war, servicing war-generated debt, and securing overseas empire. Well aware that international power depended on state finance, revenue-hungry rulers desperately searched for ways to raise money through loans and taxes. Commenting on this fiscal arms race, English economist (and former tax collector!) Charles Davenant noted in 1695 that "war is quite changed from what it was in the time of our forefathers when in a hasty expedition and a pitched field, the matter was decided by courage … [N]ow the whole art of war is in a manner reduced to money." The prince "who can best find money to feed, cloath and pay his army," rather than the one who "has the most valiant troops, is surest of success and conquest."[27] To fund ever more expensive wars, states increased customs and excise taxes and established state monopolies on certain goods in an effort to exploit the growth of consumption. Many governments of the age – notably Britain but also France, the United Provinces, Prussia, and Spain – shifted their fiscal burden from direct taxation of land and property to indirect taxation of commerce and consumption. Fiscalizing consumption in this fashion helped to sustain the growth of powerful fiscal-military states, which could borrow money on a massive scale to field armies and navies across the globe. But fiscalizing consumption also rendered the tax burden highly regressive, and conspicuously so. Taxes on everyday goods such as beer, wine, tea, tobacco, salt, soap, leather, and candles struck consumers directly or, if paid by merchants, were passed on to customers in the form of higher prices. The regressive

---

[26] In the late eighteenth century, European state ministers attempted to liberalize this antagonistic imperial system. See Jeremy Adelman, "An Age of Imperial Revolutions," *AHR* 113 (2008), 319–340. Although liberals like Adam Smith criticized the mercantilist system for impeding economic growth, peaceful, open, and free trade was a remote possibility in an era without any collective security mechanism or clearly defined hegemonic power. In such a bellicose environment, state officials were reluctant to embrace free trade unilaterally. Ronald Findlay and Kevin O'Rourke, *Power and Plenty: Trade, War, and the World Economy in the Second Millennium* (Princeton, NJ, 2007).

[27] Quoted in William J. Ashworth, *Customs and Excise: Trade, Production, and Consumption in England 1640–1845* (Oxford, 2013), 22.

nature of such taxation was compounded by the fact that debt-laden states often used the revenue from indirect taxes to make interest payments to wealthy financiers and public creditors, redistributing resources up the social hierarchy. Fiscal states functioned like welfare states in reverse.

In the eighteenth century, even before the Atlantic revolutions, the development of mercantilist and fiscal policy politicized commerce and consumption. Resistance to various mercantilist and fiscal practices took two basic forms: public debate and popular revolt. As commercial and diplomatic rivalry between European powers intensified, notably with the Seven Years' War (1756–1763), Enlightenment writers turned to political economy to assess current policies and formulate solutions to imperial crises. Writers analyzed everything from agriculture to trade to taxation, suggesting a panoply of ways in which states could build their economies, improve their finances, and thrive in an age of intense imperial and commercial rivalry. Kant was certainly aware of the explosion of print on the new "science of commerce" when he lauded the public use of reason in his 1784 essay "What Is Enlightenment?" One of his prime examples of a writer making use of public reason was the citizen-taxpayer. "The citizen cannot refuse to pay the taxes imposed on him … , but the same person does not act contrary to his duty when, as a scholar, he publicly expresses his thoughts on the appropriateness or even the injustice of these levies."[28] Indeed, Kant's protégé Johann Georg Hamann took a lucrative position in the Prussian excise administration only to become one of its fiercest critics. Hamann lambasted the government's obsession with modern finance and warned that the excise's heavy burden would throttle commerce.[29]

Fiscalizing consumption through indirect taxes also provoked rebellions. In Prussian towns, bands of smugglers and crowds of townspeople attacked excise officers.[30] In Spanish America, the Bourbon Reforms, which increased the sales tax (*alcabala*) on goods produced and sold in the colonies and reorganized state monopolies on liquor and tobacco, triggered revolt from Mexico to Peru. In Quito, the reform of the *alcabala* and the brandy monopoly gave rise to heated town meetings, strongly worded petitions, and, on May 22, 1765, the destruction of the tax bureau at the hands of a large crowd. Moreover, in the Andes, between 1780 and 1783, sales taxes prompted indigenous leader Túpac Amaru II to call for the abolition of

---

[28] Immanuel Kant, "What Is Enlightenment?" in Isaac Kramnick, ed., *The Portable Enlightenment Reader* (New York, 1995), 3.
[29] Florian Schui, *Rebellious Prussians: Urban Political Culture under Frederick the Great and His Successors* (Oxford, 2013), 118–122.
[30] Ibid., ch. 4.

colonial institutions. He mobilized an army of Native Americans and creoles to lead an insurrection against the Spanish, but the uprising was ultimately put down by royalist forces who subjected its leader to a gruesome public execution in Cuzco's main public square. Further north, the Comunero uprising of 1781 also erupted in reaction to tax increases and institutional reform. As taxes and consumer prices rose, the Comuneros of Nueva Granada openly denounced the new regent visitor general as a "rapacious tyrant."[31] This rebellion, too, was suppressed.

Such collective action often stemmed from vigorous underground economies, which had emerged as an unintended consequence of government attempts to control and tax commodity flows. From the Americas to western Europe, extralegal trade expanded dramatically in the eighteenth century as traders and consumers circumvented mercantilist trade laws and fiscal impositions. Vast clandestine markets emerged in silver, textiles, sugar, tobacco, tea, coffee, and enslaved human beings. In Chapter 3, we saw how smugglers contributed to the diffusion of consumer goods by offering low prices on taxed or prohibited merchandise, but extralegal commerce had political as well as economic repercussions. Buying and selling contraband across porous imperial or national borders unsettled rulers, who believed such trade undermined respect for the law and eroded the territorial integrity of their polities. When states attempted to crack down on underground markets, they often triggered active forms of resistance. In southeast England, the Hawkhurst gang retaliated violently against customs agents who had interfered with its illicit tea trade.[32] In France, the heavy policing of underground trade in salt and tobacco frequently ignited rebellions. Groups of villagers defended smugglers in their midst against what they took to be illegitimate fiscal and regulatory claims on their communities. As with the crowds studied by E. P. Thompson, a communal sense of economic rights and justice authorized villagers to resist outside authorities.[33]

In many cases, collective action against the regulation and taxation of consumer goods did not lead to revolution. The tax revolts in Spanish

[31] J. H. Elliot, *Empires of the Atlantic World: Britain and Spain in America, 1492–1830* (New Haven, CT, 2006), 49–50.
[32] Nicholas Rogers, *Mayhem: Post-war Crime and Violence in Britain, 1748–53* (New Haven, CT, 2012), ch. 5.
[33] Michael Kwass, *Contraband: Louis Mandrin and the Making of a Global Underground* (Cambridge, MA, 2014). Michael Kwass, "The Global Underground: Smuggling, Rebellion, and the Origins of the French Revolution," in Suzanne Desan, Lynn Hunt, and William Max Nelson, eds., *The French Revolution in Global Perspective* (Ithaca, NY, 2013), 15–31. Mandeville, the author of *The Fable of the Bees*, fled Rotterdam for England because his family had been implicated in a riot over the policing of the local wine tax.

America were severe to be sure, but they were not directly related to the Latin American independence movements that would shake the empire in the early nineteenth century.[34] Nor did unrest and public controversy in Prussia radically transform the kingdom. Frederick William eased tensions by abolishing state monopolies and reforming the excise administration. In India and the West Indies, British efforts to strengthen fiscal and commercial sovereignty ultimately consolidated imperial power.

In other cases, however, collective action and public debate about consumer goods clearly undermined the sovereignty of metropolitan centers and contributed to the outbreak of revolution. The case of the American Revolution is illustrative. To understand how consumption became politicized in the runup to American independence, it is necessary to go back to the costly global conflict of the Seven Years' War. Although Britain won the war, it was subsequently saddled with an enormous public debt and the ongoing costs of maintaining a military and political presence in America. To service the debt, the British parliament raised indirect taxes on articles of consumption in the metropole and enacted a series of laws – the Sugar Act of 1764, the Stamp Act of 1765, the Townshend Duties of 1767, and the Tea Act of 1767 – that extended the fiscal burden to the American colonies. Such legislation provoked forms of consumer protest that would give rise to the American Revolution.

Created by "authoritarian reformers" who sought to subordinate the colonies to the metropole, these fiscal and regulatory laws gave rise to active resistance movements.[35] The Stamp Act of 1765, which required colonists to pay to have documents (wills, deeds, pamphlets, and newspapers) imprinted with an official stamp, aroused intense protest. Delegates of the Stamp Act Congress claimed that only colonial assemblies, not the British parliament, had the constitutional right to tax colonists. In Boston, activists calling themselves the Sons of Liberty ransacked the home of the city's stamp distributor and encouraged crowds to hang the official in effigy. Meanwhile, merchants in ports like New York signed nonimportation agreements by which they pledged to cancel orders of British manufactured goods until the Stamp Act was repealed. Although such protest was tentative, colonists were beginning to reimagine their economic position within the British Empire. As one

[34] It was not until Napoleon occupied the Iberian Peninsula in 1808 that a major political crisis occurred, resulting in the independence of Spanish America in the 1820s. Jeremy Adelman, *Sovereignty and Revolution in the Iberian Atlantic* (Princeton, NJ, 2006).
[35] Justin du Rivage, *Revolution against Empire: Taxes, Politics, and the Origins of American Independence* (New Haven, CT, 2017).

commentator wrote in a Philadelphia newspaper, "Great Britain is in fact more dependent on us than we on her ... It is well known that by our consumption of her manufactures we maintain a large proportion of her people."[36] Colonists were coming to understand that they could leverage their power as consumers to make their voices heard in London.

The Stamp Act was soon repealed, but in 1767 parliament established the Townshend Acts, which levied taxes on a bevy of goods Americans imported from Britain (glass, lead, colors for paint, paper, and tea). The goal was to use revenue from the new taxes to pay the salaries of colonial governors and judges in the hope of weaning them away from their dependence on colonial assemblies. However, the duties encountered strong resistance from merchants in Boston, New York, and (eventually) Philadelphia, many of whom signed nonimportation agreements. But, unlike the response to the Stamp Act, protest moved beyond merchants to consumers themselves, who now vowed to boycott British imports, from pickles to playing cards. Although protesters did not use the term boycott, which would only be coined in the late nineteenth century, they began to experiment with the power derived from collectively withhold-ing acts of consumption. Picking up on the novelty of the strategy, newspapers drew on the radical Whig tradition to characterize the boy-cott as an epic struggle between liberty and tyranny. The *Virginia Gazette* declared that no imperial official "can oblige us to buy goods, which we do not choose to buy."[37] An enthusiastic Connecticut writer concurred, "We will either make our own cloaths, go naked, or augment our debt with Great Britain to a sum which will in the end enslave the country."[38] "Our All is at stake," George Mason explained to George Washington, "& the little Conveniencys & Comforts of Life, when set in Competition with our Liberty, ought to be rejected not with Reluctance but with Pleasure."[39] Growing numbers of Americans from the middle and working classes translated this language into everyday political action by steadfastly adhering to the boycott and forming extralegal associations to watch over merchants who may not be complying with nonimportation agreements. Consumption became an important site of political contestation.

Nonimportation and consumer boycotts culminated in the Boston Tea Party. Although the Townshend duties were repealed in 1770, the tax on tea remained firmly in place, a symbol of parliament's claim that it had a constitutional right to tax the colonies. Further, the Tea Act of 1773

---

[36] Quoted in Breen, *The Marketplace of Revolution*, 226. See also Steve Pincus, *The Heart of the Declaration: The Founders' Case for an Activist Government* (New Haven, CT, 2016), 33–36.

[37] Quoted in ibid., 243.   [38] Quoted in ibid., 240.   [39] Quoted in ibid., 245.

strengthened the British East India Company by permitting it to bypass customs taxes and wholesalers in Britain and sell Chinese tea directly in the American colonies. Thus, the Act put the Company in a much stronger position to compete with American smugglers who illegally stocked up on cheap tea from Dutch merchants and sold it to fellow colonists. The Tea Act immediately provoked the kinds of protest that had become familiar since the Stamp Act. Suspecting a conspiracy between the British ministry and the Company to trick them into recognizing parliament's claims to taxation, activists in New York, Charleston, and Philadelphia pressured local officials to force Company ships bearing tea to turn around and sail back to Britain. In these towns, merchants and ordinary consumers struck unusual cross-class alliances to create effective nonimportation movements. Some activists were merchant-smugglers who stood to gain financially from blocking Company ships, yet even they now couched their opposition in terms of a larger struggle for freedom. The press helped. Company tea contained "slow poison," warned Benjamin Rush in a Philadelphia newspaper, "something worse than death – the seeds of SLAVERY."[40] Well aware of the depredations inflicted upon enslaved people of African descent in the Americas, Rush and other colonists deployed the metaphor of slavery to defend their cause. They argued that unrestrained parliamentary taxation (combined with the monopolistic trade of the Company) was tantamount to a form of "tyranny" that would reduce white colonists to the abject status of political slaves. As far-fetched as the analogy was, some historians argue that using the slavery metaphor to press the cause for white American revolutionary freedom may have ultimately created possibilities for abolition in the North and emancipation in the South.[41]

In Boston, a protracted conflict ensued. On the one side stood local tea importers and high government officials who, unlike their colleagues in ports to the South, insisted on landing the Company tea, clearing it through customs, and selling it. On the other side were numerous protesters who voiced opposition in meetings, pillaged importers' homes, and posted notices decrying the "tyranny" of the Tea Act. On the moonlit night of December 16, 1773, about sixty protestors (some of whom were disguised as Native Americans, a symbol of Americanness that served as a cover under which to engage in misbehavior) boarded two tea-laden ships in Boston harbor, the *Dartmouth* and the *Eleanor*, and brought scores of tea chests up from the hold, cracked them open, and

---

[40] Quoted in Benjamin Woods Labaree, *The Boston Tea Party* (New York, 1964), 100.
[41] Peter Dorsey, *Common Bondage: Slavery as Metaphor in Revolutionary America* (Knoxville, TN, 2009).

threw the tea overboard as a crowd watched from the wharf.[42] The Tea Party successfully galvanized the movement against "unconstitutional" British taxes, which in turn triggered even sterner parliamentary legislation, the Coercive Acts, intended to punish colonists for their disobedience. The Coercive Acts confirmed many colonists' worst fears that a corrupt government in London was imposing tyranny on them. In response, they promptly formed the Continental Congress and resistance turned into revolution.

In France, too, consumer-citizens engaged in collective action to contest the taxation and regulation of certain goods. The grievance lists drafted in advance of the Estates General in 1789 denounced heavy consumption taxes on salt, wine, brandy, and tobacco, taxes which serviced the soaring war-generated public debt. Lamenting the "vexations" visited upon the population by the agents who collected such levies, petitioners called for a fairer constitutional order in which indirect taxes on "necessities" would be abolished and the privileged would finally pay their fair share through direct taxes on property. As the National Assembly moved to construct a new political order in the summer of 1789, large crowds in Paris and the provinces gathered to articulate and press for a range of political and economic claims. By far the most famous event of this popular movement was the storming of the Bastille, an iconic moment in the history of the Revolution, but historians now spotlight another important uprising that took place in July 1789: the sacking of the Parisian customs gates (see Figure 7.2).[43] From July 9 to 17, wine and tobacco smugglers joined local inhabitants to attack dozens of recently built gates along the new customs wall encircling the city. Connecting their revolt to national debates over popular sovereignty, protesters shouted "long live the Third Estate and down with customs agents!" before torching the toll houses. With the way clear, wine, tobacco, livestock, tallow, wood, and other goods moved freely into the city, to the joy of participants and spectators who could now purchase consumer goods at much lower prices. Associating the abolition of consumption taxes with the coming of a free and fair political order, many French men and women linked their material lives to the highest ideals of the Revolution. As in the case of the Bastille, deputies in the National Assembly were initially shocked by the popular violence that

[42] Philip Deloria, *Playing Indian* (New Haven, CT, 1988), 28–32.
[43] Kwass, *Contraband*, ch. 12; Momcilo Markovic, "La Révolution aux barrières: l'incendie des barrières de l'octroi à Paris en juillet 1789," AHRF 372 (April–June 2013), 27–48; Noelle Plack, "Drinking and Rebelling: Wine, Taxes and Popular Agency in Revolutionary Paris, 1789–1791" FHS 39 (2016), 599–622.

Figure 7.2 Sack of the "bons homes" customs gate, 1789. Bibliothèque nationale de France. Protesters sack the customs gates of Paris to ensure the free flow of untaxed consumer goods, such as wine and tobacco.

brought down the customs wall, but they would soon recognize it as a legitimate part of the revolutionary process.

The Creation of Revolutionary Republican Cultures

Consumption was not only politicized through contestation over taxed and regulated goods. It was also politicized by efforts to create new revolutionary material cultures. "The least things are important in revolutions," observed a French national guardsman who in 1791 was concerned about the political implications of variations in the colors of the

national cockade.[44] From the outset of the American and French revolutions, both of which entailed a radical shift from monarchical to republican forms of government, it was clear that the construction of a new
political order would involve more than simply writing new laws and
remodeling institutions. Founding or regenerating a nation required
cultivating horizontal ties of citizenship and shared visions of revolutionary transformation. Material culture was essential to this process as
legislators, producers, and consumers imbued everyday objects with
revolutionary meaning. More than merely reflecting political ideas and
aspirations, material objects mediated their very expression, enabling
citizens to participate in revolutions and express their allegiance to (or
rejection of) evolving political projects. In this way, citizens lived revolutions concretely in their daily lives.[45]

Of course, acts of consumption had had political overtones before the
revolutionary era. As we have seen, many elite and middling men and
women in prerevolutionary Europe turned against court fashion as anti-
luxury discourses proliferated in both literary and commercial spheres.
New fashions radiated Enlightenment values of neoclassical simplicity,
domesticity, nature, individuality, reason, and sentiment – all in opposition to what Rousseau and other critics portrayed as a corrupt, artificial,
and despotic world of royal courts and high society.[46] But communi-
cating civic messages through clothing, accessories, and other goods,
which social scientists define as "discursive" political consumerism,
became much more explicit and consequential in the age of Atlantic
revolutions.[47]

In the case of the American Revolution, nonconsumption and other
collective protest movements were integral to the creation of a vibrant
revolutionary material culture. Teapots bearing the inscription "No
Stamp Act" on one side and "America: Liberty Restored" on the other
adorned patriotic households (see Figure 7.3). Protest involved not only
rejecting British-made goods but valorizing American-made ones associated with principles of freedom and independence. Women, who were
vanguard consumers and producers of clothing, were at the forefront of
this movement. Over the course of the eighteenth century, even as

[44] Quoted in Wrigley, *The Politics of Appearances*, 103.
[45] Revolutionaries also expressed their opinions of the old regime though material culture, most obviously through the modification or destruction of religious, royalist, and aristocratic objects. The term *vandalism* was coined during the French Revolution by Henri Grégoire to describe the destruction of artwork.
[46] Among Protestants and Jansenists, these trends were reinforced by strong religious traditions of self-denial.
[47] Boström, Micheletti, and Oosterveer, eds., *Oxford Handbook of Political Consumerism*.

Figure 7.3 "No Stamp Act" teapot, 1766–1770.
National Museum of American History, Kenneth E. Behring Center. This teapot, made in England for sale in the American market after the 1766 repeal of the Stamp Act, is inscribed with the slogan "No Stamp Act" on one side and "America, Liberty restored" on the other

women in British America consumed large quantities of imports, they were simultaneously producing greater quantities of cloth at home; by the 1750s, the majority of rural households in New England had spinning wheels. In the wake of the patriotic boycotts against British-manufactured goods, colonial protestors proudly imbued their hearty, unrefined homespun cloth with rich political significance. From the Maine coast to Long Island, thousands of women participated in spinning bees hosted by Whig leaders and Congregational ministers to demonstrate support for the patriot cause. In the southern colony of Virginia, the fashionable wives of legislators wore clothes of locally produced fabric to a public ball in 1769. Ordinary homespun cloth became a marker of "American" political autonomy.[48]

The project to create a new material world was even more robust in the French Revolution, especially after the fall of the monarchy in 1792. Despite severe constraints on the development of the revolutionary

---

[48] Laurel Thatcher Ulrich, *The Age of Homespun* (New York, 2001); Laurel Thatcher Ulrich, "Political Protest and the World of Goods," in Jane Kamensky and Edward Gray, eds., *The Oxford Handbook of the American Revolution* (Oxford, 2012).

economy – from emigration and war to inflation and import prohibitions – certain revolutionary policies, such as the abolition of the guilds
and the sale of *biens nationaux* (confiscated property), created new oppor-
tunities for economic activity, some of which was political in orientation.[49] The brisk circulation of flags, coins, emblems, home furnishings,
paintings, clothing, uniforms, accessories, and print reflected widespread
efforts to "regenerate" the French nation.

The impetus behind this profusion of politically charged goods came
from two sources. On the one hand, elaborating on royal and Catholic
traditions of deploying material culture for the purposes of persuasion,
didactic revolutionary leaders sought to create a new political order by
legislating dress codes, organizing festivals, building monuments, and
sponsoring public art projects, all to inculcate revolutionary values in a
new citizenry – to "make a revolution in minds and hearts," in the words
of one deputy.[50] State manufactories that had once buttressed royal
power by producing visually stunning porcelain and tapestries now promoted the glory of the nation: Sèvres planted liberty trees on its grounds
and set about producing goods with revolutionary symbols such as
cockades and liberty caps.[51] In May 1794, the government called on
artist Jacques-Louis David to design a national civil uniform that would
evince the Republic's commitment to equality. Although the artist's
classically inspired tunics were never fabricated, legislators, local officials, and national guardsmen did don official costumes to legitimize
their new positions in the revolutionary state.[52]

[49] Natacha Coquery, "Luxury and Revolution: Selling High-Status Garments in
Revolutionary France," in Jon Stobart and Bruno Blondé, eds., *Selling Textiles in the
Long Eighteenth Century: Comparative Perspectives from Western Europe* (Basingstoke,
2014), 179–192, argues that although revolutionary ideology condemned luxury,
luxury goods enjoyed wide circulation in secondhand markets. The persistence of
luxury markets challenges historical clichés about pervasive republican austerity.

[50] Quoted in Cissie Fairchilds, "Fashion and Freedom in the French Revolution,"
Continuity and Change 15 (December 2000), 427. For Louis XIV's use of material
culture, see Peter Burke, *The Fabrication of Louis XIV* (New Haven, CT, 1992). For
revolutionary material culture, see Auslander, *Cultural Revolutions*, ch. 5; Antoine de
Baecque, *The Body Politic: Corporeal Metaphor in Revolutionary France, 1770–1800*, trans.
Charlotte Mandell (Stanford, CA, 1997); Lynn Hunt, *Politics, Culture, and Class in the
French Revolution* (Berkeley, CA, 1984); Mona Ozouf, *Festivals and the French Revolution*,
trans. Alan Sheridan (Cambridge, MA, 1988); and Richard Taws, *The Politics of the
Provisional: Art and Ephemera in Revolutionary France* (University Park, PA, 2013).

[51] Anne Perrin Khelissa, "De l'objet d'agrément à l'objet d'art: Légitimer les manufactures
d'État sous la Révolution," in Natacha Coquery and Alain Bonnet, eds., *Le commerce du
luxe: production, exposition et circulation des objets précieux du Moyen Âge à nos jours* (Paris,
2015), 160–167; Ashli White, *Revolutionary Things* (New Haven, CT, forthcoming).

[52] Danes and Germans also toyed with the idea of national dress around the same time.
Michael North, *"Material Delight and the Joy of Living": Cultural Consumption in the Age of
Enlightenment in Germany*, trans. Pamela Selwyn (New York, 2008), 57–60.

Figure 7.4 Cockade on national guard hat.
INTERFOTO/Alamy Stock Photo. A tricolor cockade sewn into a French National Guardsman's hat

On the other hand, citizens eager to participate in the making of a new nation crafted their own contributions to revolutionary material culture. Wealthier people hung portraits that connected the lives of family members to revolutionary events and ideas.[53] Militant "sans-culotte" men wore what would become the iconic outfit of the Revolution: loose trousers, short jacket (the carmagnole), and a red liberty cap, an ensemble that projected an image of masculine authenticity, productive labor, and popular sovereignty.[54] Rural and urban citizens decorated liberty trees with red caps, tricolor ribbons, and signs with revolutionary slogans. And enterprising traders hawked revolutionary accessories and decorative objects, such as model Bastilles carved out of stones taken from the demolished prison.[55] Officials and ordinary people alike forged a powerful revolutionary culture replete with all the promises, tensions, and contradictions of the revolutionary project itself.

Take the example of the cockade, the quintessential emblem of the Revolution (see Figure 7.4). Cockades representing different political movements appeared throughout the Atlantic world in the late eighteenth century, from Poland, Switzerland, Holland, and Ireland to North America and the Caribbean.[56] Given the general proliferation of accessories over the course of the century, it is not surprising that a small, inexpensive, and adaptable ribbon would become the most enduring patriotic symbol of the revolutionary era. In France, the cockade surfaced

[53] Amy Freund, *Portraiture and Politics in Revolutionary France* (University Park, PA, 2014).
[54] Like the term "sans-culotte," this outfit effaced the social diversity of the movement. Haim Burstin, *L'invention du sans-culotte* (Paris, 2005).
[55] Jones, "Bourgeois Revolution Revivified," 69–71; Taws, *The Politics of the Provisional*, ch. 4.
[56] White, *Revolutionary Things*.

in the summer of 1789 and would bedeck jackets, hats, scarves, lapels, and national guard uniforms for the remainder of the Revolution. A clear illustration of the ways in which leaders and citizens invested material objects with deep revolutionary meanings, the cockade also suggests how difficult it was to embody complicated revolutionary concepts such as transparency and authenticity.

The cockade became a French national symbol in July 1789. On July 12, journalist Camille Desmoulins created a green cockade (symbolizing hope) during a speech against the sudden dismissal of reformist finance minister Jacques Necker. Days later on July 17, in the aftermath of the storming of the Bastille, the mayor of Paris presented Louis XVI with a tricolor cockade befitting a day of reconciliation between the city of Paris (represented by red and blue) and the Bourbon dynasty (represented by white). This was the cockade that would stand for the revolutionary cause for years to come, a symbol of national unity and revolutionary change.

It soon became clear, however, that variations in the cockade's color could convey alternative political meanings. As we have seen, the women's march to Versailles was not merely a response to high bread prices. Also precipitating the event were newspaper reports that army officers and royal body guards at Versailles had trampled on tricolor cockades and sworn allegiance to black cockades, a gesture understood to reveal the existence of an aristocratic plot to quash the Revolution. Depending on its color, the cockade could project the specter of a royalist backlash or firm patriotic commitment to the Revolution.

During the years of radical revolution, from 1792 to 1794, the idea of transparency, which presumed that one's authentic inner political convictions could be made apparent to fellow citizens without mediation or distortion, came to a head as foreign war, economic distress, and the threat of counterrevolution raised the stakes of internal dissension.[57] In this tense environment, officials and citizens intervened repeatedly to control the display and meaning of the cockade. On June 20, 1792, a crowd of protesters concerned about the use of the royal veto invaded the Tuileries palace, where they forced the queen to wear a cockade and insisted that the king and dauphin don liberty caps (woolen red bonnets supposedly worn by emancipated slaves in ancient Rome and favored by many Parisian militants). The reigning conviction seemed to be that bearing such material manifestations of the Revolution would not only mark royal family members as revolutionaries but affect their inner

---

[57] For problems of transparency, authenticity, and revolutionary material culture, see Hunt, *Politics, Culture, and Class in the French Revolution*, part I; and Taws, *The Politics of the Provisional*.

political sentiments as well. For the next two years, as the Revolution entered its republican phase, leaders attempted to use the cockade in a similar fashion to shore up support for the revolutionary project. In July 1792, the government declared that every man in France except foreign ambassadors must either wear the tricolor cockade as a sign of loyal citizenship or face the charge of "rebellion," a crime punishable by death. Immediately after the National Convention passed the General Maximum in September 1793, the politics of the cockade intensified as fights broke out in Paris between the Dames des Halles, female food retailers whose livelihoods were threatened by the Maximum's price controls on consumer goods, and the "Society of revolutionary republican women," a leading political club that defended the Maximum's pro-consumer provisions. Although the battle between the two groups concerned economic regulation, it took the ostensible form of disputes over the cockade. The revolutionary republican women insisted that all women, as well as all men, be required to wear the ribbon, but the Dames "refused to wear an emblem that they associated more with the anti-merchant Enragés [subsistence activists] than the Republic."[58] A series of brawls ensued, leading the National Convention to decree that all women, including the Dames, must wear the national cockade or risk imprisonment. The declaration validated the republican women's pro-consumer position and emboldened them to engage in further activism (and more fights with the Dames) until the Convention "transformed a marketplace clash into generic female disorder" and shut down the republican women along with every other women's political club in France.[59] While the suppression of women's clubs has remained a black mark on the Convention, the cockade emerged from the battle unscathed to be sustained by a final piece of legislation in May 1794 that announced that anyone found not wearing one would be treated as a counterrevolutionary and judged accordingly.

Despite such initiatives, it was exceedingly difficult to control the material composition and use of the cockade, an object often fabricated at home that varied in size, shape, and color and could be worn on different parts of the body. As police agents reported, "People want to place it on the right, on the left, on the front, behind, and this frivolous question, which is not yet decided on, has already caused violent brawls."[60] It was impossible to legislate into existence a monolithic revolutionary badge with clear fixed meanings that the entire populace would use in a consistent fashion.

[58] Jarvis, *Politics in the Marketplace*, 148.   [59] Ibid., 162.
[60] Quoted in Wrigley, *The Politics of Appearances*, 108.

The idea of revolutionary transparency presumed that once the stifling hierarchical artifice of the old regime was cast off, citizens would be able to see one another's inner patriotic virtue and forge new lateral or "fraternal" bonds. As one member of the Jacobin club stated, "we don't need any more discourses or correspondence. We need mute meetings in which each person divines in the others' eyes what there is to do."[61] But, of course, inner ideas and feelings cannot help but be mediated by language, gesture, and the physical world. Material culture is all about mediation and the use of objects to express ideas and identities. Given the intense divisions of the Revolution and persistent anxieties about plots, however, no single exterior symbol of interior revolutionary virtue, not even the cockade, could effectively unify the citizenry. As a character in one revolutionary pamphlet responded when asked why he wore no cockade: "But how can that allow one to distinguish between a good and bad citizen, unless [the cockade] is a marvelous talisman which gives to others the facility of divining inner thoughts?"[62]

And yet, for all the doubt about its ability to convey political conviction, the cockade was one of the most widely shared objects of the Revolution. Wearing it enabled citizens to identify themselves with a national revolutionary movement. Unlike more radical emblems such as the liberty cap, which was associated with Jacobinism and sans-culottes militancy, the symbol of the cockade was politically capacious enough to survive the Terror and endure more conservative regimes up to and including the Napoleonic Empire. After Thermidor, however, when popular radicalism gave way to conservative forms of nationalism, the belief in the power of material culture to radically transform society waned and the cockade's association with popular sovereignty was eclipsed by its military symbolism. The emblem survived but was largely emptied of its earlier revolutionary meaning.

Slavery and Abolition

Integral to revolutionary transformation, the politics of consumption also extended to debates on slavery. As this book has stressed, the rise of consumption in eighteenth-century Europe was in large part predicated on the development of ruthlessly exploitative plantation slavery in the Americas. Enslaved men and women of African descent were forced to grow the tobacco, sugar, coffee, indigo, and cotton that Europeans ingested and wore on their backs. If these colonial products became

---

[61] Quoted in Freund, *Portraiture and Politics in Revolutionary France*, 23.
[62] Quoted in Wrigley, *The Politics of Appearances*, 114.

objects of political contestation over the course of the eighteenth century, they also stood at the center of a struggle against slavery that further defined the Age of Revolution.

The enslaved themselves launched the era's greatest attack on slavery. Long relegated by historians to second-tier status, the Haitian Revolution is now understood to be as important as, if not more important than, the American and French Revolutions in the creation of the modern world. In the late eighteenth century, the French Caribbean colony of Saint-Domingue (now Haiti) produced more sugar for European consumption than any other colony in the world, supplying the continent with 40 percent of the sweet crystal and 60 percent of the coffee it consumed. Powering a psychoactive transformation in European daily life, that high level of production was sustained by enslavers who ravaged the island's ecosystem and, tragically, drove countless enslaved men and women to an early death.

In August 1791, however, the enslaved of the Northern Plain of Saint-Domingue, the center of the colony's sugar production, staged a massive uprising against the plantation system. After destroying numerous plantations and battling European armies, the people of Haiti declared the former colony a free and independent nation in 1804, making the Haitian Revolution the only successful large-scale slave uprising in modern history. The remarkable Revolution demonstrated that enslaved men and women were capable of dynamic political and military action, imperiling the stability of the thriving plantation complex that fueled European consumption.[63] Indeed, after the Revolution, rural Haitians instituted a counter-plantation system that rejected the cultivation of export commodities (like sugar) destined for European consumption in favor of producing local subsistence crops.[64] Small wonder the Haitian Revolution shook the entire Atlantic world, spreading the hope of emancipation among enslaved people across the Americas and sowing fear among enslavers who now pursued more effective ways to control captive labor forces.

If the enslaved producers of sugar struggled to end slavery, so too did a vocal minority of its consumers in Europe and North America. While historians debate the religious, ideological, and economic origins of abolitionism, the movement to abolish the slave trade (and eventually slavery), they agree that boycotts of slave-grown sugar were an essential

---

[63] Though such agency was denied by negative depictions of Haitian military leaders produced for European viewers. See White, *Revolutionary Things*.

[64] Jean Casimir, *The Haitians: A Decolonial History*, trans. Laurent Dubois (Chapel Hill, NC, 2020); and Johnhenry Gonzales, *Maroon Nation: A History of Revolutionary Haiti* (New Haven, CT, 2019). For an overview of the Revolution, see Laurent Dubois, *Avengers of the New World: The Story of the Haitian Revolution* (Cambridge, MA, 2004).

part of the larger antislavery effort at the end of the eighteenth and beginning of the nineteenth centuries. Just as consumers in the North American British colonies initiated boycotts to transmit political signals to the metropole, and just as American and French revolutionaries tied personal acts of consumption to national political movements, so too did certain groups of consumers in Britain and the USA abstain from sugar to bring an end to slavery.[65] Although these movements differed in many respects, they all shared a strikingly new political imaginary in which specific acts of consumption or nonconsumption were understood to be capable of generating large-scale transformations in the course of human history.

In 1791–1792, the British parliament rejected a bill to abolish Britain's slave trade, prompting an outcry from an eclectic abolitionist movement composed of Quakers, women, blacks, and other radicals. In addition to petitioning and lobbying – and buying pottery, snuffboxes, and jewelry with abolitionist slogans and images – many British abolitionists (on the order of half a million according to one estimate) willfully abstained from consuming sugar produced by the enslaved in the British Caribbean (see Figure 7.5).[66] Abolitionist writers urged the public to refrain from ingesting such a morally impure product. The blood of African slaves, they avowed, tainted imported sugar both metaphorically and literally. According to William Fox, author of the most widely diffused abolitionist tract of the day, "The laws of our country ... may hold [sugar] to our lips, steeped in the blood of our fellow creatures; but they cannot compel us to accept the loathsome poison." "So necessarily connected are our consumption of the commodity, and the misery arising from it," Fox continued, "that in every pound of sugar used, ... we may be considered as consuming two ounces of human flesh."[67] As Charlotte Sussman underscores, the pamphlet sought to elicit visceral moral repugnance by hinting that British consumers of slave-produced sugar were in danger of turning into the flesh-eating "savages" they fantasized about in the Afro-Caribbean world.[68]

---

[65] No such boycotts occurred in France, where abolitionism was weaker and took different forms. The French National Convention abolished slavery throughout the empire in 1794, but Napoleon reestablished it in 1802, an act not rescinded until 1848.

[66] Julie Holcomb, "Blood-Stained Sugar: Gender, Commerce and the British Slave-Trade Debates," *Slavery and Abolition* 35 (2014), 611–628.

[67] William Fox, *An Address to the People of Great Britain, on the Propriety of Refraining from the Use of West India Sugar and Rum* (1791), 2–3.

[68] Charlotte Sussman, "Women and the Politics of Sugar, 1792," *Representations* 48 (Fall 1994), 48–69.

Figure 7.5 "Am I not a man and a brother?"
Granger Historical Picture Archive/Alamy Stock Photo. In 1787, Wedgwood designed a seal for the Society for Effecting the Abolition of the Slave Trade with an image of a kneeling slave, who asks "Am I not a man and a brother?" The image was reproduced in jasperware cameos and set in snuffboxes, bracelets, and hairpins to become an icon of the abolitionist movement. Note how the enslaved man is represented as a passive supplicant rather than an autonomous person demanding the freedom to which he is entitled. This image of passivity contrasts with what we know about resistance to slavery in the Americas

Gender was central to the boycott because it connected a major public issue to the everyday consumption of British metropolitan households, which were provisioned mainly by women. This connection explains why abolitionist literature often targeted female readers and why women figured prominently in the abolitionist movement. Women's role in the movement was understood in terms of eighteenth-century notions of feminine sensibility, according to which, women were, in the words of abolitionist Benjamin Flower, "formed to feel *more* than men are."[69] If, as purported creatures of feeling, women were considered more susceptible to disorderliness and frivolity, they were also perceived to possess the power to feel acutely the suffering of others, even distant slaves, a keen ability that equipped them for moral leadership. For many observers of the day, it was only natural that women should participate in the abolitionist movement. Although we now know that gendered ideas of sensibility were a cultural

[69] Quoted in Holcomb, "Blood-Stained Sugar," 620.

construction of the era, it is no less true that women were heavily involved in the 1791–1792 movement as well as subsequent campaigns in the 1820s. Indeed, Elizabeth Heyrick was the first white Briton to call for immediate (rather than gradual) emancipation by means of a mass movement to abstain from sugar. Women were vanguard consumer activists as well as vanguard consumers.

In making the case for boycotting sugar, abolitionist pamphleteers used current political-economic ideas of consumer sovereignty to invest the consumer with the power to effect social change. "The slave-dealer, the slave-holder, and the slave-driver, are virtually agents of the consumer," Fox wrote, "and may be considered as employed and hired by him to procure the commodity."[70] Abolitionist William Allen elaborated:

The DUTY of abstaining from the Consumption of West Indian Produce arises from the CONNECTION which subsists between the *Consumer* of that Produce and the *Means* by which it is cultivated. That connection, Sir, is more close and direct than some persons may be willing to admit. The consumer of the West India Produce, may be considered as the *Master-Spring* that gives motion and effect to the whole Machine of Cruelties … [The slave trade] involves with equal criminality THE AFRICAN TRADER – THE WEST INDIA HOLDER – AND THE BRITISH CONSUMER.[71]

This logic not only drove the British sugar boycotts of the 1790s and 1820s but also the nineteenth-century "free produce" movement in the northern USA. Activists in the latter movement urged consumers to boycott slave-produced goods (cotton, sugar, and rice) and purchase "free labor" substitutes.[72] Lawrence Glickman suggests that the origins of contemporary ethical consumption can be traced to free-produce activism, which appropriated and extended the rhetoric and tactics of the British sugar boycotts of the 1790s and American nonimportation campaigns of the 1770s.

It is important to acknowledge that none of the abolitionist boycotts succeeded, for there were limits to the effectiveness of such market-based activism. In the 1790s, the Haitian Revolution triggered the collapse of the French sugar trade, allowing British merchants to supply Europe; any drop in British demand from the boycott was more than compensated by

---

[70] Fox, *An Address to the People of Great Britain*, 3
[71] Quoted in Charlotte Sussman, *Consuming Anxieties: Consumer Protest, Gender, and British Slavery, 1713–1833* (Stanford, CA, 2000), 40. The French writer Louis-Sébastien Mercier made a similar argument against the consumption of sugar, but the French did not mount a boycott. Maud Villeret, *Le goût de l'or blanc: Le sucre en France au xviiie siècle* (Rennes, 2017), 256–257.
[72] Lawrence Glickman, "'Buy for the Sake of the Slave': Abolitionism and the Origins of American Consumer Activism," *American Quarterly* 56 (December 2004), 889–912.

new business on the continent. Nor did the 1820s and 1830s movements have much economic impact. But economic impact is not the only way to measure the significance of the boycotts, which contributed to the strength of abolitionism by bringing people into the movement, raising awareness of the violent exploitation of slave labor, and organizing public opposition. Boycotts helped to energize the larger abolitionist movement and spur the kind of collective action that led to the British Emancipation Act of 1838. In the end, it was the boycotts' political impact, not their economic impact, that made a difference.

In a widely read two-part article, Thomas Haskell argued in 1985 that British abolitionism reflected a new form of humanitarianism in which men and women began to respond to the distant suffering of others, expanding the "perceived limits of human agency and responsibility." This new moral imagination, he claimed, was due to "the emergence of a market-oriented form of life" that created "altered perceptions of causation in human affairs" as market actors learned "to attend to the remote consequences of their acts."[73] Although deeply influential, Haskell's attempt to link modern humanitarianism to the rise of capitalism has been challenged on many fronts. Richard Huzzey shows that British abolitionism was sharply bounded by the limits of the British Empire.[74] More to the point, Manisha Sinha contends that insofar as slavery in the Americas was itself a form of capitalism, antislavery was in fact anticapitalist. The abolition movement, she insightfully asserts, was a triumph of democracy, not capitalism.[75]

Building on Huzzey and Sinha, I would argue that in both metropolitan and colonial spaces, the age of democratic revolution witnessed several important experiments in consumer activism. In various ways, American, French, and Haitian revolutionaries as well as British abolitionists were reacting to the growth of markets and to the mercantilist and fiscal policies that sought to control and extract value from them. In the American and French revolutions, consumer-citizens not only opposed "despotic" state interventions through dynamic collective action and boycotts but also participated creatively in the construction of new republican cultures. In the Haitian Revolution, the enslaved rose up

---

[73] Thomas Haskell, "Capitalism and the Origins of the Humanitarian Sensibility, Part 1," AHR 90 (April 1985), 342; Thomas Haskell, "Capitalism and the Origins of the Humanitarian Sensibility, Part 2, AHR 90 (June 1985), 548.

[74] Richard Huzzey, "The Moral Geography of British Anti-slavery Responsibilities," *Transactions of the RHS* 22 (2012), 111–139.

[75] Manisha Sinha, *The Slave's Cause: A History of Abolition* (New Haven, CT, 2016); Manisha Sinha, "The Problem of Abolition in the Age of Capitalism," AHR 124 (February 2019), 144–163.

to overthrow a brutal system of production that supplied Europeans with ever greater quantities of cheap consumer goods. British abolitionists, meanwhile, sought to leverage their power as consumers to end the scourge of the slave trade and plantation slavery in the British West Indies. Of course, none of these movements was entirely new: enslaved men and women in the Caribbean had long resisted oppression through marronage and other tactics; ordinary Europeans had engaged in food revolts throughout the early modern period; and Enlightenment political economists had articulated theories of consumer sovereignty that placed the consumer at the center of the economic nervous system. But consumer activism took on new meaning and force in an age of democratic revolution when citizens connected their specific acts of consumption to unprecedented social and political transformations.

Recall that the legislators, citizens, and activists of the Age of Revolution invented the very idea of revolution "as a legitimate rising of the sovereign people."[76] In such a highly charged environment, citizens came to understand that popular politics and the invention of new material cultures could potentially produce profound structural change. It was undoubtedly this heightened sense of the possibility of durable transformation that emboldened ordinary people to experiment with new political ideas and forms of collective action. Accordingly, they improvised new ways to deploy their power as consumers (and as workers, mothers, patriots, soldiers, property-owners, and so on) to wrest sovereignty from long-entrenched institutions and establish republican polities based on contemporary ideas of liberty and equality. Although such "political consumerism" did not always achieve its immediate goals – much of it remained aspirational – it contributed significantly to the democratic politics of the age.

---

[76] William Sewell, *Logics of History: Social Theory and Social Transformation* (Chicago, 2005), 241.

Conclusion

People should think about the consequences of the little choices they make each day. What do you buy? Where did it come from? Where was it made? Did it harm the environment? Did it lead to cruelty to animals? Was it cheap because of child slave labor?[1]

The contemporary world seems obsessed with stuff: how to get it, what to do with it, how to get rid of it. Consumption across the planet has reached unprecedented levels and there is no end in sight. Although historians assumed until fairly recently that the story of rising consumption began with European industrialization, we now know that the pace of consumption quickened in certain parts of the early modern world, notably China and Europe, well before the age of mass production. In Europe between 1650 and 1800, women and men began to accumulate more clothing, carry more personal accessories, fill their households with more furnishings, and wear, smoke, snort, eat, and drink large quantities of new colonial products. Although scholars bicker about whether to call the growth of consumption in this period revolutionary or evolutionary, they all agree that is was transformational. It changed how people looked, ate, socialized, and thought, giving rise to heated debates about human civilization and moral progress and ushering in new forms of political activism.

The contours of this material transformation were defined by geography, gender, social order, and race. Northwestern Europe (the Netherlands, England, France, and parts of Germany) experienced it most intensely. The vibrant commercial culture Italians forged during the Renaissance did not disappear, though economic life of countries north of the Alps came to overshadow that of the peninsula. Parts of Spain thrived in the eighteenth century, as did certain cities in central and eastern Europe, but their levels of consumption never approached

---

[1] Jane Goodall, primatologist, quoted in David Gelles, "Corner Office," *New York Times*, September 15, 2019, 4.

those of northwestern Europe. Women spearheaded the consumption of clothing as fashion cycles accelerated, but men were also interested in the emerging consumer culture, buying big-ticket items as well as small accessories. Socially, urban nobles and middling classes participated most robustly in new forms of consumption, but, thanks to rural fairs, local shops, peddlers, and smugglers, circulation between town and country intensified and villagers purchased a greater variety of goods as well. And yet, social limits on the emerging consumer culture were real: the eighteenth century was not an age of mass consumption. The poorest of urban and rural society – countless ranks of day laborers, unemployed, indigent peasants, and homeless – were largely excluded. In the Americas, many white settlers and free people of color in busy port towns and their hinterlands shared in rising consumption, but the same cannot be said of most Native Americans and enslaved people of African descent, for whom European colonization was nothing short of catastrophic.

Unevenly distributed, consumption surged nevertheless and did so without major technological breakthroughs. The expansion of the world of goods can be attributed to incremental growth in the size of towns, agricultural specialization, changing labor practices, and the development of local, regional, and global trade. The two factors that have received most recent attention are labor and trade. With respect to labor, Jan de Vries' argument that an "industrious revolution" enabled greater consumption has been widely influential, deservedly so, but the liberal premise on which it is based – that the expansion of industriousness was fundamentally voluntary – should be questioned. To be sure, many families chose to work more in order to purchase goods they desired. But in an age defined by a wide spectrum of unfreedom, it can hardly be said that industriousness was wholly voluntary. Many laboring families in western Europe, facing stagnant wages and rising rent and food prices, had to work harder simply to stay afloat. Urban guilds sanctioned child apprenticeship. And, in the breadbasket of eastern Europe, serfdom sharply limited the rights and material lives of the peasantry. Most dramatically, the development of slavery in the Americas challenges the liberal framework of the industrious revolution thesis. Obviously, the enslaved did not choose to work in order to boost their own consumption. Enslavers brutally forced work upon them and sold the products of their labor to a separate and distant population of consumers in Europe, who took full advantage of the falling prices of colonial goods such as sugar, coffee, tobacco, and cotton. Unfree labor was therefore anything but incidental to the consumer revolution. Any assessment of

eighteenth-century industriousness needs to account for the global division of labor and the full range of conditions in which workers around
the world found themselves.

Overseas trade has also drawn recent attention. Although most consumption involved locally produced goods, colonial trade soared as
European state-sponsored trading companies and independent merchants intervened in global commercial circuits that, for the first time
in human history, directly linked the continents of Europe, Asia, Africa,
and the Americas. Chinese porcelain and Indian cotton – and European
imitations of them – shaped the material culture of the period, while the
new psychoactive products of the day (Chinese tea and American coffee,
chocolate, sugar, and tobacco) came to define elite and popular sociability. European merchants came to dominate the trade in such goods
because competing European states vigorously intervened in the global
economy by creating state-chartered companies, crafting exclusive navigation laws, and deploying blue-water navies. Fiscal, regulatory, and
military institutions of bellicose European states – what I've called the
political economy of empire – sustained large-scale global trade and
production.

The development of new forms of marketing and the acceleration of
fashion cycles also encouraged consumption. Shops proliferated, multi-
plying points of contact between retailers and consumers and, for urban
elites and middling classes, establishing shopping itself as a leisure activity. Advertising flourished in the form of newspaper announcements,
trade cards, and handbills. Opening dialogues between producers and
consumers, retailers (often women) acted as information brokers, mediating exchanges about taste and fashion and enticing customers with
shop credit. Like East India company agents who channeled knowledge
of European consumer tastes to skilled Indian weavers, metropolitan
producers and designers tailored production to customers' desires. The
flow of information between producers and consumers could make the
difference between commercial success or failure. Having accelerated in
the eighteenth century, such fast-paced, producer-consumer feedback
loops remained a mainstay of modern retail and fashion, as nineteenth-
century department stores gave way to twentieth-century big-box stores,
which are now yielding to twenty-first century online outlets. Today,
some of the most valuable companies in the world, such as Facebook and
Google, earn profits by collecting vast amounts of personal data and
selling it to advertisers, who know far more about their customers'
personal lives and tastes than most people realize. This new mode of
marketing, which Shoshana Zuboff calls "surveillance capitalism," is so

powerful that it has raised fundamental questions about the right to privacy.[2]

What all this consumption meant to eighteenth-century consumers themselves has been widely debated. The motivation for consumer desire that Neil McKendrick posited, following the work of sociologists like Thorstein Veblen, was emulation or the wish to imitate and thereby lay claim to the status of social superiors. According to the emulation thesis, new cultural practices emanated from the aristocracy and cascaded down the social hierarchy as the bourgeoisie imitated the nobility and the lower orders imitated the bourgeoisie. However, while there is no doubt that emulation occurred in the status-oriented society of eighteenth-century Europe, we must be careful not to put too much weight on an explanatory framework based largely on exaggerated accounts of social mobility written by anxiety-ridden eighteenth-century observers.

Another way historians have approached the meaning of consumption is to interpret new practices as part of a larger process of the cultural formation of the bourgeoisie. In this interpretation, the bourgeoisie, far from aping the aristocracy, was establishing itself as a distinct and powerful class in its own right with its own mores. It rejected courtly consumption as artificial and corrupt in the name of new healthier social values such as cleanliness and simplicity. Again, there is some truth to this interpretation – the middling classes were becoming more important both demographically and economically – but it fails to explain why so much of the nobility participated in the same consumer culture as the bourgeoisie. The new culture of consumption was much broader than the adjective "bourgeois" implies. Indeed, the bourgeois interpretation also fails to account for the degree to which the laboring classes adopted new modes of consumption, buying similar goods of lesser quality at lower price points. Clearly the consumer culture of the day was more widespread and complex than either the emulation thesis or the idea of bourgeois cultural formation implies.

This book has suggested two ways forward. The first is to emphasize horizontal relationships of respectability and honor as much as vertical dynamics of emulation. According to eighteenth-century anti-luxury writers, many of whom dreaded the chaos of dynamic social mobility, lower-status men and women who donned nice clothes were falsely claiming superior status. In social terms, however, it is more likely that such men and women were thinking horizontally as much as vertically as they sought to impress others in their social milieu. Elites did not hold a

---

[2] Shoshana Zuboff, *The Age of Surveillance Capitalism* (New York, 2019).

monopoly on honor in the early modern period, despite what they may have claimed. Members of all classes, even the most lowly, were concerned with maintaining honor in their local communities. Recall William Hutton's tale of how, in 1741, as a stockinger's apprentice he was able with a little overtime pay and credit to obtain a "genteel suit of clothes, fully adequate to the sphere in which I moved." He was not gunning for the nobility. Rather, he was out to impress people, especially women, in his circle: "the girls eyed me with some attention; nay, I eyed myself as much as any of them."[3] For the legions of Huttons on the streets of eighteenth-century towns, dressing up was as much about personal and familial respectability (and sex appeal!) as it was about social climbing. It also points to the development of a reflexive self, which is an essential condition of modernity. Just as Hutton could not resist eyeing himself, neither could elite cultural omnivores who experimented with more common forms of consumption to create what they understood to be authentic individual identity.

A complementary method of interpreting the meaning of eighteenth-century consumer culture is to look closely at the language and practices surrounding goods. Through the marketing, purchase, and use of new goods, eighteenth-century tastemakers and consumers constructed a material culture based on a range of values, including comfort, convenience, novelty, individuality, privacy, domesticity, nature, authenticity, simplicity, cleanliness, exoticism, and piety, not to mention national, gender, and racial identity. It is no coincidence that many of these values lined up with Enlightenment ideas found in eighteenth-century texts, for writers both reflected and promoted larger cultural changes with which they were intimately familiar. Expressing commitment to Enlightenment values through consumption involved not only distancing oneself from older courtly forms of consumption, which privileged splendor over comfort and appearance over authenticity, but also espousing what Diderot called a "modern" cultural ethos. Even Marie-Antoinette, queen of France, moved beyond restrictive courtly etiquette by subscribing to Enlightenment modes of consumption. This was even easier to do in the Netherlands and England, where court culture was relatively weak and eighteenth-century material culture grew mainly out of urban development. The evolution of consumer values in such commercial cultures was rooted more directly in sixteenth- and seventeenth-century urban antecedents.

---

[3] Quoted in John Styles, *The Dress of the People: Everyday Fashion in Eighteenth-Century England* (New Haven, CT, 2007), 1.

It is important to note, however, that the material resources and cultural competency necessary to signal one's identification with emerging Enlightenment values excluded the poor and uneducated. Those who could not afford or did not know how to become proficient in the "art" of consumption were easily stigmatized as ignorant, uncouth, and insignificant. Thus, consumption in the age of the Enlightenment could be highly exclusionary. Although elites and middling classes adopted new styles of life, whole swathes of the working classes (from low-skilled urban day laborers and small rural farmers to peasants, serfs, and the enslaved) were barred from participating in the new consumer culture. Consumption can thrive amidst the most appalling inequalities – another salient point of comparison between past and present.

Beyond the realm of material culture, historians have analyzed the relationship between consumption and Enlightenment in terms of reading practices and sociability. Following Immanuel Kant's famous essay "What Is Enlightenment?," Jürgen Habermas argued that the circulation of the printed word and the development of new spaces of sociability created a "bourgeois public sphere" capable of producing "public opinion" critical of the state.[4] Habermas has been rightly criticized for ignoring the existence of multiple publics, including plebeian ones, and for exaggerating the rational and oppositional stance of eighteenth-century readers and members of voluntary associations. Still, the profusion of books printed in the eighteenth century and the creation of new public spaces were highly significant developments. If the concept of a "reading revolution" overstates the transition from intensive to extensive reading, the increase in the number and types of printed works (periodicals, novels, and so on) encouraged a multiplicity of ways of reading, some of which did in fact open new critical perspectives on state and society. Similarly, if Habermas' claims about sociability seem overblown, it is clear that new public sites of consumption – cafés, salons, public gardens – did soften the social hierarchy and cement a broader propertied elite. To some degree, they also challenged gender divisions, enabling certain women (such as salonnières) to pursue public lives. If that wider public was not always as rational and critical as Habermas would have liked, rulers across Europe were nonetheless operating in a new political environment in which they had to appeal, at least rhetorically, to "the public" as a new source of authority.

The expansion of the world of goods did not unfold quietly. Launching a conversation that is in many ways still with us, it prompted

---

[4] Jürgen Habermas, *The Structural Transformation of the Public Sphere*, trans. Thomas Burger (Cambridge, MA, 1989).

a vigorous debate about the perils and promises of "luxury," the principal idiom through which eighteenth-century writers reflected on the moral, social, and political implications of consumption. While discussions of luxury go back to the ancient world, they took on a new sense of urgency in Enlightenment Europe when the accelerating pace of consumption drew the attention of commentators. Although most writers lamented the spread of luxury, a few daring thinkers overturned long-standing intellectual traditions and celebrated the era's changing commercial and material culture. Fénelon and Mandeville staked out the terms of the debate. Fénelon built on classical and Christian critiques of consumption to argue that luxury upended the social order, corrupted social mores, feminized men, and destroyed nations. Mandeville countered that in fact the vice of luxury bolstered prosperous and strong nations, a moral irony readers would simply have to tolerate. Over the century, the debate evolved as luxury apologists, including such celebrated philosophers as Voltaire and Hume, linked luxury to cultural progress, while a slew of interlocutors continued to warn the public of its dire consequences. Rousseau suggested that the awakening of consumer desire was an integral part of the transition from a morally pure state of nature to a morally compromised state of society in which women who dared to venture outside the domestic sphere corrupted otherwise virtuous men. After the mid-century, a number of philosophers and political economists proposed a middle path through the controversy, hoping to lead nations to enduring prosperity while avoiding the pitfalls of moral decline. Meanwhile, commercial culture shifted as some producers and retailers adapted to critiques of luxury by redesigning goods in accordance with principles of nature and authenticity – all the better to sell them. The literary attack on luxury failed to halt the rise of consumption, although the anxieties it evoked influenced commercial culture and have remained with us in various forms to this day.

If the first generation of work on eighteenth-century consumption widely ignored politics, that is beginning to change. For one, recent scholarship examines the complicated relationship between consumption and European state formation. As European fiscal-military states competed for resources and overseas colonies, they implemented trade regulations to boost imperial power (what has been controversially called "mercantilism") and fiscalized consumption. Regulating and taxing the production, movement, and sale of consumer goods, however, provoked vigorous collective action. In addition to persistent and well-studied bread riots, other forms of popular protest arose in eighteenth-century Europe and colonial America that targeted heavily taxed and regulated commodities such as salt, beer, wine, tea, and tobacco. Often these protests involved illicit traders and consumers who saw themselves as protecting local economic rights against the imposition of illegitimate fiscal and regulatory claims on their community. This emerging form of consumer activism would ultimately manifest itself in the American and French Revolutions. In the former case, nonimportation and non-consumption boycotts culminated in the famous Boston Tea Party of 1773. In the latter case, crowds of Parisians burned down the customs gates of the capital city in July 1789 before they stormed the Bastille. Consumer activism also shaped the material culture of both revolutions as citizens expressed their political convictions through the display of household goods, clothing, and accessories. Citizens lived revolutions concretely in their daily lives by producing and consuming myriad objects charged with political meaning, such as homespun cloth in America and tricolor cockades in France. Finally, in 1792, British abolitionists, mostly women, attempted to harness the power of a new form of collective protest, the boycott, to halt the Atlantic slave trade. They did not immediately succeed, but the Haitian Revolution demonstrated that the enslaved themselves were more than capable of overthrowing the brutal system of production.

Establishing a counterplantation economy, rural Haitians rejected the colonial crops that had served European consumers and embraced subsistence agriculture and local autonomy.[5]

Clearly, consumer activism in the form of collective protest, material culture, and humanitarianism flourished in Europe and its colonies in the Age of Revolution. What social scientists call "ethical" or "political" consumerism made novel yet often overlooked contributions to the democratic politics of the age.

New Directions

Since the first generation of scholarship on the "consumer revolution," the study of consumption has made great strides by more fully incorporating state formation, empire, political economy, global trade, slavery, production, exchange, material culture, social inequality, politics, revolution, and more. One important theme that remains to be more deeply investigated, however, is the relationship between consumption and the environment. The following brief sketch of the history of this relationship – or at least one important aspect of it, energy consumption – is

[5] Jean Casimir, *The Haitians: A Decolonial History*, trans. Laurent Dubois (Chapel Hill, NC, 2020); Johnhenry Gonzales, *Maroon Nation: A History of Revolutionary Haiti* (New Haven, CT, 2019).

meant to encourage students and scholars to explore new areas of research.[6]

The growth of consumption in the modern world has always depended on energy. Before industrialization in the nineteenth century, energy came primarily from human and animal power. To be sure, human beings employed technology to generate energy; they burned wood to smelt iron and bake bread, harnessed wind to sail on the high seas, and used watermills to grind grain. But the most basic and adaptable form of energy was human and animal muscle power, which derived mainly from eating plants that took their energy from the sun.[7] Under this "biological old regime," humans depended on solar energy to grow crops for food and trees for fuel.[8]

The primacy of muscle power began to ebb in the late eighteenth century, however, when a shortage of firewood in Britain led to the use of coal as a substitute. Coal warmed homes and was soon put to use in the steam engines that powered the textile factories, railroads, and steamships that defined the industrial nineteenth century.[9] Driven by worldwide consumption, the fossil fuel revolution was at hand, with the rise of coal and then, of course, petroleum for fueling cars and networked electrical infrastructures in the twentieth century, all the while emitting the greenhouse gases that have accelerated climate change in the modern era. That human beings learned how to escape the long-standing constraints of the biological old regime is a stunning achievement, but the pollution, ecological degradation, and climate change that resulted from two centuries of industrialization in the Global North and more recent economic development in the Global South now imperils much of humanity. "It is worse, much worse, than you think," David Wallace-Wells writes in his troubling book on the climate crisis. The heat, desertification, and flooding produced by emissions threaten to render uninhabitable "whole regions of Africa and Australia and the United States, parts of South America north of Patagonia, and Asia south of Siberia" by the end of the twenty-first century.[10] A recent survey of human history

[6] Other human factors besides energy use have produced climate change, such as the world's food system, particularly the production of meat and dairy, but I have chosen to focus on energy for the sake of brevity.
[7] David E. Nye, "Consumption of Energy," in Frank Trentmann, ed., *The Oxford Handbook of the History of Consumption* (Oxford, 2021), 307–325.
[8] Robert B. Marks, *The Origins of the Modern World: A Global and Environmental Narrative from the Fifteenth to the Twenty-First Century* (London, 2020), 40.
[9] Rolf Peter Sieferle, *The Subterranean Forest: Energy Systems and the Industrial Revolution,* trans. Michael P. Osman (Cambridge, 2001).
[10] David Wallace-Wells, *The Uninhabitable Earth: Life after Warming* (New York, 2019), 1, 6.

concludes that "we are destroying the foundations of human prosperity in an orgy of reckless consumption."[11] We are also devastating animal habitats in an unfathomable but ongoing sixth mass extinction.[12]

Any solution to the climate crisis requires a revolution in how humans think about – and therefore practice – consumption. One way to generate new ideas is to understand the history of consumption, including its early modern history. Breaking out of our temporal provincialism, a present-ism that ignores the deep history of humanity, can provide intellectual leverage in the fight against climate change in a number of ways. First, history exposes the environmental degradation inherent in processes of rising production and consumption. Pollution has a history, as does society's reactions to it. I have already mentioned how European coloni-alism ravaged the environment of tropical islands, leading to large-scale deforestation, soil depletion, and species extinction.[13] In Europe and its colonies, an awareness of such rapid ecological deterioration activated a nascent conservationist movement among professional scientists and colonial officials who sought to protect forests, conserve soil, and improve agriculture. In the short run, however, their conservationist efforts failed to sway metropolitan rulers.[14] Another case in point is Britain's energy conversion from wood to coal in the eighteenth century. While the use of coal may have allowed parts of England to transcend the photosynthetic constraint of plant-based fuel, it made London the smoki-est city in the world. Londoners complained about the "nuisance" of smoke in legal and scientific terms, but they ultimately accommodated themselves to it because the new energy source provided for domestic comfort, which was increasingly considered a necessity to which ordinary folk were entitled at reasonable prices. Further, it was widely understood that coal enabled British industry to thrive in a competitive international environment. Given the apparent advantages of coal in the context of imperial rivalry, Britons could not conceive of turning away from it and introducing measures for the systematic improvement of the environ-ment. Better for elites and wealthier middling folk to tolerate it by taking the occasional trip to a country retreat or pleasure garden.[15]

---

[11] Yuval Harari, *Sapiens: A Brief History of Humankind* (New York, 2015), 379.
[12] Elizabeth Kolbert, *The Sixth Extinction: An Unnatural History* (New York, 2014).
[13] J. R. McNeill, *Mosquito Empires: Ecology and War in the Greater Caribbean, 1620–1914* (Cambridge, 2010); David Watts, *The West Indies: Patterns of Development, Culture and Environmental Change since 1492* (Cambridge, 1990), 393–443.
[14] Richard Grove, *Green Imperialism: Colonial Expansion, Tropical Island Edens and the Origins of Environmentalism, 1600–1860* (Cambridge, 1995).
[15] William Cavert, *The Smoke of London: Energy and Environment in the Early Modern City* (Cambridge, 2016).

The fact that the laboring classes in London had neither the time nor the resources to escape the smoke prefigures the plight that low-income people in environmentally vulnerable areas around the world face today. A similar situation occurred across the English Channel in France, where energy remained wood-based.[16] Even without much coal, Parisians had to contend with all sorts of industrial pollution in the late eighteenth and early nineteenth centuries. An alliance between state and scientific institutions put matters of economic growth and international economic competition ahead of health concerns, enabling producers to dispose of industrial waste as they saw fit.[17] In general, European elites accommodated themselves to the environmental "nuisances" of industrial growth while ordinary people suffered the consequences, setting a dubious pattern for the modern era. Today, the populations at risk of climate disaster are laboring people who already bear the brunt of social, economic, and racial inequality, including those who live in coastal regions with the least economic development (and who have contributed least to the climate crisis in the first place). If we wish to combat climate change, therefore, we will have to attend to difficult questions of justice: who is contributing most to climate change and who is bearing the brunt of it? What does the world owe the people in the latter category?

Beyond revealing the socioenvironmental consequences of expanding consumption and production, history can help denaturalize contemporary notions of consumption. Although nothing seems more natural or inevitable today than the relentless growth of consumption, it, too, has a history. Many of the conditions of contemporary global consumption were set in the early modern period, notably but not exclusively in Europe, including the increasing acquisition of household goods through markets; the growth of world trade; the exploitation of colonial systems of labor; the use of marketing through shops, advertising, and the fashion press; the acceleration of the fashion cycle; the shift from expensive durable goods to cheaper, disposable semidurables; the creation of consumer values such as comfort, convenience, respectability, naturalness, cleanliness, selfhood, domesticity, and authenticity; the eruption of new forms of consumer activism; and the ongoing debate over consumption itself. All

---

[16] The consumption of wood put great stress on European forests, prompting the study of resource management. See Karl Appuhn, *A Forest on the Sea: Environmental Expertise in Renaissance Venice* (Baltimore, 2009); Kieko Matteson, *Forests in Revolutionary France: Conservation, Community, and Conflict, 1669–1848* (Cambridge, 2015); Paul Warde, *The Invention of Sustainability: Nature and Destiny, c.1500–1870* (Cambridge, 2018); John Wing, *Roots of Empire: Forests and State Power in Early Modern Spain*, c. 1500–1750 (Leiden, 2015).

[17] Thomas Le Roux, *Le laboratoire des pollutions industrielles: Paris, 1770–1830* (Paris, 2011).

this had to be invented; there was nothing natural about any of it. Merchants, state officials, artisans, workers, the enslaved, retailers, taste-makers, journalists, philosophers, and of course consumers of all stripes built this evolving economic and cultural system, which would ultimately be powered by fossil fuels in the nineteenth and twentieth centuries.

But any invention of human society can be reinvented. This is not to claim that changing today's practices of consumption will be easy. It will require nothing short of a revolution in consciousness. Yet, a historical awareness of the cultural constructedness of what is now considered "normal" consumption might facilitate new conversations about future consumption and energy use. There is no going back to a natural, prelapsarian world of minimal consumption – even Rousseau acknow-ledged that – but coming to grips with the history of consumption might encourage citizens to imagine the possibilities of renewable energy regimes in the future. What kind of consumer cultures are truly sustain-able? On what values should they be based? Can certain drivers of modern consumption, such as product design or the pursuit of social respectability, be used to construct an alternative, sustainable built envir-onment? What kinds of activism can most effectively combat climate change? As sociologists Riley Dunlap and Robert Brulle observe, high-profile environmental reports based solely on the natural sciences and economics "fail to analyze critically the value systems, power relation-ships, and institutional processes that have resulted in climate change."[18] History and other social scientific and humanistic disciplines have an important role to play here by examining the social, political, moral, and intellectual structures that have conditioned humanity's relationship to the natural world.

Ethical consumption movements are already trying to halt climate change as consumers look for ways to reduce their carbon footprints. Advocates for "slow fashion," for example, are raising awareness of the environmental impact of twenty-first century "fast fashion," which makes the eighteenth-century fashion cycle look positively glacial by compari-son. To the frenzied tempo of almost weekly micro-seasons, fast fashion

[18] Robert J. Brulle and Riley E. Dunlap, "Sociology and Global Climate Change: Introduction," in Riley Dunlap and Robert Brulle, eds., *Climate Change and Society: Sociological Perspectives* (Oxford, 2015), 12. See also Elisabeth Shove, *Comfort, Cleanliness and Convenience: The Social Organization of Normality* (Oxford, 2003); and Elisabeth Shove, "Comfort and Convenience: Temporality and Practice" in Trentmann, ed., *The Oxford Handbook of the History of Consumption*, 289–306. Paul Sutter, "The World with Us: The State of American Environmental History," *Journal of American History* 100 (June 2013), 94–119, suggests environmental history has moved beyond stark divisions between nature and culture to speak of a hybrid world. Any effective advocacy would have to take that hybrid world as a given.

brands like H&M and Zara relentlessly crank out new styles of clothing
that are made to be worn no more than ten times before they are thrown
away and dumped into landfills.[19] To counter the rise of such disposable
fashion, the slow fashion movement urges consumers to decelerate the
fashion cycle and buy fewer, more durable items.

Efforts to consume ethically are noble indeed, but the historical record
does not inspire a lot of confidence in their ability to transform society. In
the eighteenth century, producers adapted to critiques of luxury by
modifying the design of their goods, only to sell more of them.
Twenty-first century corporations operate in a similar fashion. "Drive
like there's a tomorrow," reads an upbeat 2019 advertisement promising
a new fleet of electric cars that will supposedly alleviate the climate crisis –
and this from Volkswagen, a German car giant caught cheating on
emissions tests in 2015. The practice of deceptively marketing consumer
goods as environmentally friendly is called "greenwashing." We can
expect to see a lot more advertising of this type in the coming years.

One precedent from the late eighteenth and early nineteenth centuries
provides a ray of hope. Although the boycott of sugar by British abolitionists, one of the first major ethical consumer movements in Europe, failed
to end plantation slavery in the British Caribbean, it did galvanize a
movement that would eventually force parliament to abolish the British
slave trade. There may be a lesson here. Ethical consumption movements based on personal conscience and consumer choice may only have
limited economic impact; green consumerism may be better at forging
cultural identities than changing underlying patterns of consumption.[20]
But in moments of political or moral urgency such movements *can*
contribute to the organization of consequential grassroots political movements that exert pressure on governments to change public policy. In
turn, public policy measures such as education campaigns, high carbon
taxes, strong emissions regulations, the adoption of indigenous practices
of resource management, and substantial support for renewable energy
(to name but a few tools in the kit) can do more to shape collective
practices of consumption and reduce emissions than voluntary acts of
personal (non)consumption.[21] Robust public policy can be effective, but
it remains to be seen whether movements for an environmentally

[19] Louise Morgan and Grete Birtwistle, "An Investigation of Young Fashion Consumers'
Disposal Habits," *International Journal of Consumer Studies* 33 (2009), 190–198.
[20] Matthew Klingle, "The Nature of Desire: Consumption in Environmental History" in
Andrew Isenberg, ed., *The Oxford Handbook of Environmental History* (Oxford, 2014),
467–512.
[21] More extreme measures, such as individual consumption quotas, are explored in
Dominique Bourg et al., *Retour sur Terre: 35 propositions* (Paris, 2020).

sustainable economy based on the consumption of renewable energy will become powerful enough to pressure governments to address climate change and climate injustice in a decisive fashion.

As a problem of study, the "consumer revolution" has flourished well beyond its initial outlines. Historians have not only elaborated on its social and economic implications but also broadened the approach to the subject by incorporating political, cultural, imperial, and global history. Thanks to what has become a large and sophisticated corpus of work on eighteenth-century consumption, we can more clearly understand why and how Europe and the wider world experienced fundamental historical transformations before the age of industrialization. It now remains to incorporate more fully into the history of consumption not only the study of interactions between humans and the environment but also how a changing natural world has mediated human relations past and present.

Select Bibliography

General

Appadurai, Arjun, ed., *Social Life of Things: Commodities in Cultural Perspective* (Cambridge, 1986).

Berg, Maxine, *Luxury and Pleasure in Eighteenth-Century Britain* (Oxford, 2005).

Brewer, John, and Roy Porter, eds., *Consumption and the World of Goods* (London, 1993).

Crowston, Clare Haru, *Credit, Fashion, Sex: Economies of Regard in Old Regime France* (Durham, NC, 2013).

de Vries, Jan, *The Industrious Revolution: Consumer Behavior and the Household Economy, 1650 to the Present* (Cambridge, 2008).

Duplessis, Robert, *The Material Atlantic: Clothing, Commerce, and Colonization in the Atlantic World, 1650–1800* (Cambridge, 2016).

Erlin, Matt, *Necessary Luxuries: Books, Literature, and the Culture of Consumption in Germany, 1770–1815* (Ithaca, NY, 2014).

Lemire, Beverly, *Global Trade and the Transformations of Consumer Cultures: The Material World Remade, c. 1500–1820* (Cambridge, 2018).

McKendrick, Neil, John Brewer, and J. H. Plumb, *The Birth of a Consumer Society: The Commercialization of Eighteenth-Century England* (Bloomington, IN, 1982).

North, Michael, *"Material Delight and the Joy of Living": Cultural Consumption in the Age of Enlightenment in Germany*, trans. Pamela Selwyn (New York, 2016).

Overton, Mark, Jane Whittle, Darron Dean, and Andrew Hann, *Production and Consumption in English Households, 1600–1750* (New York, 2012).

Peck, Linda Levy, *Consuming Splendor: Society and Culture in Seventeenth-Century England* (Cambridge, 2005).

Riello, Giorgio, *Cotton: The Fabric That Made the Modern World* (Cambridge, 2013).

Roche, Daniel, *A History of Everyday Things: The Birth of Consumption in France, 1600–1800*, trans. Brian Pearce (Cambridge, 2000).

Rublack, Ulinka, *Dressing Up: Cultural Identity in Renaissance Europe* (Oxford, 2010).

Styles, John, *The Dress of the People: Everyday Fashion in Eighteenth-Century England* (New Haven, CT, 2007).

Styles, John, and Amanda Vickery, eds., *Gender, Taste, and Material Culture in Britain and North America, 1700–1830* (New Haven, CT, 2006).

Trentmann, Frank, *Empire of Things: How We Became a World of Consumers, from the Fifteenth Century to the Twenty-First* (New York, 2016).

Introduction

Clunas, Craig, *Superfluous Things: Material Culture and Social Status in Early Modern China* (Cambridge, 1991).

de Vries, Jan, "The Industrial Revolution and the Industrious Revolution," *The Journal of Economic History* 54 (June 1994), pp. 249–270.

Frank, Robert, *Luxury Fever: Money and Happiness in an Era of Excess* (New York, 1999).

McKendrick, Neil, John Brewer, and J. H. Plumb, *The Birth of a Consumer Society: The Commercialization of Eighteenth-Century England* (Bloomington, IN, 1982).

Pomeranz, Kenneth, *The Great Divergence: China, Europe, and the Making of the Modern World Economy* (Princeton, NJ, 2000).

Roche, Daniel, *The Culture of Clothing: Dress and Fashion in the Ancien Regime*, trans. Jean Birrell (Cambridge, 1996).

A History of Everyday Things: The Birth of Consumption in France, 1600–1800, trans. Brian Pearce (Cambridge, 2000).

Schama, Simon, *The Embarrassment of Riches: An Interpretation of Dutch Culture in the Golden Age* (New York, 1987).

Schor, Juliet, *The Overspent American: Upscaling, Downshifting, and the New Consumer* (New York, 1998).

Thirsk, Joan, *Economic Policy and Projects: The Development of a Consumer Society in Early Modern England* (Oxford, 1978).

Trentmann, Frank, ed., *The Oxford Handbook of the History of Consumption* (Oxford, 2012).

Chapter 1

Berg, Maxine, *Luxury and Pleasure in Eighteenth-Century Britain* (Oxford, 2005).

Blondé, Bruno, and Natacha Coquery, eds., *Retailers and Consumer Changes in Early Modern Europe: England, France, Italy and the Low Countries* (Tours, 2005).

Brown, Kathleen, *Foul Bodies: Cleanliness in Early America* (New Haven, CT, 2009).

Claverías, Belén Moreno, "L'inégalité comme norme: Modèles de consommation dans l'Espagne préindustrielle," in *Consommateurs & consommation XVIIe – XXIe siècle: Regards franco-espagnols* (Perpignan, 2015), pp. 15–46.

Coquery, Natacha, *L'hôtel aristocratique: Le marché du luxe à Paris au XVIIIe siècle* (Paris, 1998).

Tenir Boutique à Paris au XVIIIe siècle (Paris, 2011).

Crowston, Clare Haru, *Fabricating Women: The Seamstresses of Old Regime France, 1675–1791* (Durham, NC, 2001).

Credit, Fashion, Sex: Economies of Regard in Old Regime France (Durham, NC, 2013).

da Vinha, Mathieu, Catherine Lanoë, and Bruno Laurioux, eds., *Cultures de cour, cultures du corps, XIVe–XVIIIe siècle* (Paris, 2011).

de Vries, Jan, *The First Modern Economy: Success, Failure, and Perseverance of the Dutch Economy, 1500–1815* (Cambridge, 1997).

The Industrious Revolution: Consumer Behavior and the Household Economy, 1650 to the Present (Cambridge, 2008).

DuPlessis, Robert, *The Material Atlantic: Clothing, Commerce, and Colonization in the Atlantic World, 1650–1800* (Cambridge, 2016).

Earle, Rebecca, *The Body of the Conquistador: Food, Race and the Colonial Experience in Spanish America, 1492–1700* (Cambridge, 2012).

Elias, Norbert, *The Civilizing Process: The History of Manners*, trans. Edmund Jephcott (Oxford, 2000).

Fairchilds, Cissie, "The Production and Marketing of Populuxe Goods in Eighteenth-Century Paris," in John Brewer and Roy Porter, eds., *Consumption and the World of Goods* (London, 1993), pp. 228–248.

Farge, Arlette, *Fragile Lives: Violence, Power, and Solidarity in Eighteenth-Century Paris*, trans. Carol Shelton (Cambridge, MA, 1993).

Finn, Margot, "Men's Things: Masculine Possession in the Consumer Revolution," *Social History* 25 (May 2000), pp. 133–155.

Fox, Robert, and Anthony Turner, eds., *Luxury Trades and Consumerism in Ancien Régime Paris* (Aldershot, 1998).

Goldthwaite, Richard, *Wealth and the Demand for Art in Italy, 1300–1600* (Baltimore, 1993).

Grafe, Regina, *Distant Tyranny: Markets, Power, and Backwardness in Spain, 1650–1800* (Princeton, NJ, 2012).

Hoffman, Philip, David S. Jacks, Patricia A. Levin, and Peter H. Lindert, "Sketching the Rise of Real Inequality in Early Modern Europe," in Robert Allen, Tommy Bengtsson, and Martin Dribe, eds., *Living Standards in the Past: New Perspectives on Well-Being in Asia and Europe* (Oxford, 2005), pp. 131–172.

Jones, Jennifer, *Sexing la Mode: Gender, Fashion, and Commercial Culture in Old Regime France* (Oxford, 2004).

Kwass, Michael, "Big Hair: A Wig History of Consumption in Eighteenth-Century France," *The American Historical Review* 111 (June 2006), pp. 631–659.

Margairaz, Dominique, "City and Country," in Frank Trentmann, ed., *The Oxford Handbook of the History of Consumption* (Oxford, 2012).

Martin, Anne Smart, *Buying into the World of Goods: Early Consumers in Backcountry Virginia* (Baltimore, 2008).

McCants, Anne, "Exotic Goods, Popular Consumption, and the Standard of Living: Thinking about Globalization in the Early Modern World," *Journal of World History* 18 (Dec. 2007), pp. 433–462.

Mintz, Sydney, *Sweetness and Power: The Place of Sugar in Modern History* (New York, 1985).

Morgan, Philip, *Slave Counterpoint: Black Culture in the Eighteenth-Century Chesapeake and Lowcountry* (Chapel Hill, NC, 1998).

North, Michael, *"Material Delight and the Joy of Living": Cultural Consumption in the Age of Enlightenment in Germany*, trans. Pamela Selwyn (New York, 2016).

Overton, Mark, Jane Whittle, Darron Dean, and Andrew Hann, *Production and Consumption in English Households, 1600–1750* (New York, 2012).

Pardailhé-Galabrun, Annik, *The Birth of Intimacy: Privacy and Domestic Life in Early Modern Paris*, trans. Jocelyn Phelps (Philadelphia, 1991).

Peck, Linda Levy, *Consuming Splendor: Society and Culture in Seventeenth-Century England* (Cambridge, 2005).

Roche, Daniel, *The Culture of Clothing: Dress and Fashion in the Ancien Regime*, trans. Jean Birrell (Cambridge, 1996).

  A History of Everyday Things: The Birth of Consumption in France, 1600–1800, trans. Brian Pearce (Cambridge, 2000).

Rublack, Ulinka, *Dressing Up: Cultural Identity in Renaissance Europe* (Oxford, 2010).

Sarti, Raffaella, *Europe at Home: Family and Material Culture 1500–1800*, trans. Allan Cameron (New Haven, CT, 2002).

Schama, Simon, *The Embarrassment of Riches: An Interpretation of Dutch Culture in the Golden Age* (New York, 1987).

Shammas, Carole, *The Pre-industrial Consumer in England and America* (Los Angeles, 1990).

Smith, Woodruff, *Consumption and the Making of Respectability* (New York, 2002).

Sombart, Werner, *Luxury and Capitalism*, trans. W. R. Dittmar (Ann Arbor, MI, 1967).

Stobart, Jon, *Sugar and Spice: Grocers and Groceries in Provincial England, 1650–1830* (Oxford, 2013).

Styles, John, *The Dress of the People: Everyday Fashion in Eighteenth-Century England* (New Haven, CT, 2007).

Styles, John, and Amanda Vickery, eds., *Gender, Taste, and Material Culture in Britain and North America, 1700–1830* (New Haven, CT, 2006).

Thomas, Keith, *In Pursuit of Civility: Manners and Civilization in Early Modern England* (New Haven, CT, 2018).

Veblen, Thorstein, *The Theory of the Leisure Class* (1899; New York, 1975).

Walker, Tamara J., *Exquisite Slaves: Race, Clothing, and Status in Colonial Lima* (Cambridge, 2017).

Weatherill, Lorna, *Consumer Behaviour and Material Culture in Britain, 1660–1760* (London, 1988).

White, Sophie, "Geographies of Slave Consumption: French Colonial Louisiana and a World of Goods," *Winterthur Portfolio* 45 (June 2011), pp. 229–248.

Chapter 2

Allen, Robert, "Progress and Poverty in Early Modern Europe," *The Economic History Review* 56 (August 2003), pp. 403–443.

Baily, C. A., *The Birth of the Modern World, 1780–1914* (Malden, MA, 2004).

Berg, Maxine, "Asian Luxuries and the Making of the European Consumer Revolution," in Maxine Berg and Elizabeth Eger, eds., *Luxury in the Eighteenth Century* (New York, 2003), pp. 228–244.

Luxury and Pleasure in Eighteenth-Century Britain (Oxford, 2005).

Berg, Maxine, Felicia Gottman, Hanna Hodacs, and Chris Nierstrasz, eds., *Goods from the East, 1600–1800: Trading Eurasia* (Houndmills, 2015).

Burbank, Jane, and Frederick Cooper, *Empires in World History: Power and the Politics of Difference* (Princeton, NJ, 2010).

Burnard, Trevor, and John Garrigus, *The Plantation Machine: Atlantic Capitalism in French Saint-Domingue and British Jamaica* (Philadelphia, 2016).

Butel, Paul, *Histoire du thé* (Paris, 1989).

Claverías, Belén Moreno, "L'inégalité comme norme: Modèles de consommation dans l'Espagne préindustrielle," in Antonio Escudero and Nicolas Marty, eds., *Consommateurs & consommation XVIIe–XXIe siècle: Regards franco-espagnols* (Perpignan, 2015), pp. 15–46.

de Vries, Jan, "Connecting Europe and Asia: A Quantitative Analysis of the Cape-Route Trade, 1497–1795," in Dennis Flynn, Arturo Giráldez, and Richard von Glahn, eds., *Global Connections and Monetary History, 1470–1800* (Aldershot, 2003), pp. 35–106.

The Industrious Revolution: Consumer Behavior and the Household Economy, 1650 to the Present (Cambridge, 2008).

de Zwart, Pim, and Jan Luiten van Zanden, *The Origins of Globalization: World Trade in the Making of the Global Economy, 1500–1800* (Cambridge, 2018).

Findlay, Ronald, and Kevin O'Rourke, *Power and Plenty: Trade, War, and the World Economy in the Second Millennium* (Princeton, NJ, 2007).

Flynn, Dennis, and Arturo Giráldez, "Born with a 'Silver Spoon': The Origin of World Trade in 1571," *Journal of World History* 6 (1995), pp. 201–221.

Gerritsen, Anne, and Giorgio Riello, eds., *The Global Lives of Things: The Material Culture of Connections in the Early Modern World* (New York, 2016).

Goodman, Jordan, "Excitantia: Or, How Enlightenment Europe Took to Soft Drugs," in Jordan Goodman, Paul E. Lovejoy, and Andrew Sherratt, eds., *Consuming Habits: Drugs in History and Anthropology* (London, 1995), pp. 126–147.

Grafe, Regina, *Distant Tyranny: Markets, Power, and Backwardness in Spain, 1650–1800* (Princeton, NJ, 2012).

Hardwick, Julie, "Fractured Domesticity in the Old Regime: Families and Global Goods in Eighteenth-Century France," *The American Historical Review* 124 (October 2019), pp. 1267–1277.

Haudrère, Philippe, *La Compagnie française des Indes au XVIIIe siècle* (Paris, 2005).

Hoffman, Philip, *Growth in a Traditional Society: The French Countryside, 1450–1815* (Princeton, NJ, 1996).

Hopkins, A. G., ed., *Globalization in World History* (New York, 2002).

Inikori, Joseph E., "English versus Indian Cotton Textiles: The Impact of Imports on Cotton Textile Production in West Africa," in Giorgio Riello and Tirthankar Roy, eds., *How India Clothed the World: The World of South Asian Textiles, 1500–1800* (Leiden, 2009), pp. 85–114.

Klein, Herbert S., *The Atlantic Slave Trade* (Cambridge, 1999).

Kriger, Colleen E., "Guinea Cloth: Production and Consumption of Cotton Textiles in West Africa before and during the Atlantic Slave Trade," in Giorgio Riello and Prasannan Parthasarathi, eds., *The Spinning World: A Global History of Cotton Textiles, 1200–1850* (Oxford, 2011), pp. 105–126.

Kwass, Michael, *Contraband: Louis Mandrin and the Making of a Global Underground* (Cambridge, MA, 2014).

Lemire, Beverly, *Global Trade and the Transformation of Consumer Cultures: The Material World Remade, c. 1500–1820* (Cambridge, 2018).

Liu, Andrew B., *Tea War: A History of Capitalism in China and India* (New Haven, CT, 2020).

McCabe, Ina Baghdiantz, *A History of Global Consumption, 1500–1800* (New York, 2015).

McCants, Anne, "Poor Consumers as Global Consumers: The Diffusion of Tea and Coffee Drinking in the Eighteenth Century," *The Economic History Review* 61 (2008), pp. 172–200.

McNeill, J. R., *Mosquito Empires: Ecology and War in the Greater Caribbean, 1620–1914* (Cambridge, 2010).

Mintz, Sydney, *Sweetness and Power: The Place of Sugar in Modern History* (New York, 1985).

Muldrew, Craig, *Food, Energy, and the Creation of Industriousness: Work and Material Culture in Agrarian England, 1550–1780* (Cambridge, 2011).

Nierstrasz, Chris, *Rivalry for Trade in Tea and Textiles: The English and Dutch East India Companies (1700–1800)*, trans. Pamela Selwyn (New York, 2015).

O'Rourke, Kevin, and Jeffrey Gale Williamson, "When Did Globalisation Begin?" *European Review of Economic History* 6 (April 2002), pp. 23–50.

Ogilvie, Sheilagh, "Consumption, Social Capital, and the 'Industrious Revolution' in Early Modern Germany," *Journal of Economic History* 70 (June 2010), pp. 287–325.

Paquette, Gabriel, *The European Seaborne Empires from the Thirty Years' War to the Age of Revolutions* (New Haven, CT, 2019).

Pomeranz, Kenneth, *The Great Divergence: China, Europe, and the Making of the Modern World Economy* (Princeton, NJ, 2000).

Potofsky, Allan, *Constructing Paris in the Age of Revolution* (Basingstoke, 2009).

Riello, Giorgio, and Tirthankar Roy, eds., *How India Clothed the World: The World of South Asian Textiles, 1500–1800* (Leiden, 2009).

Riello, Giorgio and Prasannan Parthasarathi, eds., *The Spinning World: A Global History of Cotton Textiles, 1200-1850* (Oxford, 2011).

Rothschild, Emma, "Isolation and Economic Life in Eighteenth-Century France," *The American Historical Review* 119 (October 2014), pp. 1055–1082.

Ruderman, Anne Elizabeth, "Supplying the Slave Trade: How Europeans Met African Demand for European Manufactured Products, Commodities and Re-exports, 1670–1790" (Dissertation, Yale University, 2016).

Shammas, Carole, *The Pre-industrial Consumer in England and America* (Los Angeles, 1990).

"Changes in English and Anglo-American Consumption from 1550 to 1800," in John Brewer and Roy Porter, eds., *Consumption and the World of Goods* (London, 1994), pp. 177–205.

Stobart, Jon, *Sugar and Spice: Grocers and Groceries in Provincial England, 1650–1830* (Oxford, 2016).

Thomson, J. K. J., *A Distinctive Industrialization: Cotton in Barcelona 1728–1832* (Cambridge, 1992).

van Nederveen Meerkerk, Elise, "Couples Cooperating? Dutch Textile Workers, Family Labour and the 'Industrious Revolution,' c. 1600–1800," *Continuity and Change* 23 (August 2008), pp. 237–266.

van Zanden, Jan Luiten, "Early Modern Economic Growth: A Survey of the European Economy, 1500–1800," in Maarten Prak, ed., *Early Modern Capitalism: Economic and Social Change in Europe, 1400–1800* (London, 2001), pp. 69–87.

Vicente, Marta, *Clothing the Spanish Empire: Families and the Calico Trade in the Early Modern Atlantic World* (New York, 2006).

Villeret, Maud, *Le goût de l'or blanc: Le sucre en France au xviiie siècle* (Rennes, 2017).

Voth, Hans-Joachim, "Work and the Sirens of Consumption in Eighteenth-Century London," in Marina Bianchi, ed., *The Active Consumer: Novelty and Surprise in Consumer Choice* (London, 1998), pp. 143–173.

Watts, David, *The West Indies: Patterns of Development, Culture and Environmental Change since 1492* (Cambridge, 1990).

Chapter 3

Berg, Maxine, and Helen Clifford, "Selling Consumption in the Eighteenth Century: Advertising and the Trade Card in Britain and France," *Cultural and Social History* 4 (2007), pp. 145–170.

Blondé, Bruno, and Natacha Coquery, eds., *Retailers and Consumer Changes in Early Modern Europe: England, France, Italy and the Low Countries* (Tours, 2005).

Collins, James, "Women and the Birth of Modern Consumer Capitalism," in Daryl Hafter and Nina Kushner, eds., *Women and Work in Eighteenth-Century France* (Baton Rouge, LA, 2015), pp. 152–176.

Coquery, Natacha, "Language of Success: Marketing and Distributing Semi-luxury Goods in Eighteenth-Century Paris," *Journal of Design History* 17 (2004), pp. 71–89.

Tenir Boutique à Paris au XVIIIe siècle (Paris, 2011).

"Selling India and China in Eighteenth-Century Paris," in Maxine Berg, Felicia Gottmann, Hanna Hodacs, and Chris Nierstrasz, eds., *Goods from the East, 1600–1800: Trading Eurasia* (Houndmills, 2015), pp. 229–244.

Cox, Nancy, *The Complete Tradesman: A Study of Retailing, 1550–1820* (New York, 2000).

Crowston, Clare Haru, *Fabricating Women: The Seamstresses of Old Regime France, 1675–1791* (Durham, NC, 2001).
   Credit, Fashion, Sex: Economies of Regard in Old Regime France (Durham, NC, 2013).
Fairchilds, Cissie, "The Production and Marketing of Populuxe Goods in Eighteenth-Century Paris," in John Brewer and Roy Porter, eds., *Consumption and the World of Goods* (London, 1993), pp. 228–248.
Finn, Margot, "Women, Consumption and Coverture in England, c. 1760–1860," *Historical Journal* 39 (September 1996), pp. 703–722.
   "Men's Things: Masculine Possession in the Consumer Revolution," *Social History* 25 (2000), pp. 133–155.
Fontaine, Laurence, *History of Pedlars in Europe* (Durham, NC, 1996).
   ed., *Alternative Exchanges: Second-Hand Circulations from the Sixteenth Century to the Present* (New York, 2008).
   Le Marché: Histoire et usages d'une conquête sociale (Paris, 2014).
Hardwick, Julie, *Family Business: Litigation and the Political Economies of Daily Life in Early Modern France* (Oxford, 2009).
   "Fractured Domesticity in the Old Regime: Families and Global Goods in Eighteenth-Century France," *The American Historical Review* 124 (October 2019), pp. 1267–1277.
Jones, Colin, "The Great Chain of Buying: Medical Advertisement, the Bourgeois Public Sphere, and the Origins of the French Revolution," *The American Historical Review* 101 (February 1996), pp. 13–40.
Jones, Jennifer, *Sexing la Mode: Gender, Fashion, and Commercial Culture in Old Regime France* (Oxford, 2004).
Kaplan, Steven L., *The Bakers of Paris and the Bread Question, 1700–1775* (Durham, NC, 1996).
Kowaleski-Wallace, Elizabeth, *Consuming Subjects: Women, Shopping, and Business in the Eighteenth Century* (New York, 1997).
Kwass, Michael, "Big Hair: A Wig History of Consumption in Eighteenth-Century France," *The American Historical Review* 111 (June 2006), pp. 631–659.
   Contraband: Louis Mandrin and the Making of a Global Underground (Cambridge, MA, 2014).
Lanoë, Catherine, *Le Poudre et le fard: Une histoire des cosmétiques de la Renaissance aux Lumières* (Seyssel, 2008).
Lemire, Beverly, "Peddling Fashion: Salesmen, Pawnbrokers, Taylors, Thieves and the Second-Hand Clothes Trade in England, c. 1700–1800," *Textile History* 22 (1991), pp. 67–82.
Lyon-Caen, Nicolas, "Les marchands du temple. Les boutiques du Palais de justice de Paris aux xvie–xviiie siècles," *Revue historique*, 674 (2015), pp. 323–352.
Margairaz, Dominique, *Foires et marchés dans la France préindustrielle* (Paris, 1988).
Martin, Ann Smart, *Buying into the World of Goods: Early Consumers in Backcountry Virginia* (Baltimore, 2008).
Martin, Morag, *Selling Beauty: Cosmetics, Commerce, and French Society, 1750–1830* (Baltimore, 2009).

Miller, Lesley, "Paris–Lyon–Paris: Dialogue in the Design and Distribution of Patterned Silks in the Eighteenth Century," in Robert Fox and Anthony Turner, eds., *Luxury Trades and Consumerism in Ancien Régime Paris* (Farnham, 1998), pp. 139–167.

Mitchell, Ian, *Tradition and Innovation in English Retailing, 1700 to 1850* (London, 2016).

Mui, Hoh-Cheung, and Lorna H. Mui, *Shops and Shopkeeping in Eighteenth-Century England* (Montreal, 1989).

Muldrew, Craig, *An Economy of Obligation: The Culture of Credit and Social Relations in Early Modern England* (New York, 1998).

Navarro, Daniel Muñoz, ed., *Comprar, vender y consumir. Nuevas aportaciones a la historia del consumo en la España moderna* (València, 2011).

Ogilvie, Sheilagh, *A Bitter Living: Women, Markets, and Social Capital in Early Modern Germany* (Oxford, 2003).

"Consumption, Social Capital, and the 'Industrious Revolution' in Early Modern Germany," *The Journal of Economic History* 70 (June 2010), pp. 287–325.

Poni, Carlo, "Fashion as Flexible Production: The Strategies of the Lyons Silk Merchants in the Eighteenth Century," in Charles Sabel and Jonathan Zeitlin, eds., *World of Possibilities: Flexibility and Mass Production in Western Industrialization* (Cambridge, 1977), pp. 37–74.

Sargentson, Carolyn, *Merchants and Luxury Markets: The Marchands Merciers of Eighteenth-Century Paris* (London, 1996).

Sewell, William, "The Empire of Fashion and the Rise of Capitalism in Eighteenth-Century France," *Past & Present* 206 (February 2010), pp. 81–120.

Stobart, Jon, *Sugar and Spice: Grocers and Groceries in Provincial England, 1650–1830* (Oxford, 2016).

Styles, John, "Product Innovation in Early Modern London," *Past & Present* 168 (August 2000), pp. 124–169.

Torra, L., "Las botigues de teles de Barcelona: aportación al estudio de la oferta de tejidos y del crédito al consumo (1650–1800)," *Revista de Historia Económica* 21 (2003), pp. 89–105.

van den Heuvel, Danielle, "Policing Peddlers: The Prosecution of Illegal Street Trade in Eighteenth-Century Dutch Towns," *The Historical Journal* 58 (June 2015), pp. 367–392.

van den Heuvel, Danielle, and Sheilagh Ogilvie, "Retail Development in the Consumer Revolution: The Netherlands, c. 1670–c. 1815," *Explorations in Economic History* 50 (January 2013), pp. 69–87.

Vickery, Amanda, "His and Hers: Gender, Consumption, and Household Accounting in Eighteenth-Century England," in Lyndal Roper and Ruth Harris, eds., *The Art of Survival: Essays in Honor of Olwen Hufton* (Oxford, 2006), pp. 12–38.

Walsh, Claire, "Shop Design and the Display of Goods in Eighteenth-Century London," *Journal of Design History* 8 (1995), pp. 157–176.

Welch, Evelyn, *Shopping in the Renaissance: Consumer Cultures in Italy, 1400–1600* (New Haven, CT, 2005).

Chapter 4

Bennett, Tony, Mike Savage, Elizabeth Silva, et al., *Culture, Class, Distinction* (New York, 2009).

Bourdieu, Pierre, *Distinction: A Social Critique of the Judgement of Taste*, trans. Richard Nice (Cambridge, MA, 1984).

Brown, Kathleen, *Foul Bodies: Cleanliness in Early America* (New Haven, CT, 2009).

Cavallo, Sandra, *Artisans of the Body in Early Modern Italy: Identities, Families and Masculinities* (Manchester, 2007).

Crowley, John, "The Sensibility of Comfort," *The American Historical Review* 104 (June 1999), pp. 749–782.

The Invention of Comfort: Sensibilities and Design in Early Modern Britain and Early America (Baltimore, 2001).

da Vinha, Mathieu, Catherine Lanoë, and Bruno Laurioux, eds., *Cultures de cour, cultures du corps, XIVe–XVIIIe siècle* (Paris, 2011).

DeJean, Joan, *The Age of Comfort: When Paris Discovered Casual – And the Modern Home Began* (New York, 2009).

Dobie, Madeleine, *Trading Places: Colonization and Slavery in Eighteenth-Century French Culture* (Ithaca, NY, 2010).

Edelstein, Dan, *The Enlightenment: A Genealogy* (Chicago, 2010).

Elias, Norbert, *The Civilizing Process: The History of Manners*, trans. Edmund Jephcott (Oxford, 2000).

Fairchilds, Cissie, "Marketing the Counter-Reformation," in Christine Adams, Jack R. Censer, and Lisa Jane Graham, eds., *Visions and Revisions of Eighteenth-Century France* (University Park, PA, 1997), pp. 31–59.

Garrioch, David, "Varieties of Religious Behavior in Eighteenth-Century Paris: The Material Culture of Leaders of Confraternities," in Mita Choudhury and Daniel J. Watkins, eds., *Belief and Politics in Enlightenment France* (Oxford, 2019), pp. 181–196.

Goodman, Dena, *Becoming a Woman in the Age of Letters* (Ithaca, NY, 2009).

Jones, Colin, *The Smile Revolution in Eighteenth-Century Paris* (Oxford, 2014).

Jones, Jennifer, *Sexing La Mode: Gender, Fashion, and Commercial Culture in Old Regime France* (Oxford, 2004).

Kopytoff, Igor, "The Cultural Biography of Things: Commoditization as Process," in Arjun Appadurai, ed., *Social Life of Things: Commodities in Cultural Perspective* (Cambridge, 1986), pp. 64–92.

Kwass, Michael, "Big Hair: A Wig History of Consumption in Eighteenth-Century France," *The American Historical Review* 111 (June 2006), pp. 653–656.

Lemire, Beverly, "Domesticating the Exotic: Floral Culture and the East India Calico Trade with England, c. 1600–1800," *Textile* 1 (2003), pp. 64–85.

Lilti, Antoine, *The World of the Salons*, trans. Lydia G. Cochrane (Oxford, 2006).

Martin, Ann Smart, "Material Things and Cultural Meanings: Notes on the Study of Early American Material Culture," *The William and Mary Quarterly* 52 (1996), pp. 5–12.

Miller, Daniel, *Stuff* (Cambridge, 2010).

Norton, Marcy, *Sacred Gifts, Profane Pleasures: A History of Tobacco and Chocolate in the Atlantic World* (Ithaca, NY, 2008).

Pardailhé-Galabrun, Annik, *The Birth of Intimacy: Privacy and Domestic Life in Early Modern Paris*, trans. Jocelyn Phelps (Philadelphia, 1991).

Porter, Roy, *The Creation of the Modern World: The Untold Story of the British Enlightenment* (New York, 2000).

Purdy, Daniel, *The Tyranny of Elegance: Consumer Cosmopolitanism in the Era of Goethe* (Baltimore, 1998).

Rappaport, Erika, *The Thirst for Empire: How Tea Shaped the Modern World* (Princeton, NJ, 2017).

Roche, Daniel, *A History of Everyday Things: The Birth of Consumption in France, 1600–1800*, trans. Brian Pearce (Cambridge, 2000).

Rublack, Ulinka, *Dressing Up: Cultural Identity in Renaissance Europe* (Oxford, 2010).

Schmidt, Benjamin, *Inventing Exoticism: Geography, Globalism, and Europe's Early Modern World* (Philadelphia, 2015).

Sewell, William, *Capitalism and the Emergence of Civic Equality in Eighteenth-Century France* (Chicago, 2021).

Simmel, Georg, "Fashion," *American Journal of Sociology* 62 (1957), pp. 541–558.

Smith, Woodruff, *Consumption and the Making of Respectability* (New York, 2002).

Spang, Rebecca, *The Invention of the Restaurant: Paris and Modern Gastronomic Culture* (Cambridge, MA, 2001).

Spary, Emma, *Eating the Enlightenment: Food and the Sciences in Paris, 1670-1760* (Chicago, 2012).

Styles, John, and Amanda Vickery, eds., *Gender, Taste, and Material Culture in Britain and North America, 1700–1830* (New Haven, CT, 2006).

Thomas, Keith, *In Pursuit of Civility: Manners and Civilization in Early Modern England* (New Haven, CT, 2018).

Veblen, Thorstein, *The Theory of the Leisure Class* (1899; New York, 1975).

Vigarello, Georges, *Concepts of Cleanliness: Changing Attitudes in France since the Middle Ages*, trans. Jean Birrell (Cambridge, 1988).

Chapter 5

Armory, Hugh, and David Hall, eds., *A History of the Book in America, vol. 1, The Colonial Book in the Atlantic World* (Cambridge, 2000).

Blanning, T. C. W., *The Culture of Power and the Power of Culture: Old Regime Europe 1660–1789* (Oxford, 2002).

Brewer, John, *Pleasures of the Imagination: English Culture in the Eighteenth Century* (New York, 1997).

Brophy, James, *Popular Culture and the Public Sphere in the Rhineland 1800–1850* (Cambridge, 2007).

Burke, Peter, *Popular Culture in Early Modern Europe* (New York, 1978).

Cavallo, Guglielmo, and Roger Chartier, "Introduction," in Guglielmo Cavallo and Roger Chartier, eds., *A History of Reading in the West*, trans. Lydia Cochrane (Cambridge, 1999), pp. 1–36.

Chartier, Roger, *The Cultural Origins of the French Revolution*, trans. Lydia Cochrane (Durham, NC, 1991).

Cowan, Brian, *The Social Life of Coffee: The Emergence of the British Coffeehouse* (New Haven, CT, 2005).

Engelsing, Rolf, *Der Bürger als Leser: Lesergeschichte in Deutschland, 1500–1800* (Stuttgart, 1974).

Farge, Arlette, *Subversive Words: Public Opinion in Eighteenth-Century France*, trans. Rosemary Morris (Cambridge, 1994).

Goodman, Dena, *The Republic of Letters: A Cultural History of the French Enlightenment* (Ithaca, NY, 1994).

Habermas, Jürgen, *The Structural Transformation of the Public Sphere*, trans. Thomas Burger (Cambridge, MA, 1989).

Isherwood, Robert, *Farce and Fantasy: Popular Entertainment in Eighteenth-Century Paris* (Oxford, 1986).

Jones, Colin, "Bourgeois Revolution Revivified: 1789 and Social Change," in Colin Lucas, ed., *Rewriting the French Revolution* (Oxford, 1991), pp. 69–118.

"The Great Chain of Buying: Medical Advertisement, the Bourgeois Public Sphere, and the Origins of the French Revolution," *The American Historical Review* 101 (February 1996), pp. 13–40.

Lilti, Antoine, *The World of the Salons: Sociability and Worldliness in Eighteenth-Century Paris*, trans. Lydia G. Cochrane (Oxford, 2006).

The Invention of Celebrity, 1750–1850, trans. Lynn Jeffress (Cambridge, 2017).

North, Michael, *"Material Delight and the Joy of Living": Cultural Consumption in the Age of Enlightenment in Germany*, trans. Pamela Selwyn (New York, 2016).

Pettegree, Andrew, *The Invention of News: How the World Came to Know About Itself* (New Haven, CT, 2014).

Pincus, Steve, "'Coffee Politicians Does Create': Coffeehouses and Restoration Political Culture," *The Journal of Modern History* 67 (December 1995), pp. 807–834.

Porter, Roy, *The Creation of the Modern World: The Untold Story of the British Enlightenment* (New York, 2000).

Raven, James, "The Book as a Commodity," in Michael Suarez and Michael Turner, eds., *The Cambridge History of the Book in Britain* (Cambridge, 2009), pp. 83–117.

Rigogne, Thierry, "Readers and Reading in Cafés, 1660–1800," *French Historical Studies* 41 (2018), pp. 473–494.

Roche, Daniel, *France in the Enlightenment*, trans. Arthur Goldhammer (Cambridge, MA, 1998).

Sewell, William, "Connecting Capitalism to the French Revolution: The Parisian Promenade and the Origins of Civic Equality in Eighteenth-Century France," *Critical Historical Studies* 1 (Spring 2014), pp. 5–46.

Capitalism and the Emergence of Civic Equality in Eighteenth-Century France (Chicago, 2021).

Spary, Emma, *Eating the Enlightenment: Food and the Sciences in Paris, 1670–1760* (Chicago, 2014).

Suarez, Michael, "Towards a Bibliometric Analysis of the Surviving Record, 1701–1800," in Michael Suarez and Michael Turner, eds. *The Cambridge History of the Book in Britain* (Cambridge, 2009), pp. 37–65.

van Horn Melton, James, *The Rise of the Public in Enlightenment Europe* (Cambridge, 2001).

Williams, Abigail, *The Social Life of Books: Reading Together in the Eighteenth-Century Home* (New Haven, CT, 2017).

Wittmann, Reinhard, "Was There a Reading Revolution at the End of the Eighteenth Century?" in Guglielmo Cavallo and Roger Chartier, eds., *A History of Reading in the West*, trans. Lydia Cochrane (Cambridge, 1999), pp. 284–312.

Chapter 6

Berg, Maxine, and Helen Clifford, eds., *Consumers and Luxury: Consumer Culture in Europe 1650–1850* (Manchester, 1999).

Berg, Maxine, and Elizabeth Eger, eds., *Luxury in the Eighteenth Century: Debates, Desires and Delectable Goods* (New York, 2002).

Berry, Christopher, *The Idea of Luxury: A Conceptual and Historical Investigation* (Cambridge, 1994).

Brewer, Anthony, "Luxury and Economic Development: David Hume and Adam Smith," *Scottish Journal of Political Economy* 45 (1998), pp. 78–98.

Claverías, Belén Moreno, "L'inégalité comme norme: Modèles de consommation dans l'Espagne préindustrielle," in *Consommateurs & consommation XVIIe–XXIe siècle: Regards franco-espagnols* (Perpignan, 2015), pp. 15–46.

Coleman, Charly, *The Spirit of French Capitalism: Economic Theology in the Age of Enlightenment* (Stanford, CA, 2021).

Crowston, Clare Haru, *Credit, Fashion, Sex: Economies of Regard in Old Regime France* (Durham, NC, 2013).

Hilton, Mathew, "Legacy of Luxury: Moralities of Consumption since the 18th Century," *Journal of Consumer Culture* 4 (2004), pp. 101–123.

Hirschman, Albert O., *The Passions and the Interests: Political Arguments for Capitalism before Its Triumph* (Princeton, NJ, 1977).

Hont, Istvan, "The Early Enlightenment Debate on Commerce and Luxury," in Mark Goldie and Robert Wokler, eds., *The Cambridge History of Eighteenth-Century Political Thought* (Cambridge, 2006), pp. 379–418.

Hundert, E. G., *The Enlightenment's Fable: Bernard Mandeville and the Discovery of Society* (Cambridge, 1994).

Jones, Jennifer, "Repackaging Rousseau: Femininity and Fashion in Old Regime France," *French Historical Studies* 18 (Fall 1994), pp. 939–961.

Sexing La Mode: Gender, Fashion, and Commercial Culture in Old Regime France (Oxford, 2004).

Kwass, Michael, "Ordering the World of Goods: Consumer Revolution and the Classification of Objects in Eighteenth-Century France," *Representations* 82 (Spring 2003), pp. 87–116.

"Consumption and the World of Ideas: Consumer Revolution and the Moral Economy of the Marquis de Mirabeau," *Eighteenth-Century Studies* 37 (Winter 2004), pp. 187–214.

"Big Hair: A Wig History of Consumption in Eighteenth-Century France," *The American Historical Review* 111 (June 2006), pp. 631–659.

"'Le superflu, chose très nécessaire': Physiocracy and Its Discontents in the Eighteenth-Century Luxury Debate," in Steven L. Kaplan and Sophus Reinert, eds., *The Economic Turn: Recasting Political Economy in Enlightenment Europe* (London, 2019), pp. 117–138.

Maza, Sarah, "Luxury, Morality, and Social Change: Why There Was No Middle-Class Consciousness in Prerevolutionary France," *The Journal of Modern History* 69 (June 1997), pp. 199–229.

Morize, André, *L'Apologie du luxe au XVIIIe siècle et "Le Mondain" de Voltaire* (Geneva, 1970).

Perrot, Philippe, *Le luxe: une richesse entre faste et confort, XVIIIe–XIX siècle* (Paris, 1995).

Pocock, J. G. A., *The Machiavellian Moment: Florentine Political Thought and the Atlantic Republican Tradition* (Princeton, NJ, 1975).

Virtue, Commerce, and History (Cambridge, 1985).

Provost, Audrey, *Le luxe, les Lumières et la Révolution* (Seyssel, 2014).

Reinert, Sophus, and Steven L. Kaplan, eds., *The Economic Turn: Recasting Political Economy in Enlightenment Europe* (London, 2019).

Ross, Ellen, "Mandeville, Melon, and Voltaire: The Origins of the Luxury Controversy in France," *Studies on Voltaire and the Eighteenth Century* 155 (1976), pp. 1897–1912.

Rothschild, Emma, *Economic Sentiments: Adam Smith, Condorcet, and the Enlightenment* (Cambridge, MA, 2001).

Sekora, John, *Luxury: The Concept in Western Thought, Eden to Smollett* (Baltimore, 1977).

Shovlin, John, "The Cultural Politics of Luxury in Eighteenth-Century France," *French Historical Studies* 23 (2000), pp. 577–606.

The Political Economy of Virtue: Luxury, Patriotism, and the Origins of the French Revolution (Ithaca, NY, 2006).

Terjanian, Anoush Fraser, *Commerce and Its Discontents in Eighteenth-Century French Political Thought* (Cambridge, 2016).

Winch, Donald, "Adam Smith: Scottish Moral Philosopher as Political Economist," *The Historical Journal* 35 (1992), pp. 91–113.

Chapter 7

Adelman, Jeremy, *Sovereignty and Revolution in the Iberian Atlantic* (Princeton, NJ, 2006).

"An Age of Imperial Revolutions," *The American Historical Review* 113 (2008), pp. 319–340.

Auslander, Leora, *Cultural Revolutions: Everyday Life and Politics in Britain, North America, and France* (Berkeley, CA, 2009).

Bohstedt, John, *The Politics of Provisions: Food Riots, Moral Economy, and Market Transition in England, c. 1550–1850* (New York, 2016).

Boström, Magnus, Michele Micheletti, and Peter Oosterveer, eds., *The Oxford Handbook of Political Consumerism* (Oxford, 2019).

Bouton, Cynthia, *The Flour War: Gender, Class, and Community in Late Ancien Régime French Society* (University Park, PA, 1993).

Breen, T. H., *The Marketplace of Revolution: How Consumer Politics Shaped American Independence* (Oxford, 2004).

Casimir, Jean, *The Haitians: A Decolonial History*, trans. Laurent Dubois (Chapel Hill, NC, 2020).

Cheney, Paul, *Revolutionary Commerce: Globalization and the French Monarchy* (Cambridge, MA, 2010).

Coquery, Natacha, "Luxury and Revolution: Selling High-Status Garments in Revolutionary France," in Jon Stobart and Bruno Blondé, eds., *Selling Textiles in the Long Eighteenth Century: Comparative Perspectives from Western Europe* (Basingstoke, 2014), pp. 179–192.

Desan, Suzanne, "Gender, Radicalization, and the October Days: Occupying the National Assembly," *French Historical Studies* 43 (2020), pp. 359–390.

Dubois, Laurent, *Avengers of the New World: The Story of the Haitian Revolution* (Cambridge, MA, 2004).

du Rivage, Justin, *Revolution against Empire: Taxes, Politics, and the Origins of American Independence* (New Haven, CT, 2017).

Fairchilds, Cissie, "Fashion and Freedom in the French Revolution," *Continuity and Change* 15 (December 2000), pp. 419–433.

Findlay, Ronald, and Kevin O'Rourke, *Power and Plenty: Trade, War, and the World Economy in the Second Millennium* (Princeton, NJ, 2007).

Freund, Amy, *Portraiture and Politics in Revolutionary France* (University Park, PA, 2014).

Glickman, Lawrence, "'Buy for the Sake of the Slave': Abolitionism and the Origins of American Consumer Activism," *American Quarterly* 56 (December 2004), pp. 889–912.

Gonzales, Johnhenry, *Maroon Nation: A History of Revolutionary Haiti* (New Haven, CT, 2019).

Gross, Jean-Pierre, *Fair Shares for All: Jacobin Egalitarianism in Practice* (Cambridge, 1997).

Haskell, Thomas, "Capitalism and the Origins of the Humanitarian Sensibility, Part 1" *The American Historical Review* 90 (April 1985), pp. 339–361.

"Capitalism and the Origins of the Humanitarian Sensibility, Part 2" *The American Historical Review* 90 (June 1985), pp. 547–566.

Holcomb, Julie, "Blood-Stained Sugar: Gender, Commerce and the British Slave-Trade Debates," *Slavery and Abolition* 35 (2014), pp. 611–628.

Huzzey, Richard, "The Moral Geography of British Anti-Slavery Responsibilities," *Transactions of the RHS* 22 (2012), pp. 111–139.

Jarvis, Katie, *Politics in the Marketplace: Work, Gender, and Citizenship in Revolutionary France* (Oxford, 2019).

Jones, Colin, "Bourgeois Revolution Revivified: 1789 and Social Change," in Colin Lucas, ed., *Rewriting the French Revolution* (Oxford, 1991), pp. 69–118.

"The Great Chain of Buying: Medical Advertisement, the Bourgeois Public Sphere, and the Origins of the French Revolution," *The American Historical Review* 101 (February 1996), pp. 13–40.

Jones, Colin, and Rebecca Spang, "*Sans-culottes, sans café, sans tabac*: Shifting Realms of Necessity and Luxury in Eighteenth-Century France," in Maxine Berg and Helen Clifford, eds., *Consumers and Luxury: Consumer Culture in Europe 1650–1850* (Manchester, 1999), pp. 37–62.

Kaplan, Steven L., *The Famine Plot Persuasion in Eighteenth-Century France* (Philadelphia, 1982).

Bread, Politics, and Political Economy in the Reign of Louis XV (London, 2014).

The Stakes of Regulation (London, 2015).

Khelissa, Anne Perrin, "De l'objet d'agrément à l'objet d'art: Légitimer les manufactures d'État sous la Révolution," in Natacha Coquery and Alain Bonnet, eds., *Le commerce du luxe: production, exposition et circulation des objets précieux du Moyen Âge à nos jours* (Paris, 2015), pp. 160–167.

Kwass, Michael, "The Global Underground: Smuggling, Rebellion, and the Origins of the French Revolution," in Suzanne Desan, Lynn Hunt, and William Max Nelson, eds., *The French Revolution in Global Perspective* (Ithaca, NY, 2013), pp. 15–31.

Contraband: Louis Mandrin and the Making of a Global Underground (Cambridge, MA, 2014).

Margairaz, Dominique, and Philippe Minard, "Marché des subsistances et économie morale: ce que 'taxer' veut dire," *Annales historiques de la Révolution française* 352 (2008), pp. 53–99.

Markoff, John, *The Abolition of Feudalism: Peasants, Lords, and Legislators in the French Revolution* (University Park, PA, 1996).

Markovic, Momcilo, "La Révolution aux barrières: l'incendie des barrières de l'octroi à Paris en juillet 1789," *Annales historiques de la Révolution française* 372 (April–June 2013), pp. 27–48.

Mathiez, Albert, *La vie chère et le mouvement social sous la Terreur* (Paris, 1973).

Nicolas, Jean, *La Rébellion française: Mouvements populaires et conscience sociale, 1661–1789* (Paris, 2002).

Pincus, Steve, "Rethinking Mercantilism: Political Economy, the British Empire, and the Atlantic World in the Seventeenth and Eighteenth Centuries," *The William and Mary Quarterly* 69 (January 2012), pp. 3–34.

Plack, Noelle, "Drinking and Rebelling: Wine, Taxes and Popular Agency in Revolutionary Paris, 1789–1791," *French Historical Studies* 39 (2016), pp. 599–622.

Randall, Adrian, and Andrew Charlesworth, eds., *Moral Economy and Popular Protest: Crowds, Conflict and Authority* (London, 2000).

Sewell, William, "The Sans-Culottes Rhetoric of Subsistence," in Keith Baker, ed., *The French Revolution and the Creation of Modern Political Culture, vol. 4, The Terror* (Oxford, 1994), pp. 249–270.

"The Empire of Fashion and the Rise of Capitalism in Eighteenth-Century France," *Past & Present* 206 (February 2010), pp. 81–120.

"Connecting Capitalism to the French Revolution: The Parisian Promenade and the Origins of Civic Equality in Eighteenth-Century France," *Critical Historical Studies* 1 (Spring 2014), pp. 5–46.

Capitalism and the Emergence of Civic Equality in Eighteenth-Century France (Chicago, 2021).

Sinha, Manisha, *The Slave's Cause: A History of Abolition* (New Haven, CT, 2016).

"The Problem of Abolition in the Age of Capitalism," *The American Historical Review* 124 (February 2019), pp. 144–163.

Spang, Rebecca, "What Is Rum? The Politics of Consumption in the French Revolution," in Martin Daunton and Mathew Hilton, eds., *The Politics of Consumption: Material Culture and Citizenship in Europe and America* (Oxford, 2001), pp. 33–49.

Stern, Philip, and Carl Wennerlind, eds., *Mercantilism Reimagined: Political Economy in Early Modern Britain and Its Empire* (Oxford, 2014).

Sussman, Charlotte, *Consuming Anxieties: Consumer Protest, Gender, and British Slavery, 1713–1833* (Stanford, CA, 2000).

Taws, Richard, *The Politics of the Provisional: Art and Ephemera in Revolutionary France* (University Park, PA, 2013).

Thompson, E. P., "The Moral Economy of the English Crowd in the Eighteenth Century," *Past & Present* 50 (February 1971), pp. 76–136.

Ulrich, Laurel Thatcher, "Political Protest and the World of Goods," in Jane Kamensky and Edward Gray, eds., *The Oxford Handbook of the American Revolution* (Oxford, 2012), pp. 64–84.

Walton, Charles, "Why the Neglect? Social Rights and the French Revolutionary Historiography," *French History* 33 (December 2019), pp. 503–519.

White, Ashli, *Revolutionary Things* (New Haven, CT, forthcoming).

Wrigley, Richard, *The Politics of Appearances: Representations of Dress in Revolutionary France* (Oxford, 2002).

Conclusion

Appuhn, Karl, *A Forest on the Sea: Environmental Expertise in Renaissance Venice* (Baltimore, 2009).

Bourg, Dominique, Gauthier Chapelle, Johann Chapoutot, et al., *Retour sur Terre: 35 propositions* (Paris, 2020).

Brulle, Robert J., and Riley E. Dunlap, "Sociology and Global Climate Change: Introduction," in Riley Dunlap and Robert Brulle, eds., *Climate Change and Society: Sociological Perspectives* (Oxford, 2015), pp. 1–31.

Casimir, Jean, *The Haitians: A Decolonial History*, trans. Laurent Dubois (Chapel Hill, NC, 2020).

Cavert, William, *The Smoke of London: Energy and Environment in the Early Modern City* (Cambridge, 2016).

Gonzales, Johnhenry, *Maroon Nation: A History of Revolutionary Haiti* (New Haven, CT, 2019).

Grove, Richard, *Green Imperialism: Colonial Expansion, Tropical Island Edens and the Origins of Environmentalism, 1600–1860* (Cambridge, 1995).

Harari, Yuval, *Sapiens: A Brief History of Humankind* (New York, 2015).

Klingle, Matthew, "The Nature of Desire: Consumption in Environmental History" in Andrew Isenberg, ed., *The Oxford Handbook of Environmental History* (Oxford, 2014), pp. 467–512.

Kolbert, Elizabeth, *The Sixth Extinction: An Unnatural History* (New York, 2014).

Le Roux, Thomas, *Le laboratoire des pollutions industrielles: Paris, 1770–1830* (Paris, 2011).

Marks, Robert B., *The Origins of the Modern World: A Global and Environmental Narrative from the Fifteenth to the Twenty-First Century* (London, 2020).

Matteson, Kieko, *Forests in Revolutionary France: Conservation, Community, and Conflict, 1669–1848* (Cambridge, 2015).

McNeill, J. R., *Mosquito Empires: Ecology and War in the Greater Caribbean, 1620–1914* (Cambridge, 2010).

Morgan, Louise, and Grete Birtwistle, "An Investigation of Young Fashion Consumers' Disposal Habits," *International Journal of Consumer Studies* 33 (2009), pp. 190–198.

Nye, David E., "Consumption of Energy," in Frank Trentmann, ed., *The Oxford Handbook of the History of Consumption* (Oxford, 2021), pp. 307–325.

Shove, Elisabeth, *Comfort, Cleanliness and Convenience: The Social Organization of Normality* (Oxford, 2003).

   "Comfort and Convenience: Temporality and Practice" in Frank Trentmann, ed., *The Oxford Handbook of the History of Consumption* (Oxford, 2021), pp. 289–306.

Sieferle, R.-P., *The Subterranean Forest: Energy Systems and the Industrial Revolution* (Cambridge, 2001).

Sutter, Paul, "The World with Us: The State of American Environmental History," *Journal of American History* 100 (June 2013), pp. 94–119.

Wallace-Wells, David, *The Uninhabitable Earth: Life after Warming* (New York, 2019).

Warde, Paul, *The Invention of Sustainability: Nature and Destiny, c.1500–1870* (Cambridge, 2018).

Watts, David, *The West Indies: Patterns of Development, Culture and Environmental Change since 1492* (Cambridge, 1990).

Wing, John, *Roots of Empire: Forests and State Power in Early Modern Spain, c. 1500–1750* (Leiden, 2015).

Zuboff, Shoshana, *The Age of Surveillance Capitalism* (New York, 2019).

Index

Page numbers for illustrations are in *italics*.